1992

THE QUOTE SLEUTH

The
Quote Sleuth

A Manual for
the Tracer of
Lost Quotations

Anthony W. Shipps

UNIVERSITY OF ILLINOIS PRESS
Urbana and Chicago

This book is printed on acid-free paper.

Library of Congress Cataloging-in-Publication Data

Shipps, Anthony W., 1926–
    The quote sleuth : a manual for the tracer of lost quotations /
Anthony W. Shipps.
        p.   cm.
    Includes bibliographical references.
    ISBN 0-252-01695-5 (alk. paper).
    1. Quotations, English—Handbooks, manuals, etc. 2. Reference
books—Bibliography—Handbooks, manuals, etc. 3. Research—
Methodology—Handbooks, manuals, etc.   I. Title.
PN6081.S44   1990
080′.72—dc20   89-77126
                                                                    CIP

To Jan
and to Steve and Teri

Like all Holmes's reasoning the thing seemed
simplicity itself when it was once explained.
                    "The Stock-broker's Clerk"

Contents

Preface

The readers I had in mind while writing this book were such people as these: reference librarians; students and teachers of English and American literature; students and teachers of English and American history; researchers in other fields in which quotations abound, such as American studies, religious studies, forensic studies, and political science; editors and editorial researchers; trivia buffs; journalists; public speakers and their ghostly assistants; creative writers; general readers; and any other persons who often need to identify the sources or verify the wording of quotations.

I have attempted to write the book I wish I could have read and consulted many years ago as a graduate student, as an English teacher, and as a reference librarian. In the absence of such a manual for the quotation tracer, it was necessary for me to learn on my own the art and science of identifying the sources of quotations. I did this because I needed to learn it and also because I wanted to learn it, for the subject has long fascinated me. My apprenticeship included the years spent doing research on my dissertation, a critical edition of an old book of essays made up of quotations; a few years as an English instructor; a few years as a reference librarian; two decades as Librarian for English in a major university library; many years of attempting to find answers to queries published in scholarly journals and national publications; and some time spent serving as a consultant to scholars working on critical editions of literary or historical works.

I am still learning my trade, but unfortunately I am also beginning to forget a few things. In this book I have written down all I can remember of what I have learned about the subject. Most of that consists of fairly obvious things in the public domain that were not obvious to me when I set about learning them and that may not be obvious to the reader of this book. "Perhaps," said Poe's Dupin, "the mystery is a little *too* plain." What I want to accomplish is to acquaint the reader with these obvious things and with obvious methods and to make the learning process easier for him or her than it has been for me. The book will achieve its goal if you will assist me by paying close attention and by verifying my solutions whenever they are not self-evident.

The person who is just now beginning to need to know how to identify the sources of quotations will benefit from reading attentively this book of facts and principles, from rereading sections of it from time to time, and from consulting the index and the bibliography when problems involving quotations present themselves. The inexperienced quotation tracer who is willing to study this book and to spend some time getting acquainted with at least the basic reference materials discussed will discover that a respectable level of competence as a quote sleuth can be reached in a very short time. The experienced reader, editor, reference librarian, or professor who is already an able finder of sources will not benefit so markedly, but even for such a person this book should provide a useful review of helpful materials, some information about reference tools not yet examined or long since forgotten, and a handy bibliography.

If, as Sheridan noted, "easy writing's vile hard reading," this book should be easy reading indeed. Writing it has not been easy for me; and I have spent more years in its composition than anyone with any character and self-discipline would have spent. That I have finally completed it is due mainly to the assistance, the encouragement, and the support I have received from my good wife. Throughout the years of research and writing, Jan encouraged me in my endeavors, shielded me from distractions and temptations, and gave me just the right amount of advice.

Indiana University awarded me two sabbatical leaves during the long gestation of this work—the second one, I think, to keep the first one from being wasted—and the University Library gave me a research leave in addition. Moreover, as the final revision of the manuscript was nearing completion, Acting Dean of Libraries Carolyn Snyder gave me even more time off from my regular duties so that I could finish the undertaking. I am profoundly grateful to her and to other university administrators for research time formally and informally granted and to the university trustees for giving to librarians at Indiana the privileges accorded to members of the teaching faculty. The university also awarded me, through its Office of Research and Graduate Development, a grant in aid of research that enabled me to visit several university libraries outside Indiana. "For this relief much thanks."

During the preparation of this manual, I made use of general and special collections of the libraries of several universities—Indiana University, primarily, but also Yale University, the University of Texas, and Harvard University. I am grateful to their staffs for privileges and courtesies. At Indiana University and elsewhere, I was assisted by a number of professors, reference librarians, bibliographers, booksellers, and other persons who shared with me the fruits of their knowledge and experience or who furthered my research in other ways. I cannot name all of these fine people, but I must mention J. Albert Robbins, Ann Bristow, Barbara Halporn, Ralph Loomis, Tom Glastras, Betty Jarboe, Fred Musto, David Frasier, Jeff Graf, Ron Luedemann, Frank Quinn, Ian Jackson, Pauline Spulber, Marilyn Halkovic, Pat Riesenman, Rhonda Stone, Fred Beaty, Robert Merriam, Donald Hawthorne, Goldia Hester, and the late Philip Wikelund.

Three persons of distinguished professional accomplishment read the manuscript and offered invaluable suggestions: Justin Kaplan, Eugene P. Sheehy, and Roger G. Clark. This book owes much to their diagnoses and prescriptions. Needless to say, these three are not responsible for the deficiencies, infelicities, and errors that remain—concerning any of which I must say with Coriolanus, "Alone I did it."

I also want to thank various editors at the University of Illinois Press for their encouragement, cooperation, and assistance. When he was the associate director of the Press, the aforementioned Roger Clark welcomed my modest proposal to write a little book about tracing quotations, and in later years he gave me helpful and wise advice about organization and style. Assistant Director Elizabeth Gjelsness Dulany (whose father was dean of the library school I attended) helped immeasurably in getting the manuscript approved for publication and transformed into a book. Director Richard Wentworth suggested a better subtitle for the work than the one I had given it. And Associate Editor Theresa L. Sears has copyedited the manuscript with great care, skill, and understanding, remolding it nearer to the heart's desire.

Finally, I hope I shall be forgiven for the presence of a few unidentified quotations here and there in the text, some in quotation marks and some in disguise. In the unlikely event that there are any quotes you do not recognize and immediately recall, I think you will know how to trace them by the time the last page has been reached.

THE QUOTE SLEUTH

1 | Introduction

Some, for *renown*, on scraps of learning doat,
And think they grow immortal as they *quote*.
Edward Young[1]

For many centuries writers and speakers have been quoting other writers and speakers in their writings and speeches and in their everyday conversations. One thinks of the New Testament's many quotations from the Old; of the literary quotations and allusions in congressional speeches; of the chapter mottoes in the novels of George Eliot and Sir Walter Scott; of the literary quotations that adorn the works of Burton, Montaigne, Walpole, Hazlitt, Lamb, Howells, Thoreau, Emerson, Hardy, Woolf, and Wolfe; and of the innumerable book titles and play titles taken from the King James Bible and from the works of English poets and dramatists—*The Little Foxes, The Voice of the Turtle, East of Eden, The Silver Cord, Giants in the Earth, The Sun Also Rises, The Cricket on the Hearth, Ladies Whose Bright Eyes, Precious Bane, In Dubious Battle, Look Homeward, Angel, Eyeless in Gaza,* and so on.

Until fairly recently the use of illustrative quotations from literary works or from other sources has been a major feature of English, American, and Continental prose writing; and, although at a reduced level, it still characterizes much writing today. The practice has never been limited to what we call literary contexts. In times when readers and writers in all subjects have shared a familiarity with a basic corpus of both old and contemporary literature, writings and utterances in many fields other than belles lettres have also been characterized by the use of literary passages and allusions and of quotations from the Bible. Abraham Lincoln, for example, was quoting when he made the celebrated remark about "a house divided."

Leafing through many a quaint and curious volume of forgotten lore, as well as a few recent books and periodicals, in search of quotes to add to a collection I am compiling, I have found examples of illustrative or ornamental quotations not only in such literary journals as the *Atlantic Monthly, Blackwood's Edinburgh Magazine, Fraser's Maga-*

zine, and *Graham's Magazine* but also in publications not primarily literary, such as the *American Farmer,* the *Examiner,* the *Merchants' Magazine,* the *Lady's Book,* the *International Journal of Ethics,* the *National Anti-Slavery Standard, Newsweek,* the *Congressional Record,* the *Lancet, Scientific American,* and *Sunday at Home.* I have found them in the correspondence and speeches of major historical and political figures, as well as in writings of sociologists, philosophers, psychologists, novelists, essayists, journalists, and preachers. Since most of my reading has been in works in the English language, most of the quotations I have seen occur in works written in English, though the quotes themselves have been in several languages. I have found quotations also in large numbers in French and German periodical literature, and I assume that they occur in Spanish, Chinese, Russian, and Polish works as well. With regard to various kinds of writings of past times, I would risk the generalization that the quotations occurring in them have usually come from literary works, even when the writings in which they appear are historical or religious or political or agricultural.

Literary quotations have appeared in periodicals, in novels, in speeches, in sermons, in personal letters, in historical works, in collections of essays, and in writings representative of virtually any discipline or any genre. Even plays and poems have contained quotations from other plays and poems. In writings of our day, we find quotations from old literary works along with familiar or unfamiliar contemporary utterances from sports, politics, news stories, movies, and popular song, fiction, and poetry. Today's readers, moreover, are not limited to the works of today's writers. Anyone who reads or studies or edits any kind of writing from earlier centuries or even earlier decades is likely to encounter a large number of unfamiliar or no longer familiar quotations. These may appear as epigraphs to books, as chapter mottoes, as titles, as space fillers, as supporting statements, as illustrations of aspects of topics being discussed, or as ornament and decoration in writings "from grave to gay, from lively to severe." They range from lengthy passages in prose or verse to the more usual line or two. Sometimes only two or three words are quoted, challenging you to recall additional words and original contexts.

That a quotation is a quotation is usually quite obvious. An indirect quotation customarily begins with something like "Emerson says that" and then goes on to give a paraphrased or somewhat modified rendering of the words the quoter has in mind. The new wording may closely resemble the old wording, or the wording may be mainly that of the quoter. Direct quotations, too, are often preceded or followed by tags that identify the purported author or give the name of the work quoted. Moreover, the fact that a passage is a direct quotation is usually indicated by some combination of special signals. A quotation may be put within quotation marks (double or single); it may be printed in italics; it may be indented and set off from the text; and, if set off and indented, it may be printed in a typeface different from that of the main text. Verse passages especially—even single lines—are often, but not always, set off from the words that precede and follow them. When such conventions have been used, you know immediately that a passage is a quotation.

On the other hand, some quotations do not announce themselves as quotations at all. They are not put in quotation marks or printed in italics or set off from the text or preceded or followed by the name of the author or the title of the source. You know that they are quotations only if they sound familiar or if they differ stylistically from the passages in which they occur. In many cases, of course, you recognize the quote and appreciate its aptness, but a careless reader or one who is not thoroughly familiar with the work quoted may fail to realize that an unannounced quotation of the words of an author has been perpetrated. Such persons may read right through the unheralded quotation, perhaps wondering in passing why a sentence makes so little sense or why a few words in it are so different from their surroundings.

Sometimes a quoted passage is intentionally modified to increase its aptness or to produce a certain effect or simply to make it fit the syntax of the sentence in which it occurs; even an unannounced quotation may be altered for some purpose. Correctly quoted, the verse from Hebrews 11 that appears in the touching conclusion to Edward Everett Hale's story "The Man without a Country" would not have belonged in the story at all. Among other changes, Hale omitted the word "better" from "a better country." One of the characters relates,

> "We looked in his Bible, and there was a slip of paper at the place where he had marked the text:—
> " 'They desire a country, even a heavenly: wherefore God is not ashamed to be called their God: for he hath prepared for them a city.' "[2]

An unannounced quotation that has been altered occurs in Edward Newhouse's short story "The Day Before." In *As You Like It*, a well-known passage reads:

> And this our life, exempt from public haunt,
> Finds tongues in trees, books in the running brooks,
> Sermons in stones, and good in every thing.[3]

Without any reference to Shakespeare at all, Newhouse writes: "Tomorrow, Martin would begin *his* de-education. All right, make it re-education then—tongues in tanks, books in bombs, sermons in sergeants, and good in everything."[4] More common than intentional modifications, however, are slight or serious misquotations that are due to ignorance or faulty memory. For example, Herbert Spencer writes of "a feeling akin to that named by Shakespeare as shown by those who counted it 'a meanness to write fair.' " The proper word, of course, is "baseness."[5]

As they quote or misquote, writers or speakers may refer to sources in many ways, or they may not refer to them at all. As I have noted, the name of the author of a quoted passage is sometimes supplied by the quoter; sometimes only the name of the work quoted from is given; sometimes both the author and the title are named; sometimes the name of a fictional character associated with the quotation is provided; sometimes a different sort of clue occurs in the quotation's context; sometimes, particularly in writings of periods earlier than our own, a quotation is not accompanied by an author attribution or by any kind of source citation at all; and sometimes, alas, a quotation is attributed to the wrong author. In an old periodical we find this statement:

> . . . we were forcibly impressed with the truth of Wordsworth's impassioned outburst—
>
> "God made the country, but man the town."[6]

The impassioned outburst, slightly misquoted here, is actually from Cowper.[7]

These various characteristics of quotations will become more clear as you look at some quotes I have assembled. The following passages taken from my reading are more or less typical of the quotations that the scholarly reader of the writings of yesterday and today is likely to encounter. They are given here just as I found them, with all their imperfections on their heads. Some of them are quotations or misquotations; others contain quotations or misquotations. The notes to this chapter indicate, for the curious, where I happened to read the passages; the notes do not indicate the original sources of the quotations, which will be identified during the course of this book.

1. Alas! that journals so voluminously begun should come to so lame and impotent a conclusion as most of them did![8]

2. The world was now all before Mr. Sponge where to choose; and not being the man to keep hack-horses to look at, we must be setting him a-going.[9]

3. It was at the theatre and at Carnegie Hall that Paul really lived; the rest was but a sleep and a forgetting.[10]

4. The Memoirs were never intended for publication, and that fact should be kept in mind by the few who might otherwise resent

their candour as well as by the many whose withers are unwrung.[11]

5. Some St. Louisans have seen "Twain" steadily and seen it whole and have seen enough of it.[12]

6. And that we are of the earth, earthy, goes without saying: else we would not be glued to it by our feet all our lives.[13]

7. Roy Cohn does not go gentle into that good night.[14]

8. We need hardly say that decorum reigned supreme, for want of decency is want of sense, and the society was something more than sensible.[15]

9. ... and the critics ... will find in this brilliant Frenchman a foeman worthy of their steel.[16]

10. ... and I notice that even the clergy who come my way ... no longer insist upon the point, but, at the worst, faintly trust the larger hope.[17]

11. The crowning fortune of a man is to be born to some pursuit which finds him in employment and happiness, whether it be to make baskets, or broadswords, or canals, or statues, or songs.
EMERSON[18]

12. Many of our best poets

    "Are cradled into poetry by wrong,
    And learn in suffering what they teach in song."[19]

13. "The best of men are moulded out of faults."[20]

14. A man with a long memory is a troublesome companion; he veers about like a weathercock, and

    "Is every thing by fits, and nothing long."[21]

15. Lady Kicklebury remarked that Shakespeare was very right in stating how much sharper than a thankless tooth it is to have a serpent child.[22]

16. John Wesley was a most devout believer in witchcraft, and said on one occasion that, if witchcraft was not to be believed, we could not believe in the Bible.[23]

17. Of course, adultery is impossible, if you only assume a license to take your neighbour's wife. It is DIDO's old apology:

    Conjugium vocat, hoc praetexit nomine culpam.[24]

18. "The bellman writes better verses," said Mr. Osbaldistone, when he threw poor Frank's away.[25]

19. The battle occupies a considerable area of paper, but seems a mere academic battle or diagram of a battle, without life, or force, or fire; as it were, a military thesis—

"Wherein the toga'd consuls can propose
As masterly,"

to say the least, as Mr. Rider Haggard.[26]

20. Old Knowell laments that his son neglects his other studies
"To dream of naught but idle poetry."[27]

21. The curse of growing factions and divisions
Still vex your councils!
Venice Preserved.[28]

22. "The Dyer's Hand"[29]

23. "To-morrow to *fresh* fields and pastures *new*."[30]

24. On Wednesday, Mr. S. extended his walk into the city, whither
"His faithful *bird* still bore him Company."[31]

25. *Quandoque bonus dormitat Homerus*.[32]

26. . . . I ventured to repeat the line from Horace at the top of this
memorandum, to which I was immediately answered by the
following well-known line from Roscommon:

It is not Homer nods, but we that dream.[33]

27. Mosquitos "murder sleep;"[34]

28. To paraphrase my beloved e. e. cummings, there are some things
I will not eat.[35]

29. But these are animals

"Fruges consumere nati."

They live only for themselves, and fill a space which better
beings ought to occupy.[36]

30. Their personal experience would have led them to ratify the
verdict of the Laureate—

"Each man walks with his head in a cloud of poisonous flies."[37]

31. "Calm or convulsed, in breeze, or gale, or storm."[38]

32. Edward and Alfred

closed their long Glories with a Sigh to find
th' unwilling Gratitude of base Mankind.[39]

33. He will proceed, with this banner flying, to the custom-house in
Charleston,

"All the while,
Sonorous metal blowing martial sounds."[40]

The first ten items contain quotations that, in context, were not set
off in any of the usual ways. Those who recognize a hidden quotation
and already know its correct wording and its original context, or de-

termine that it sounds vaguely familiar, will probably find the task of identifying and citing the exact source very easy. If a dictionary of quotations is consulted for the source of a hidden quote, the passage is ordinarily identified almost immediately, for unheralded quotations are or used to be familiar quotations. The difficulty, if there is one, is in recognizing that a quotation is present when there are no outward and visible signs to attract our attention.

What if you fail to recognize the quotations hidden in the first ten excerpts? What is there about these passages that should make you suspect that they contain quotations at all? Well, for one thing, most of the excerpts contain prose that sounds like verse. Note the following iambic passages:

> so lame and impotent . . . conclusion
> the world was . . . all before . . . Sponge where to choose
> the rest was but a sleep and a forgetting
> have seen "Twain" steadily and seen it whole
> does not go gentle into that good night
> for want of decency is want of sense
> a foeman worthy of their steel
> but . . . faintly trust the larger hope

One or two of my examples of iambic stretches are not very striking or very convincing, but most of them, as presented, really do stand out as verse. Six of the passages are (at least as I have given them) in iambic pentameter, a line basic to poetry in English, and two are in iambic tetrameter, another standard meter of English verse. The presence of a metrical line in a prose passage is strong circumstantial evidence indeed, "as when you find a trout in the milk," that the passage contains a quotation.

But to leave these iambic elements and return to all of the first ten passages, in what other ways are you warned that they may contain quotations? I suggest that they all contain elements or sequences of words that are different from their surroundings, not only in rhythm, but also in vocabulary, in diction, in tone, or, to put all of this more briefly, in style. Also, in the first ten excerpts these stylistically different elements do not have much or any meaning in their present contexts if considered alone and without reference to any other contexts. For example, when we see the words "whose withers are unwrung" in their present context, we suspect that a quotation is being used. We must, then, be ever alert in our reading to notice sustained metrical passages occurring in prose contexts, to recognize two different styles of writing occurring within the same sentence, and to stop and wonder about phrases and clauses that have little or no meaning for us. Any or all of these things may serve to indicate that silent quotations are present.

The eleventh passage is both a quotation used as a chapter motto and a motto followed by an author attribution. (Incidentally, it is also a misquotation, with "statues" occurring in place of "statutes.") In the twelfth and fourteenth passages, the quotations are indented and set off from the text; they are also enclosed in quotation marks. The second of these (" 'Is every thing by fits . . .' ") is, like a great many other quotations, worded incorrectly. The thirteenth, another misquotation, is the motto to a story. The fifteenth contains a humorous alteration of a quotation, while the sixteenth is an indirect quotation whose verification I found to be a foeman worthy of my steel.

The seventeenth passage contains a Latin quotation and a clue to its authorship. The eighteenth and twentieth supply the names of the speakers, but who are they? The nineteenth is shortened to fit the needs of the sentence in which it occurs. The twenty-first, another chapter motto, gives us not the name of the author but the title of the work quoted. The twenty-second is an essay title that you should suspect is a quotation because, taken by itself, it hardly seems suitable as a title of an essay on anything. The twenty-third is a common misquotation. (Ay, madam, it is common.)

The twenty-fourth quotation contains an intentional modification of a line, with a substituted word appearing in italics. (Such use of italics does not always indicate substitution, but it often does.) The twenty-fifth is a Latin quotation, printed in italics, used as a motto to a magazine article. The twenty-sixth contains a line attributed to the wrong author; the twenty-seventh contains an example of a short quotation whose very brevity warns us that it will be difficult to locate in an index to a dictionary of quotations. The twenty-eighth passage is an example of an indirect quotation and a paraphrase, with the quoter warning us up front that the quotation has been altered. The twenty-ninth contains a once-familiar Latin quotation, and the thirtieth contains a line attributed to the person who was the English poet laureate in 1890. The thirty-first and thirty-second quotations occur without attribution, the former in a letter of William Lloyd Garrison and the latter in the diary of John Adams. The thirty-third is taken from a speech by Daniel Webster. The last three quotes, by the way, serve to remind us that the student of history, like the student of literature, needs to be able to identify the sources of literary quotations.

These thirty-three quotations plus dozens more will be traced to their origins as I discuss various reference materials that may be used in the pursuit of quotation sources. Some of the quotes will not yield until this neglected reference work or that one is employed or until, together, we follow the leads that the quoter has given us. Most of the passages, however, may be traced by careful use of general dictionaries of quotations.

NOTES

1. Edward Young, *Love of Fame*, "Satire 1," ll. 89–90.
2. Edward Everett Hale, *"The Man without a Country" and Other Tales* (Boston, 1868; reprint, Freeport, N.Y.: Books for Libraries Press, 1971), 46.
3. William Shakespeare, *As You Like It*, 2.1.15–17.
4. Edward Newhouse, *Many Are Called: Forty-two Short Stories* (New York: William Sloane Associates, 1951), 135.
5. Herbert Spencer, *The Study of Sociology* (New York and London: D. Appleton and Co., 1910), 71; *Hamlet*, 5.2.34.
6. *Bradshaw's Manchester Journal* 1 (28 August 1841): 274.
7. William Cowper, *The Task*. Book 1, *The Sofa*, 749.
8. Mark Twain, *The Innocents Abroad*, 2 vols. (New York: Harper and Brothers, n.d.), 1:69.
9. Robert Smith Surtees, *Mr. Sponge's Sporting Tour*, ed. Virginia Blain (London: Batsford Academic and Educational, 1981), 17.
10. Willa Cather, "Paul's Case," in *Willa Cather's Collected Short Fiction, 1892–1912*, rev. ed., ed. Virginia Faulkner (Lincoln: University of Nebraska Press, 1970), 251.
11. *Blackwood's Edinburgh Magazine* 163 (April 1898): 539.
12. George F. Will, "Giving Art a Bad Name," *Newsweek* 106 (16 September 1985): 80.
13. *Current Literature* 34 (January 1903): 34.
14. Aric Press, "A Tough Guy Down But Not Yet Out: Roy Cohn Battles Both Cancer and the Bar," *Newsweek* 106 (9 December 1985): 78.
15. *Blackwood's Edinburgh Magazine* 148 (July 1890): 60.
16. Ibid. 146 (December 1889): 794.
17. *Nineteenth Century* 5 (May 1879): 818.
18. Motto to chapter 10 in Orison Swett Marden, *Pushing to the Front* (Petersburg, N.Y.: Success Co., 1911), 125.
19. Ibid., 355.
20. Motto to story in *Leisure Hour*, (1886): 752.
21. *Fraser's Magazine* 10 (July 1834): 37.
22. William Makepeace Thackeray, "The Kickleburys on the Rhine," *The Works of William Makepeace Thackeray*, Biographical Edition, 13 vols. (New York: Harper and Brothers, 1899), 9:207.
23. *Popular Science Monthly* 2 (November 1872): 25.
24. *Saturday Review* 2 (6 September 1856): 414.
25. *Fortnightly Review* 50 (1 July 1888): 33.
26. Ibid., (1 September 1888): 335.
27. *European Magazine* 57 (April 1810): 257.
28. Motto to chapter 30 of Sir Walter Scott's *Old Mortality*.

29. Title of essay in W. H. Auden, *"The Dyer's Hand" and Other Essays* (London: Faber and Faber, 1963).

30. *Blackwood's Edinburgh Magazine* 43 (April 1838): 521.

31. *Farmer's Magazine* 1 (June 1834): 146.

32. Motto to article in *European Magazine* 9 (April 1786): 238.

33. Ibid., 239.

34. *Athenaeum*, no. 1215 (8 February 1851): 165.

35. Ed Hofmann, " 'Thieves' at the Auto Shop," *Newsweek* 110 (28 September 1987): 10.

36. *Fraser's Magazine* 10 (December 1834): 731.

37. *Contemporary Review* 57 (February 1890): 180.

38. William Lloyd Garrison, *The Letters of William Lloyd Garrison*, ed. Walter M. Merrill and Louis Ruchames, 6 vols. (Cambridge: Belknap Press of Harvard University Press, 1971–81), 3:462.

39. John Adams, *Diary and Autobiography of John Adams*, ed. L. H. Butterfield, 4 vols. (Cambridge: Belknap Press of Harvard University Press, 1961–62), 2:35.

40. Daniel Webster, *The Writings and Speeches of Daniel Webster*, National Edition, 18 vols. (Boston: Little, Brown and Co., 1903), 6:70.

2 | General Dictionaries of Quotations

It is a good thing for an uneducated man to read
books of quotations. Bartlett's *Familiar Quotations*
is an admirable work, and I studied it intently.

Churchill[1]

Major Collections

Ideally, a dictionary of quotations should contain tens of
thousands of passages that have actually been used from time to time
as illustrative quotations; it should contain reliable texts of quotations
in their original languages; it should contain reliable English translations of quotations from classical or foreign languages; it should supply
full and correct source citations; it should be equipped with a generous
word index to the passages it includes; it should be organized logically,
either by author or by subject, so that it can serve us even if we fail
to find our quarry in the index; it should be reasonably up to date—
and therefore should be revised periodically, for the addition of current
quotations and for the correction of mistakes; and it should be a pleasure to use. Although this is asking a great deal, a few compilations
do meet all or most of these criteria.

Three quotation dictionaries that approach the ideal may be found
in most library reference collections: the second edition of the *Oxford
Dictionary of Quotations* (*ODQ2*); the fifteenth edition of Bartlett's *Familiar Quotations*; and any fairly recent edition of Stevenson's *Home
Book of Quotations*. An individual scholar's own reference collection
should, I suggest, contain one or two of these books. Other dictionaries
of quotations, both general and specialized, may be used as supplements, and various sorts of reference books may be used as supplements to the supplements. For now, let us concentrate on these three.

One of the best collections of quotations is the *ODQ2*, though, with
its mid-century publication date, it is necessarily weak in recent materials. Superbly indexed and containing almost twenty thousand well-
chosen quotations, it is a great collection and a wieldy one. The compilation is made up of quotations likely to be sought after; each appears

in reliable wording, and almost all source citations are complete. Quotations are arranged alphabetically by author, which is very useful if you are trying to trace a paraphrased or garbled or vaguely remembered quotation attributed to a certain author.

The index to the *ODQ2* is self-explanatory and easy to use. Every quotation appearing in the body of the book is represented in the index under several keywords, though of course not under every possible word. Under each word entry in the index, short passages from all the quotes indexed under that word are listed alphabetically. With a little experience you can develop an ability to determine the most likely words to look for in the index and the most likely places to look for the passage desired in an alphabetical column of short passages. Once you have located the quote, or part of it, in the index, you are referred to a page and an item number on that page.

Since 1855 John Bartlett's *Familiar Quotations* has been one of the leading reference works in its field. Now in its fifteenth edition, it is a scholarly compilation of some 22,500 quotations from both old and recent sources. The index is excellent, and the entire book is handsomely printed. The quotations are arranged by author, but the chronological arrangement of the authors adds the additional step of consulting an author index if you want to turn to all the quotations from a certain author. An important feature is the anglicizing of many of the classical and foreign quotations, both in the body of the collection and in the index. This is an excellent feature to keep in mind for tracing present-day English renderings of passages from foreign and classical authors. A quotation appears in the index under several keywords, and like the *ODQ2*'s index, Bartlett's supplies both a page and an item number.

The largest of the three collections is Burton Stevenson's *Home Book of Quotations*. First published in 1935, and appearing with corrections and small numbers of additional quotations in several subsequent editions, it contains about fifty thousand quotations, the majority of which originated before 1940. The compilation is often very useful to source hunters, but it contains no recent material and is not easy to consult. It is big and unwieldy, and the index is like no other. As the compiler points out, "the word selected for the index entry is always the noun— if there is a noun—which is the subject of the sentence. . . ." "Where there is no noun," he goes on, "the principal adjective or verb is used."[2] This makes for a much weaker index than the indexes to Bartlett and the *ODQ2*. In addition, some quotations in the collection do not appear in the index at all but may be found in the book under the appropriate subject heading. Once you locate a passage in the index, you are referred to a page number and an item number on that page. In the body of the book, quotations appear under subjects arranged in alphabetical order. Thus, if the index fails you, you can easily scan all the quotations in the book having to do with a certain subject. Because of the subject arrangement, the collection also gives assistance to those who simply need to find a good quote on a given subject. The texts of the quotations seem to be accurate enough generally, but source citations, though presumably correct, vary in completeness. Too many references fail to enable you to find the passage easily in the source cited, and some source citations are mere author attributions.

A wise rule in most cases is routinely to consult the three basic collections, one after another, until the solution is found or until all three have failed. Tracers with limited resources at hand should of course begin with the quotation-finding tools immediately available, whatever they may be. However, in a library setting you should ordinarily begin with either the *ODQ2* or the fifteenth edition of Bartlett and go on to the others if necessary. Because of its weak index, Stevenson, if it is needed, should be third in line. If the quotation you are working on is already known to be of quite recent origin, you should eliminate the *ODQ2* and Stevenson at the start and check the most recent edition of Bartlett, and then, if they are needed, go on to a few other works I shall discuss later. (The sixteenth edition of Bartlett, edited by Justin Kaplan, is scheduled for publication in 1992.) But since most of the quotes you will need to trace are not of recent vintage or at least are not known to be, it is usually best not to eliminate any of the basic collections at the beginning.

To get some practice using all three of the basic collections, and to learn firsthand how they are alike and how they differ from one another, let us now try to trace the thirty-three quotations listed in chapter 1. This time we shall not follow the wise rule suggested above—to consult one dictionary of quotations after another until the solution is found; rather, we shall consult each index under every likely word from each quotation and not stop until we have exhausted these indexes and ourselves.

If hidden quotations are seen to be quotations, it is, as I have already stated, usually a simple matter to identify their sources. The first one on the list ("Alas! that . . . lame and impotent a conclusion . . ."), a modified passage from *Othello*, is easy enough. We find it in the indexes to the *ODQ2* and to Bartlett under each of the likely words "conclusion," "lame," and "impotent." We also find it in Stevenson, but only under "conclusion." (Remember, in Stevenson the policy is to index mainly under nouns.) The second quotation ("The world was now all before Mr. Sponge where to choose . . ."), most of which is from *Paradise Lost*, is very easy to trace if we use the *ODQ2*, where we find it under "before" and "world." It is also listed under "choose" ("where to c. their place of rest"), though not easily recognized there. In Bartlett and in Stevenson we find it indexed under "world."

The third passage (". . . the rest was but a sleep and a forgetting") is from Wordsworth's "Ode. Intimations of Immortality" and can be found in any of the three dictionaries. In the *ODQ2* we find it under "sleep" and "forgetting"; in Bartlett and in Stevenson we find it only under "forgetting." In all three it is also indexed under "birth," though not everyone will know to look for it there. The fourth item on the list (". . . whose withers are unwrung"), from *Hamlet*, is not difficult. In all three compilations we find it indexed under "withers"; and in Bartlett it is indexed also under "unwrung." The fifth (". . . have seen 'Twain' steadily and seen it whole . . ."), from Matthew Arnold's "To a Friend," is difficult to trace because of the alterations that have been made in it; however, we can identify it if we consult the *ODQ2* or Bartlett, where parts of the line are indexed under "steadily" and "whole," and if we realize that what we find is what we are seeking. All three collections index this quote under "life," and Bartlett and Stevenson index it under "saw" as well, if only we somehow know in advance to look under these words. The sixth quote (". . . of the earth, earthy . . ."), from 1 Corinthians, is not at all troublesome. In all three dictionaries it is indexed under "earth" and "earthy." The seventh (". . . does not go gentle into that good night"), from Dylan Thomas's "Do Not Go Gentle into That Good Night," is not to be found in the *ODQ2* or in Stevenson; in Bartlett it is listed under "gentle," "go," "good," and "night."

The eighth quotation (". . . for want of decency is want of sense . . ."), from the Earl of Roscommon's "Essay on Translated Verse," is plentifully indexed: it is listed under "want," "decency," and "sense" in Bartlett and in the *ODQ2*; in Stevenson it is indexed only under "decency." In tracing the ninth phrase (". . . a foeman worthy of their steel"), from *The Lady of the Lake*, we discover that "foeman" has been substituted for "foemen," but this creates no difficulty for us. Bartlett indexes it under "worthy," "steel," and "foemen"; the *ODQ2*, under "steel" and "foemen"; and Stevenson, only under "foemen." Alas, the tenth (". . . faintly trust the larger hope") defeats us for the time being, since it seems not to appear in any of the three collections.

The eleventh quotation ("The crowning fortune of a man . . ."), from Emerson's "Considerations by the Way" in his *Conduct of Life*, is not easy to locate, as it does not occur in Bartlett or in the *ODQ2*. But it is solvable, thanks to Stevenson, where it is indexed under "fortune," "bias" (a word that does not appear in the stated version of the quotation), and "pursuit." By contrast, the twelfth item on the list (" 'Are cradled into poetry by wrong . . .' "), from Shelley's "Julian and Maddalo," is quite simple to trace. In the *ODQ2* it is indexed under five words: "cradled," "poetry," "wrong," "suffering," and "song"; in Bartlett it is indexed under six: "cradled," "wrong," learn," "suffering," "teach," and "song"; and in Stevenson it is indexed under three: "cradled," "poetry," and "suffering."

The thirteenth passage (" 'The best of men are moulded out of faults' "), a misquotation from *Measure for Measure,* can be found in the *ODQ2* under "best," "moulded," and "faults," and in Bartlett under "best," "men," "molded," and "faults"—a good reminder that if a word has two spellings, you should check the index for both. (Ordinarily, the American spelling will be in Bartlett and the British in the *ODQ2.*) At first glance it appears not to be in Stevenson, but you can find it by scanning the items under the keyword "men" until you come to "best m. moulded of faults." The fourteenth (" 'Is every thing by fits, and nothing long' "), a misquotation—with "fits" substituted for "starts"—from Dryden's *Absalom and Achitophel,* is hard to trace. Bartlett indexes it only under the word "starts," but this helps us not at all, since few of us will know that "starts" occurs in the quotation until we have successfully traced it. In Stevenson, part of the quotation is indexed under "everything," but it is unrecognizable if you do not already know the correct wording of the quotation. In the *ODQ2* it is indexed under "everything," "nothing," "long," and "starts." Of these, the most satisfactory information occurs under "long."

The fifteenth item on the list (". . . how much sharper than a thankless tooth . . ."), Lady Kicklebury's garbled quotation from *King Lear,* presents no problem, except perhaps to someone who is a stranger in a strange land. In the *ODQ2* we find the correctly worded passage by checking the index under "sharper," "serpent," "tooth," "thankless," and "child." The same is true of Bartlett's index, except that "serpent's" is a separate entry. In Stevenson's index the words are "sharper," "serpent's," "tooth," and "child." In searching for the source of the sixteenth quotation, Wesley's statement about witchcraft, we are disappointed by Bartlett and by the *ODQ2.* However, Stevenson provides two versions, both of them credited to Wesley's journal of 1768 but with no references to edition, page, or the date of entry. Neither of these is absolutely definitive, but we shall accept them until we find something better. One is located in Stevenson by checking the index under "witchcraft"; the other, by turning to the subject "witch, witchcraft" in the body of the compilation. A somewhat similar path is taken to trace the Latin quotation in the seventeenth item ("Conjugium vocat . . ."), which is from the *Aeneid.* Bartlett and the *ODQ2* do not list the quotation, but it is included in Stevenson, where it is indexed under "conjugium."

The eighteenth (" 'The bellman writes better verses . . .' "), nineteenth (" 'Wherein the toga'd consuls . . .' "), twentieth ("Old Knowell . . . 'To dream of naught . . .' "), and twenty-first quotes ("The curse of growing factions and divisions . . ."), like the tenth (". . . faintly trust the larger hope"), defeat us for the present, since they cannot be found in any of the three collections. The defeat, however, is only temporary.

The twenty-second item (" 'The Dyer's Hand' "), the essay title from Shakespeare's Sonnet 111, is easily solved. In the *ODQ2* it is indexed under "dyer"; in Stevenson, under "hand"; and in Bartlett, under "hand" and "dyer's." Equally easy is the twenty-third (" 'To-morrow to *fresh* fields and pastures *new*' "), a common misquotation from Milton's *Lycidas*, with "fields" substituted for "woods." As usual, Bartlett's index is the most thorough. The quote is found there under "tomorrow," "fresh," "woods," "pastures," and "new." In Stevenson and the *ODQ2* the words indexed are "tomorrow," "woods," and "pastures." Of course, the quote is not listed under "fields" anywhere; and the listings under "woods" do not help us unless we know in advance to look there. Another altered quotation, the twenty-fourth (" 'His faithful *bird* still bore him Company' "), which comes originally from Pope's *Essay on Man*, is difficult to trace. The italicizing of "bird" indicates that there has probably been a substitution, and we eventually discover that there have been other modifications as well. We proceed cautiously, since we are not sure what we are looking for, trying all three indexes for "faithful," "still," "bore," "company," and "bird." In Bartlett's superb index we find the quote under "faithful." Of course, we can also find it under "dog" in all three collections, once we know to look for it there.

The twenty-fifth quotation on the list ("*Quandoque bonus dormitat Homerus*"), from Horace's *Ars Poetica*, is not difficult to trace. In all three collections it is indexed under "Homerus," and in the *ODQ2* it is indexed under "dormitat" as well. A related quotation, the twenty-sixth ("*It is not Homer nods, but we that dream*"), is attributed to Roscommon but is really from Pope's *Essay on Criticism*. It does not occur in the *ODQ2*, and to find it in Stevenson we must turn to the section on Homer in the body of the book. But in the index to Bartlett we find it under "Homer," "nods," and "dream." The twenty-seventh item ("Mosquitos 'murder sleep' ") is difficult to trace because it is a very short quotation—or a very small part of one. But if we check all three indexes for both words, we eventually succeed in finding the quotation and recognizing it. Like a hidden quote, a short quote usually is or was a very familiar one or part of a very familiar one; therefore, you should assume that it is to be found somewhere in any standard book of quotations. Since this particular quote is so short that we cannot know its original context, we must look at every line occurring in the various indexes under the two words until we come upon the passage. In the indexes to Bartlett and the *ODQ2* we find it under "murder" and "sleep," as well as under the name that is omitted, "Macbeth." To find it in Stevenson we must turn to the section on "sleep" in the book itself, unless we know to look in the index under "Macbeth."

The twenty-eighth quotation, paraphrased from E. E. Cummings (". . . there are some things I will not eat"), presents an interesting problem. It does not occur in Stevenson or in the *ODQ2*, and to find it in Bartlett we must read carefully every line indexed under "eat" until we come to the line we are seeking, or else we must turn to the E. E. Cummings section in the body of the collection and scan every quotation until we find the passage, which comes from Cummings's "i sing of Olaf glad and big." Like the writer in *Newsweek*, the editors of the fifteenth edition of Bartlett have presented the Cummings quotation without using or spelling out the word that would have offended some readers. Their omission has not delayed us in our pursuit of the quotation, however, since we start the search without knowing that anything has been left out. The fact that the offending word appears in Bartlett only as an abbreviation, both in the index under "eat" and in the quotation itself, may mislead some quote sleuths into believing that Cummings himself used the abbreviation. Rest assured that he did not.

Item twenty-nine ("Fruges consumere nati"), another quotation from Horace, occurs in the *ODQ2*, where it is indexed under "fruges," but it seems not to occur in Bartlett or in Stevenson. We are unable, at this time, to trace the thirtieth quotation (" 'Each man walks with his head . . .' "), the exquisite line attributed to the poet laureate, since it is not in any of the three dictionaries of quotations we are using.

The thirty-first quote (" 'Calm or convulsed . . .' ") seems not to occur in the *ODQ2* or in Bartlett or in Stevenson and must be added to our list of failures. The thirty-second (". . . closed their long Glories . . ."), from Pope's *Imitations of Horace*, is not in Bartlett or in the *ODQ2*, but we find it in Stevenson if we check the index under "gratitude." The thirty-third item (" '. . . Sonorous metal blowing martial sounds' "), from *Paradise Lost*, can be found in Bartlett under "sonorous," "metal," "martial," and "sounds"; in the *ODQ2* it appears under "sonorous," "metal," and "martial"; and in Stevenson, only under the noun "metal."

Of the three collections, Bartlett gets credit for locating twenty of the quotations,[3] though perhaps it should not be given full credit for number 28; grading generously, I would credit Stevenson with twenty also,[4] though it would not be unfair to mark that collection down for numbers 16, 26, and 27; and the *ODQ2* earns a score of eighteen.[5] Of the thirty-three quotations, we have succeeded with all but numbers 10, 18, 19, 20, 21, 30, and 31, though we really should not be satisfied with the answers to items 16 and 28. Eventually we shall have all of the needed solutions.

After going through this exercise, you should be more aware than ever before of the kinds of hidden, altered, modified, truncated, incorrectly recalled, and mistakenly attributed quotations with which our reading world is filled and with which we quote sleuths must deal. You should also be acquainted with the three standard dictionaries of quotations, having acquired some idea of their relative strengths in this and that area and having discovered how their indexes should be used. You have seen that some quotation collections are indexed much more generously than others, and you have had the experience of using one index that is unlike all others, namely, Stevenson's. You also have seen that different indexers go about their function in different ways, not only in deciding which keywords to use as entries, but in deciding which parts of a quotation should be listed under those keywords. Remember, too, that the index to a book of quotations must be checked carefully for every main word of the quotation you are trying to trace before you can say for certain that the compilation has failed you. And while a goodly percentage of the quotations you try to trace can be identified or verified by means of the expert use of one or another of Bartlett, the *ODQ2*, or Stevenson, you must also realize that a disappointing number of them cannot.

By now you should have some idea of the likelihood that a certain compilation will contain a certain quotation or that a certain index will turn it up on the first attempt. Also, anyone who has performed these thirty-three searches with me or after me has almost certainly chosen an all-around favorite dictionary of quotations.

Other Basic Collections

You can deal successfully and satisfactorily with perhaps the majority of your quotation problems by carefully checking one or more of the great dictionaries of quotations. When your use of these does not lead you to the solution, you may be tempted either to surrender or to proceed to one or another of the various kinds of reference works that will be discussed in other chapters; on the other hand, it is often the wiser course to continue for the time being to consult general compilations. If knowing what you know about the problem and the tools makes it seem at all likely that you will be able to identify the passage by doing some checking in some of the members of a second group of dictionaries of quotations, and if time and stamina permit, you should of course proceed in that direction.

In the second group of references are Bergen Evans's *Dictionary of Quotations;* the third edition of the *Oxford Dictionary of Quotations (ODQ3);* the still very useful *Benham's Book of Quotations, Proverbs, and Household Words* of Sir William Gurney Benham; *Hoyt's New Cyclopedia of Practical Quotations,* as revised by Kate Louise Roberts; several outdated editions of Bartlett; H. L. Mencken's *New Dictionary of Quotations on Historical Principles;* George Seldes's *Great Quotations;* Stevenson's *Home Book of Proverbs, Maxims, and Familiar Phrases;* Rhoda Tripp's *International Thesaurus of Quotations;* Franklin P. Adams's *FPA Book of Quotations;* the *Penguin Dictionary of Modern Quotations;* the *Reader's Digest Treasury of Modern Quotations; Simpson's Contemporary Quotations;* and Suzy Platt's *Respectfully Quoted.* You will doubtless wish to add two or three other works to this list, and you may even choose to subtract one or two. I may eventually do some subtracting myself, since Adams and Seldes barely made the cut.

A good place to look for the source of any English passage that strikes you as wise, witty, urbane, or memorable is Bergen Evans's *Dictionary of Quotations,* a collection of perhaps thirteen to fourteen thousand well-chosen passages. Although many of these are from the standard corpus of well-known words of tongue or pen, quite a few are not likely to be found in the three major compilations. The number of quotations included in this work is much smaller than you would expect, considering the book's size and weight, but the collection has some real strengths, the chief ones being the quality of its selections and the thoroughness of its index. The quotations, all of which are in English, are representative of many periods and many literatures. The book is well stocked with really fine illustrative quotations from all periods and with fairly recent quotations from literary and political figures. Also, it is a book to consult when tracing a classical or foreign passage by means of its English rendering.

The twelve hundred–page index to the eight hundred pages of quotations in Evans's compilation is doubly generous, in the number of index entries used for each quotation and in the length of the passages given under these keywords. With the help of this index I was able to trace eighteen of the thirty-three passages.[6] (Remember, I also found eighteen in the *ODQ2,* twenty in Stevenson, and twenty in Bartlett.) The tenth quotation (". . . faintly trust the larger hope"), which comes from *In Memoriam,* was found in Evans though not in any of the three major tools; and though not in Evans's index, Wesley's statement in the sixteenth item turns up correctly worded and with three complete source citations in a note to another quotation on witchcraft. Moreover, the long passages included in the index under the keywords in the second ("The world was now all before Mr. Sponge where to choose . . ."), fifth (". . . have seen 'Twain' steadily and seen it whole . . ."), and fourteenth (" 'Is every thing by fits, and nothing long' ") passages make recognition of the quotes instantaneous.

Evans's book is not a large collection, despite its bulk. It takes longer to locate things in Evans than it does to find things in Bartlett or the *ODQ2*, and Evans does not include Latin, Greek, French, German, or Italian quotations in their original languages—quotations we do have to trace from time to time. Over the years, if we quote sleuths see the Evans book steadily, and if we see it whole, I think we shall appreciate it more as a supplement than as a first source. I recommend it as ordinarily the first place to check after the *ODQ2*, Bartlett, and Stevenson, but I will not quarrel with anyone who consults it sooner than that.

Although considerably weaker, numerically speaking, than the *ODQ2*, the third edition of the *Oxford Dictionary of Quotations* is a fine collection of almost seventeen thousand quotations. It omits thousands of quotes included in the earlier work and contains thousands not included in the *ODQ2*. It is organized like the *ODQ2*, with author sections in alphabetical order. However, the index to the *ODQ3*, while very easy to read and convenient to use, is significantly weaker than the indexes of the *ODQ2* and Bartlett; as a result, someone trying to trace a short quotation or a misquotation or a quotation that has only a few words in common with a passage in the *ODQ3* may fail to discover that the *ODQ3* does indeed contain the passage sought. For example, if we used the *ODQ3* to trace the quotations listed in chapter 1, we would fail to solve the second ("The world was now all before Mr. Sponge . . ."), fifth (". . . have seen 'Twain' steadily and seen it whole . . ."), fourteenth ("Is every thing by fits, and nothing long"), twenty-fourth (" 'His faithful *bird* . . .' "), twenty-fifth ("*Quandoque bonus* . . ."), and twenty-ninth ("Fruges consumere nati") quotes, *even though the collection contains all of them*. The second item is indexed only under "choose" ("c. their place of rest"); the fifth is indexed only under "life," which does not occur in the version being traced, as is the case with the fourteenth, indexed only under "starts," and the twenty-fourth, indexed only under "dog." The twenty-fifth item occurs in the *ODQ3* in Latin and in English but is indexed only in English; similarly, the twenty-ninth is indexed under "numerus," which does not occur in the version being traced, and under two English words. We can compensate somewhat for the weakness of the index by checking under every possible keyword before giving up and by scanning the quotes in the author section when the name of the author is already known; but these maneuvers would not have been successful in the above instances.

Dr. Johnson's Hodge was not his all-time favorite feline, but he still considered him "a very fine cat, a very fine cat indeed." Although not as strong or as well indexed as the *ODQ2* or Bartlett, the *ODQ3* is still a very fine dictionary of quotations, and even by means of its weak index we are able to find fourteen of the thirty-three quotations.[7] Being a recent publication, the *ODQ3* is very helpful in tracing twentieth-century quotations, and it is strong in quotations from women writers of many centuries. It is a good supplement to the three collections of the first group, especially in its areas of strength. And in all areas it is scholarly, reliable, and authoritative.[8]

Unlike any other dictionary of quotations is *Benham's Book of Quotations, Proverbs, and Household Words,* by Sir William Gurney Benham, which has also been published as *Putnam's Dictionary of Thoughts.* This marvelous collection contains thousands of quotations, including a large selection from English and American authors, though access is somewhat limited. Each quotation is, as a rule, indexed only once: all or part of it is listed under one keyword or one subject. Also, the index heading is not necessarily a word that appears in the quotation. Classical and foreign quotations are not represented in the index, but quotes in each foreign language section are arranged in alphabetical order by initial word. Despite limited access to the quotations, I managed to find and recognize seventeen of the thirty-three items on my list, though the twelfth (" 'Are cradled into poetry by wrong . . .' "), twenty-third (" 'To-morrow to *fresh* fields and pastures *new*' "), and twenty-seventh ("'Mosquitos 'murder sleep' ") were not immediately obvious.[9]

Another four of the quotes are contained in *Benham's,* but they cannot be found by using the information given in the quotations; nor can they be recognized from the short phrase found in the index: the third quote (". . . the rest was but a sleep . . .") is indexed under "birth"; the fourteenth (" 'Is every thing by fits . . .' ") appears in the index, correctly, as "Everything by starts," but most searchers would not recognize it; the twenty-fourth ("His faithful *bird* . . .") is indexed, again correctly, under "dogs"; and the passage corresponding to the twenty-ninth quote (" 'Fruges consumere nati' ") begins with "Nos." On the other hand, *Benham's* did help out with two of our earlier failures: the tenth quotation (". . . faintly trust the larger hope"), from *In Memoriam,* which we also found in Evans; and the twentieth ("To dream of naught but idle poetry"), a misquotation from Jonson's *Every Man in His Humour.*

Despite its outstanding success rate, few literary detectives would wish to begin a quote search with *Benham's*, with its one-chance index and its small sections of one-chance alphabetized classical and foreign quotations. Still, there is a strong possibility that it will help you locate the source of a quotation not found in Bartlett, the *ODQ2*, or Stevenson, so it must rank very high as a supplement to those works in tracing quotations that antedate 1900.

An early twentieth-century collection of great value is Kate Louise Roberts's *Hoyt's New Cyclopedia of Practical Quotations*. Of course, you should not begin with this work, even if the quotation being traced is obviously an old one, for among general dictionaries of quotations older usually means less reliable. In the wording of passages, in the quality of source citations, and in the choice of texts upon which quotations and citations are based, the best recent collections are far superior to the best collections of past years. However, as a supplement to other compilations, *Hoyt's* is an important resource for Latin quotations and for those quotations in English originating earlier than about 1920. Of the thirty-three quotations, twelve can be found easily and quickly by means of the fine index in *Hoyt's*.[10] Also, I was able to locate the thirty-second quote (". . . closed their long Glories . . .") by looking under "gratitude" in the body of the book. Despite *Hoyt's* less than outstanding showing in our exercise, I recommend it highly.

Just as *Benham's* and *Hoyt's* are useful when we are tracing older quotations, old editions of Bartlett may also serve us on occasion. For over a century Bartlett's editors have been dropping as well as adding, and quotations not in the latest edition may be retrieved without effort or loss of time by means of the excellent indexes of the old editions. The fourteenth, thirteenth, twelfth, eleventh, and even earlier editions can be consulted, sometimes with some success, whenever the need arises.

As compiler H. L. Mencken wrote, *A New Dictionary of Quotations on Historical Principles* "confines itself to authors who really had something to say, and said it to some effect."[11] There is no index in this work, but thousands of quotations are found under hundreds of rubrics, and there are references from one rubric to another. To find Lady Kicklebury's Shakespeare quotation (the fifteenth item on the list), I tried "ingratitude" first and then "thankless," which referred me to "child," which led me to the information I sought. Tracing the fourth quote (". . . the many whose withers are unwrung"), I tried "withers" and was referred to "jade" and from there to the solution. In all, I located nine of the thirty-three quotations and would have found two more if I had known to look for the third under "birth" and for the twenty-fourth under "dog."[12] No one who does much work with quotations will want to use Mencken's book early in the search process, but its wealth of well-selected utterances is bound to help the quote sleuth eventually. It should be kept in mind and consulted now and then for quotations from "authors who really had something to say, and said it to some effect."

Occasionally helpful in the pursuit of sources is George Seldes's *Great Quotations*, a compilation of statements of ideas from influential thinkers. Most of the quotations are in prose, and most do not appear in other compilations. In the original hardbound edition the arrangement of quotations is by author; a very short subject index lists authors and page numbers. In the paperback edition quotes are arranged by subject. In both, source citations are minimal—author and title or merely author. Although Seldes is not a work to be used routinely, the weary searcher should consult it when the passage being traced contains an idea of some significance and the name of the thinker is known or suspected.

Not to be forgotten by the quotation tracer is Burton Stevenson's *Home Book of Proverbs, Maxims, and Familiar Phrases*. Even if you are not actually looking for a proverb, bear in mind that the book contains maxims and familiar phrases, both of which concern the quote sleuth very much, and also proverbs and restatements of proverbs. Many of the quotations you will be called upon to trace belong to one or more of these categories and thus qualify for inclusion in this collection. To my surprise I succeeded in locating in this work ten of the thirty-three quotations on the list.[13]

In Rhoda Thomas Tripp's *International Thesaurus of Quotations*, prose or poetical statements about some aspect of life are arranged according to subject categories. Over one-third of the passages come from the twentieth century. With a generous keyword index, the work is easy to use. An older, less scholarly collection is Franklin P. Adams's *FPA Book of Quotations*, an assemblage of some fifteen thousand quotations appearing under more than a thousand rubrics. Regrettably, there is no keyword index, and source citations lack detail. I faintly recommend this book, mainly as a supplementary source of twentieth-century quotations. When it was published in 1952, it was said to contain the most extensive representation of quotations from major political and literary figures of the twentieth century.

A useful little collection of quotations of fairly recent vintage is the *Penguin Dictionary of Modern Quotations*, compiled by J. M. Cohen and M. J. Cohen. The quotes are well chosen, but documentation and indexing are not sufficiently detailed. Since each quotation is listed in the index under only one keyword, you should check it for several likely words before giving up. The book includes the two modern quotations from our list, those from Dylan Thomas and E. E. Cummings. The latter quote appears in the book, but we miss it in the one-chance index because we do not know the catchword. We find the quote easily enough under the author, though the source given is not a poem title but a page number in a collection. (A better tool for tracing Cummings quotations is mentioned in chapter 6 and in the corresponding section of the bibliography.)

Another collection of quotes of fairly recent origin is the *Reader's Digest Treasury of Modern Quotations,* which contains about six thousand quotations listed under about seventy broad headings, all traceable by means of a keyword index of sorts. Typically, the only source citation is the name of the author followed by the title of a book or a reference to the issue of a periodical, such as *Reader's Digest,* in which the quote appeared. If a magazine is named, be sure to locate the quote in the periodical itself, where you may also find a helpful reference to a source. This work is especially valuable when the authorship of the modern quotation being traced is already known or when the quotation simply seems to be something likely to have appealed to the editors of *Reader's Digest.*

Still another dictionary of modern passages is *Simpson's Contemporary Quotations.* This collection of about ten thousand quotations from almost four thousand people is based largely on media coverage of the years 1950 to 1987 and should prove to be a powerful aid to the tracer of recent quotations, especially when authorship is already known and when the quotation being traced seems unlikely to have had its origin in a book.

The most attractive and probably the most interesting book of quotations published in recent years is Suzy Platt's *Respectfully Quoted: A Dictionary of Quotations Requested from the Congressional Research Service.* The two thousand or so quotations included may be variously characterized as political or historical or judicial or literary or presidential or modern, and all of them have been of interest to political leaders. Most of the source citations are scholarly and detailed; some of the quotations have not yet been traced or verified, but authenticity has not been claimed for these. There is a good index of subjects, authors, and keywords.

For quotations thought to have their origin in the twentieth century, I suggest you consult some such sequence of general collections as this one before going on to other resources: the latest edition of Bartlett; the *ODQ3;* the *Penguin Dictionary of Modern Quotations;* Tripp; *Simpson's;* the *Reader's Digest Treasury;* Evans; Platt; Stevenson; the *ODQ2;* and Adams. You should, of course, eliminate any that seem especially unlikely at the moment. Other resources include likely single-author and single-subject quotation books, to be discussed in later chapters, and indexes to newspapers, both printed and computerized. Recent or contemporary sayings may be located, I am told, by full-text computer searches of the *New York Times* or the *Washington Post* databases available on the NEXIS system.

Before leaving the second group of collections, let us look at what remains to be identified from our list of thirty-three quotations. Since we have successfully traced the tenth, sixteenth, twentieth, and twenty-eighth items with the aid of some of these works, only five can still be considered problems: the eighteenth (" 'The bellman writes better verses . . .' "), nineteenth (" 'Wherein the toga'd consuls . . .' "), twenty-first ("The curse of growing factions . . ."), thirtieth (" '. . . a cloud of poisonous flies' "), and thirty-first ("Calm or convulsed . . .").

Older Collections

A third group of quotation compilations consists of some repositories of information that can be consulted from time to time if they are available and if the conditions seem right. Some of these are quite ancient, but most appeared between 1850 and 1930. The majority of those mentioned are organized by subject and do not include a keyword index. Two interesting features of many of these are the large amount of material they have in common and their similarities in organization of contents and references to sources. (One might even suspect that compilers borrowed from one another, but I make no such accusation.) The typical source citation in many of these collections is the name of the purported author of a quotation. With only an alphabetical subject arrangement as a guide, consulting one of these books is a real chore; and if by chance you succeed in locating the quotation you seek, you still must attempt to determine just where in the works of a voluminous author that passage occurs. Still, it is a great relief to be directed to the works of one author, as this eliminates, at least for a time, hundreds or even thousands of other possibilities.

A heavy nineteenth-century tome still found on the reference shelves of some libraries, as indeed it should be, is *Day's Collacon: An Encyclopaedia of Prose Quotations*, by Edward Parsons Day, a book of maxims and words of wisdom arranged alphabetically by subject. Similarly organized and similarly characterized by undocumented author attributions is Charles Noel Douglas's *Forty Thousand Sublime and Beautiful Thoughts*, also published as *Forty Thousand Quotations, Prose and Poetical*. Comparable in organization and documentation is Tryon Edwards's *Dictionary of Thoughts*; the edition I occasionally use is the *New Dictionary of Thoughts*, revised and enlarged by C. N. Catrevas.

Different from the collections mentioned above and from one another are works by Sarah Josepha Hale, James Wood, and Samuel
Austin Allibone. Hale's *Complete Dictionary of Poetical Quotations* contains quotes arranged by subject, from the "old British poets" and from
authors who were in 1849 the modern British and American poets.
There is, unfortunately, no keyword index. Wood's *Dictionary of Quotations from Ancient and Modern, English and Foreign Sources,* also published as the *Nuttall Dictionary of Quotations,* is organized alphabetically by initial word. Authors are named, but works are not. Allibone's
Prose Quotations from Socrates to Macaulay lacks a keyword index but
is at least organized by subject. Generally, long passages are accompanied by relatively complete citations; short passages are traced only
to their authors. A companion volume, Allibone's *Poetical Quotations
from Chaucer to Tennyson,* is also organized by subject. While it, too,
lacks a keyword index, it does contain a helpful first-line index to the
quotations. Source citations consist of only the names of the authors.

Also useful on occasion are some still older collections. Edward
Bysshe's *Art of English Poetry,* first published in 1702, contains poetical
and dramatic quotations, largely from the seventeenth century, arranged by subject and with incomplete and abbreviated documentation. A similar collection is Thomas Hayward's *British Muse; or, A
Collection of Thoughts Moral, Natural, and Sublime, of Our English Poets
Who Flourished in the Sixteenth and Seventeenth Centuries,* which was
also published as *The Quintessence of English Poetry.* Another eigh-
teenth-century quotation compilation is *A Poetical Dictionary; or, The
Beauties of the English Poets.* Similar to all of these but limited to dramatic excerpts is *The Beauties of the English Stage,* also published as
The Beauties of the English Drama. Each is characterized by a subject
arrangement of quotations, by the absence of a keyword index, and
by incomplete and abbreviated source citations. Even if you succeed
in finding what you seek in one of these works, you still have far to
go. However, these works can be helpful in turning up sources of old
quotations; and occasionally you will discover that there is a concordance to the works of the author so identified.

I have solved a number of quotations by using these and other old
dictionaries of quotations. Once I needed to trace these lines, which
had been quoted without attribution in 1768:

Who can behold such beauty and be silent!
Desire first taught us words—
Man when created, wander'd up and down,
But when a heav'n-born maid like you appear'd,
Strange pleasure fill'd his eyes, and seiz'd his heart,
Unloos'd his tongue, and his first talk was love.

Using Bysshe's *Art of English Poetry* (though *The Beauties of the English Stage* would have done as well), I was able to identify the source of the lines as Otway's play *The Orphan*.[14] A more correct version of the passage than the one given above appeared in Bysshe under the subject "love—protestations of love," though not under "beauty." Of course, I still had to locate the lines in the play.

In this chapter we have looked at a large number of compilations of several centuries, proceeding from the very useful to the only occasionally useful. There are still others for you to discover independently. Ordinarily, you should begin with the first group of quotation dictionaries; if these do not work, consult likely works from the second group. If these do not work either, and if the passage being traced is an old one that fits clearly under a standard topic from "ability" to "zeal" or seems at all likely to be found in the alphabetical listing of old quotations in James Wood's collection, then proceed to certain books in the third class, if they are available. Special tools and more imaginative approaches, to be discussed in future chapters, may be used next if needed.

All of this is good general advice, but it should not be followed too literally. The tracer's goals are to identify the source of a quotation, to find or to produce a detailed citation based on a reliable edition of the work, to find an authoritative text of the passage being traced, and to do all this in the shortest time possible and with the least possible amount of effort. If an approach discussed in another chapter seems very likely to enable you to achieve these goals, and if the temptation to bypass most of the compilations discussed here is very great, then by all means strike off in other directions. But return to the compilations if other methods fail.

NOTES

1. Sir Winston Churchill, *My Early Life: A Roving Commission* (London: Thornton Butterworth, 1930), 130.

2. Burton Stevenson, comp., *The Home Book of Quotations*, 10th ed. (New York: Dodd, Mead and Co., 1967), 2420.

3. Nos. 1–9, 12–13, 15, 22–28, 33.

4. Nos. 1–4, 6, 8–9, 11–13, 15–17, 22–23, 25–27, 32–33.

5. Nos. 1–6, 8–9, 12–15, 22–23, 25, 27, 29, 33.

6. Nos. 1–10, 12–16, 22–23, 33.

7. Nos. 1, 3–4, 6–9, 12–13, 15, 22–23, 27, 33.

8. The *ODQ3* does contain mistakes, however. See my review in *Notes and Queries* 227 (February 1982): 86–88.

9. Nos. 1–2, 4, 6, 8–10, 12–13, 15, 17, 20, 22–23, 25–27.

10. Nos. 1–2, 5, 8–9, 12, 15, 23, 25–27, 33.

11. H. L. Mencken, comp., *A New Dictionary of Quotations on Historical Principles* (New York: Alfred A. Knopf, 1942), vi.

12. Nos. 1, 4, 9, 12–13, 15, 23, 25, 27.

13. Nos. 1–2, 4, 6, 8–9, 12–13, 23, 25.

14. *Notes and Queries* 223 (February 1978): 71; ibid., (December 1978): 541.

3 | Single-Subject and Special-Category Quotation Books

If the resources discussed so far fail to supply the information you need, then it is time to consider using other tools and other methods. One approach is to consult a book made up of quotations about a certain subject, or quotations from a certain genre, or quotations representative of a certain type of human utterance, or quotations from persons belonging to a certain classification. There are books of quotations on such subjects as America and American life, authors, authorship, books and reading, business and economics, communism, education, law, medicine, military matters, music, persons, places, politics, religion, science, and sports. There are quotation collections limited to such special categories or such literary forms as aphorisms, last words, proverbs, and similes. There are collections that consist entirely of quotations from Australians, blacks, Canadians, Catholics, the Irish, Jews, or presidents; and there are others that contain quotations from movies or from novels. There are also collections that are limited to quotations in classical or foreign languages, but these will be dealt with in a later chapter. In the pages that follow, we shall examine a number of special compilations. Some of them are very useful indeed, some will prove to be helpful from time to time, and a few others may possibly be of service someday.

The main purpose of most of these single-subject and special-category compilations is to provide a small collection of apt quotations on certain subjects for the embellishment of speeches and articles and for the entertainment or the education of the interested user or reader. Although many of these books are as scholarly as one could wish, many others seem to have been hastily assembled, and most of them lack satisfactory documentation and adequate indexing. However, these special collections often contain information that the standard quotation dictionaries fail to provide. A source reference consisting only of the name of an author may lead the tracer of a quotation to the source of a passage—or the attribution may be enough to satisfy the casual inquirer.

A book devoted to one subject or to one category of utterance should never be the very first thing you consult, even if a quotation is recognized as an aphorism or a deathbed statement, or if it is clearly about economics or music, or if you are sure that the author was a president. No, you must first plod through the resources discussed in chapter 2, leaving these special tools unopened until you conclude that the time to consult them has finally come.

Subject Collections

AMERICA. Clifton Fadiman's well-known *American Treasury, 1455–1955* is a collection of quotable passages about the United States—its government, its history, and its people—as well as a collection of quotations by notable Americans about practically anything. Source citations are incomplete, some lamentably so. The book has indexes to subjects, authors, and familiar words and phrases. A more recent work on America is Mike Edelhart and James Tinen's *America the Quotable*, which contains thousands of quotations about America, American life, and individual states, cities, and regions. Source citations lack the details that facilitate verification of information. There is an author index but no keyword index, forcing the tracer of a quote of unknown authorship to scan the appropriate section. The book is harder to use than *The American Treasury*, but it does include a number of interesting quotations, based on recent sources as well as old ones. Other works that contain quotations about America will be considered under "Places."

AUTHORS. Quotations about individual authors occur in dozens of general, subject, and special compilations. Perhaps the most useful of these is the collection of Kenin and Wintle, which will be mentioned in the section on "Persons." An old work that can be used in tracing or verifying quotations about authors of earlier centuries than ours is Charles Wells Moulton's *Library of Literary Criticism of English and American Authors*.

AUTHORSHIP. Quotations on authorship occur even in the standard general collections. The passages in these well-indexed books are authoritatively worded and definitively documented, and you should begin with them when a quote about authorship (or about anything else) is to be traced. If these prove unsuccessful, a book of quotations on writing may supply an author attribution that will serve as the beginning of another search. Jon Winokur's *Writers on Writing* contains about fifteen hundred interesting quotes accompanied by author ascriptions. The subject index is in some cases a keyword index. James Charlton's *Writer's Quotation Book* contains perhaps six hundred statements on the subject of writing that are attributed to twentieth-century writers. Since there is no index, the only way to locate any of these sparkling quotations is to leaf through the book.

BOOKS AND READING. Although not a book of quotations, Holbrook Jackson's *Anatomy of Bibliomania* is filled with well-documented quotations about books and reading. Joseph Shaylor's *Pleasures of Literature and the Solace of Books* contains approximately seventy-five classic prose extracts about books and reading from important nineteenth-century English and American writers and statesmen. A similar collection is John Alfred Langford's *Praise of Books*, which consists of passages in prose and verse from English authors.

BUSINESS AND ECONOMICS. There are not many collections of quotes in the area of business and economics that are of much value to the quotation tracer. Outstanding, however, is Simon James's *Dictionary of Economic Quotations*, a well-indexed collection of about two thousand carefully chosen, admirably referenced quotes. Robert W. Kent's *Money Talks* contains about twenty-five hundred undocumented quotations occurring under about fifteen broad topics. There is an author index but no subject or keyword index. A bit easier to use than *Money Talks* is Michael Jackman's *Macmillan Book of Business and Economic Quotations*. In it some three thousand undocumented quotations occur under about sixty topics. There is a keyword index, but since not all the quotations appear in it, scanning of likely sections is also necessary. George Thomas Kurian's *Handbook of Business Quotations*, a potpourri of some nine hundred quotations appearing under some three hundred fifty topics, contains unverifiable (or not easily verifiable) author attributions. A table of contents lists the many subjects, and there is a name index. The books by Kent, Jackman, and Kurian, while lacking any real authoritativeness, may nonetheless be of possible use to the quotation tracer.

Jerry Rosenberg's *Dictionary of Business and Management* is not itself a book of quotations, but it does contain an appendix of almost four hundred "relevant quotations," ordered alphabetically by author. Source citations lack many details, and there is no keyword index, although there is a subject index to the quotations.

COMMUNISM. Albert L. Weeks's *Brassey's Soviet and Communist Quotations* contains more than two thousand quotes, all of them in English, from communist theorists and leaders of the past and present. Documentation is excellent, and there are subject and keyword indexes.

EDUCATION. The best collection of quotations on education is Bernard E. Farber's *Teacher's Treasury of Quotations*. Some five thousand passages appear under six hundred or so alphabetically arranged rubrics. Source citations are relatively complete, and there are indexes to authors and subjects. Only the absence of a keyword index keeps this book from being an excellent reference work for our purposes.

August Kerber's *Quotable Quotes on Education* is useful to the tracer of quotations, despite its deficiencies. It includes about twenty-five hundred minimally referenced passages under a broad range of topics. There are indexes to authors and subjects but not keywords. Somewhat more literary in content is N. B. Sen's *Glorious Thoughts on Education*. Quotes appear under several broad subjects, listed alphabetically by author. Here, too, the source citations are minimal.

LAW. Three excellent collections of well-chosen, well-documented, and well-indexed law quotations are M. Frances McNamara's *Ragbag of Legal Quotations*, republished as *2,000 Famous Legal Quotations*; Eugene C. Gerhart's *Quote It! Memorable Legal Quotations*; and Simon James and Chantal Stebbings's *Dictionary of Legal Quotations*. Less useful is David Shrager and Elizabeth Frost's *Quotable Lawyer*, a collection of twenty-five hundred or so quotations accompanied by source citations that lack many details needed for easy verification of information. The latter has an author index and a subject index but no keyword index.

Percival E. Jackson's *Wisdom of the Supreme Court* is a noteworthy collection of quotations from judicial opinions and other writings of members of our highest tribunal. An old but scholarly collection of quotations from English chancellors and judges is James William Norton-Kyshe's *Dictionary of Legal Quotations*. Paul C. Cook's *Treasury of Legal Quotations* contains a small number of lengthy excerpts from judicial opinions. Leon Mead and F. Newell Gilbert's *Manual of Forensic Quotations*, which was published around the turn of the century, is a small collection of quotations taken from English and American trials and speeches.

MEDICINE. *Medical Quotes*, a recent work by John Daintith and Amanda Isaacs, is a slim collection of some two thousand interesting quotations, old and new, in topical arrangement. Source citations lack detail, but many of them can be verified with a little effort. Access is provided by a keyword and key phrase index and a name index. Maurice Benjamin Strauss's *Familiar Medical Quotations* is a fine collection of more than seven thousand quotes arranged by subjects and indexed by keywords. Source citations vary in the amount of detail provided, but most of them give author, title, and chapter or section.

MILITARY MATTERS. Robert Debs Heinl's *Dictionary of Military and Naval Quotations* is a collection, in English, of some six thousand well-chosen passages. Authors include poets, dramatists, generals, presidents, historians, and novelists. Source citations lack detail, but they are more complete than those in most other single-subject collections. There is no keyword access, but there are indexes to subjects and authors.

MUSIC. Ian Crofton and Donald Fraser's *Dictionary of Musical Quotations* contains some three thousand first-rate quotes on all aspects of traditional music. Citations lack chapter or page references, but in other respects this is a fine collection. There are an author index and an index of subjects and keywords. Also useful is Nat Shapiro's *Encyclopedia of Quotations about Music*, which contains nearly two thousand quotes accompanied by source citations that vary in quality. There are good indexes to names and sources and to keywords and phrases. Nicolas Slonimsky's *Lexicon of Musical Invective* is an anthology of unflattering judgments about composers, arranged by composer and indexed by vituperative or deprecatory words and phrases.

PERSONS. Many collections contain some quotations about individuals, but Richard Kenin and Justin Wintle's *Dictionary of Biographical Quotation of British and American Subjects* consists only of this type of quote. Included in this large volume are quotations from a variety of sources on more than a thousand famous or infamous British or American persons no longer living. Source citations usually lack some desirable details. Miriam Ringo's *Nobody Said It Better* is a small collection of interesting quotations about famous people. The citations are adequate, and there are subject, author, and keyword indexes.

PLACES. The *Travellers' Dictionary of Quotation*, by Peter Yapp, is a monumental collection of thousands of quotes about places and peoples. The arrangement is alphabetical under place-names—countries, continents, oceans, and so on—and then alphabetical again under these headings for lesser place-names. Source citations are incomplete, and there is no keyword index, but the book does include an index of places and peoples as well as an index of persons quoted. *The City: A Dictionary of Quotable Thought on Cities and Urban Life*, compiled by James A. Clapp, consists of some five thousand passages on specific cities and on urban living in general. Documentation varies in quality from poor to fair. There are indexes to cities and to subjects but not to keywords.

Although quotations about any place-name on the map may be sought in Clapp or in Yapp, still other resources exist. Quotes about Australia appear in a book of Australian quotations to be discussed below; quotations about the United States appear in the books discussed under "America." In addition to using books of quotations, the adventurous tracer can look for and look at anthologies about places.

POLITICS. If the large general collections of quotations do not identify the source of a political quotation, a good book to consult is Robert MacKenzie Stewart's *Dictionary of Political Quotations*, a scholarly, well-documented, well-indexed collection of some twenty-three hundred political statements. Jonathon Green's *Book of Political Quotes* contains three thousand or so not very accessible quotations arranged under about twenty general topics. Source citations lack detail, and since the only index is an author index, it is difficult to locate a quotation unless you already know the name of the author. Michael Jackman's *Crown's Book of Political Quotations* contains twenty-five hundred short statements arranged by subject. Source references mention only the names of the purported authors.

Of value in tracking short phrases used by or applied to English political figures of the nineteenth and early twentieth centuries is Hugh Montgomery and Philip G. Cambray's *Dictionary of Political Phrases and Allusions*. Still other places to look for sources of quotations on politics are the dictionaries of legal quotations, the books about America already discussed, Suzy Platt's *Respectfully Quoted*, the collections of presidential quotations to be considered later in this chapter, and likely single-author quotation books.

RELIGION. In trying to identify the source of a religious quotation, you should always begin with basic and supplemental general collections of quotations. If these do not work, then proceed to dictionaries of religious quotations, with the understanding that success is unlikely. So far as I know, there is no large, scholarly, well-organized, well-indexed collection of carefully chosen, correctly worded, well-referenced religious quotations; however, the compilations that do exist may be of some help.

The two best-known collections of quotations in this area are Frank S. Mead's *Encyclopedia of Religious Quotations* and Ralph Woods's *World Treasury of Religious Quotations*. Mead's book contains about twelve thousand quotes arranged topically. Poetical and biblical source citations are detailed, but others are undocumented author attributions or author and title references lacking specificity. A weak index of topics, which in some cases is a keyword index, refers to page numbers in the dictionary. The Woods collection contains more than fifteen thousand passages arranged by topic. Biblical and poetical passages are excluded, source citations are incomplete, and the only index is an author index. Looking for a quotation in either of these collections is a weariness of the flesh; and even if the quotation sought is located, the task of verification remains.

Recently published collections that I have seen do not merit our attention, but one of the older compilations perhaps does. A classic used by old-time preachers was F. B. Proctor's *Classified Gems of Thought*, recently republished as the *Treasury of Quotations on Religious Subjects*, which consists of short and long quotes arranged under about three thousand topics. Source citations supply only the names of the authors. There is a good subject index.

John Chapin's important compilation from Catholic sources is discussed under "Catholics"; collections from Jewish sources are discussed under "Jews." In tracing quotations thought to be biblical in origin, you should ordinarily begin with the standard dictionaries of quotations and then, if necessary, consult specialized works. A good book of quotations from the Good Book is Burton Stevenson's *Home Book of Bible Quotations*. If this reference work fails, then a biblical concordance is the next step. Some tracers, I hasten to add, prefer to use a biblical concordance as the second step, or even as the first.

SCIENCE. Alan L. Mackay's *Harvest of a Quiet Eye* is a charming collection of perhaps fifteen hundred passages in prose and verse on various scientific subjects. Documentation is good, though usually chapter and page references are lacking, and there is a helpful keyword index.

SPORTS. Collections on sports are a disappointing lot. These books lack keyword indexes, making it difficult to locate a particular quotation if you do not already know the name of the purported author. In addition, source citations in most of these compilations consist merely of author attributions. Perhaps the least unsatisfactory general sports collections are by Barry Liddle and by Bob Abel and Michael Valenti. Liddle's *Dictionary of Sports Quotations* is a well-documented assortment of about twelve hundred somewhat bookish, largely British quotes. Liddle includes subject and author indexes. Abel and Valenti's *Sports Quotes* consists of some thirteen hundred relatively long passages on fifty aspects of sport. Citations accompanying the quotes give few details, but a chapter on sources provides a media reference for almost every quotation.

Better quotations, and quotations you are more likely to need to identify, are found in Andrew J. Maikovich's *Sports Quotations*, a collection of almost eighteen hundred undocumented quotes on various sporty topics. The book has subject and name indexes but no keyword index; to look for a quotation whose author is unknown to you, you must scan the appropriate section. Fortunately, scanning in this book is a pleasure. Another general sports collection deficient in documentation is Lee Green's *Sportswit*, a handsome book of about twenty-five hundred sports quotations arranged under some one hundred rubrics. Two books of quotations about the national pastime are Bob Chieger's *Voices of Baseball* and Kevin Nelson's *Baseball's Greatest Quotes*. Another collection pertaining to a single sport is Bob Chieger and Pat Sullivan's *Inside Golf*. Documentation in the latter three is weak or nonexistent, and the indexes are helpful only if you know the name of the sports figure thought to be the author of the quotation.

Genre Categories

APHORISMS. Collections of aphorisms may be of occasional use to the quotation tracer. W. H. Auden and Louis Kronenberger's compilation, *The Viking Book of Aphorisms,* also published as *The Faber Book of Aphorisms,* contains more than three thousand pithy statements arranged under general topics. Unfortunately, source citations consist only of the names of authors. The book has an author index and a subject index. *The Oxford Book of Aphorisms,* edited by John Gross, lists about thirty-five hundred maxims, arranged by topic. Source citations usually supply author, title, and date but no page references. There is an author index but no subject or keyword index. An older collection is Logan Pearsall Smith's *Treasury of English Aphorisms.* Here, too, quotations appear under scattered topics and are not indexed except by author. However, the source citations are excellent. Since keyword indexes are lacking in all three collections, you should ordinarily use these books only to trace a quotation already attributed to a certain author. Finding a quote in Auden and Kronenberger would not constitute a definitive identification, since documentation is lacking in that book, but it would add some support to the attribution and to the wording. The collections of Gross and Smith, however, contain useful references to printed sources.

LAST WORDS. There are several collections of the putative last words of the dying and of spoken or written pronouncements made by persons contemplating death. However, in tracing or in trying to verify such purported quotations, you should begin with the standard dictionaries of quotations, where indexing is very good and where standards of transcription and citation are high. Bartlett and the *ODQ2* should come first, followed by Stevenson and a few others, with books of last words being consulted only after the others have failed. Incidentally, Stevenson prefaces a list of last words with a warning that we should all remember: "The reputed last words of famous men are always open to suspicion."[1]

Of the books of last words, the only scholarly collection is Edward S. Le Comte's *Dictionary of Last Words.* It contains 1,664 ultimate utterances arranged by author. In a separate chapter, which should not be overlooked, printed sources are indicated for each quotation. There is no keyword index, but for once this is not a serious deficiency since, in tracing or verifying last words, we almost always begin with the name of the deceased. A popular recent collection is Barnaby Conrad's

Famous Last Words, which contains about eight hundred fifty dying pronouncements arranged by purported author. There are no references to sources and no indexes. Still another recent compilation is Herbert Lockyer's *Last Words of Saints and Sinners,* which contains some seven hundred undocumented examples.

PROVERBS. Many quotations are either proverbs or statements that resemble or restate proverbs. In tracing such passages to collections of proverbs or to literary works, several books may prove to be of value. An excellent compilation is Burton Stevenson's *Home Book of Proverbs, Maxims, and Familiar Phrases,* also published as *The Macmillan Book of Proverbs, Maxims, and Famous Phrases.* For our purposes this is probably the most useful compilation, although other collections should not be disregarded. An old classic is W. Carew Hazlitt's *English Proverbs and Proverbial Phrases,* in which many adages are traced to early appearances. Two later and more detailed works are George L. Apperson's *English Proverbs and Proverbial Phrases: A Historical Dictionary* and *The Oxford Dictionary of English Proverbs,* both of which provide many illustrative quotations from literature. Archer Taylor and Bartlett Jere Whiting's *Dictionary of American Proverbs and Proverbial Phrases, 1820–80* is a useful index to passages appearing in the works of American writers of the nineteenth century.

SIMILES. Frank J. Wilstach's *Dictionary of Similes* contains about nineteen thousand similes from the works of twenty-four hundred authors. Since source citations are merely the names of the authors, considerable searching may remain after a quotation's author has been identified. This unusual reference work should be consulted when the standard sources have been used without success and when the quotation to be traced includes a comparison introduced by "like" or "as." Wilstach's book can provide information that will not be found in other collections.

Author Categories

AUSTRALIANS. Stephen Murray-Smith's *Dictionary of Australian Quotations* contains about four thousand quotes by Australians or about Australia. The documentation in this scholarly book is excellent, and there is a good keyword index as well as an index of subjects and ideas.

BLACKS. Anita King's useful *Quotations in Black* contains some eleven hundred quotes by more than two hundred blacks from all over the world. There are indexes to subjects and keywords and to authors.

CANADIANS. Robert M. Hamilton and Dorothy Shields's *Dictionary of Canadian Quotations and Phrases* lists about ten thousand passages under almost two thousand topics and provides excellent source citations. Although the book has an author index and a list of subjects, the lack of a keyword index makes access to this fine collection somewhat difficult.

CATHOLICS. More than ten thousand quotations on many subjects from approved Catholic sources are presented in John Chapin's *Book of Catholic Quotations*. Both prose and verse quotations are included, and Latin quotations are given in English. Authors include popes, saints, poets, playwrights, and critics. The citations are scholarly, and there is a very good keyword index as well as an index of sources.

THE IRISH. Sean McMahon's *Book of Irish Quotations* is a fine collection of perhaps five thousand quotations arranged by author. The level of documentation varies. There is a keyword index.

JEWS. A useful compilation of Jewish quotes is Joseph L. Baron's lifework, *A Treasury of Jewish Quotations*, which classifies some eighteen thousand entries under more than a thousand subjects. There are author and subject indexes. Authors and sources range from the Talmud and the Bible to Spinoza, Freud, and Einstein. *Leo Rosten's Treasury of Jewish Quotations* is a considerably less substantial collection of about forty-five hundred Jewish proverbs, folk sayings, and epigrams, most of which are not traced to individual authors.

PRESIDENTS. Caroline Harnsberger's *Treasury of Presidential Quotations* includes twenty-eight hundred or so quotes from America's leaders, from George Washington to Lyndon Johnson. The documentation is excellent. An author index refers to quotations on specific subjects by each president; there is also a subject index but no keyword index. A more recent book of this kind is Elizabeth Frost's *Bully Pulpit: Quotations from America's Presidents*, whose coverage extends to Ronald Reagan. It lists about three thousand interesting quotes under some two hundred subjects. Citations range from undocumented ascriptions to dated letters and speeches. Other resources containing presidential quotations are the general dictionaries of quotations, Suzy Platt's *Respectfully Quoted*, the books discussed under the heading "America," books of political quotations, and single-author quotation books.

Literary and Artistic Forms

QUOTATIONS FROM MOVIES. Harry Haun's *Movie Quote Book* contains three thousand or so quotations from about six hundred motion pictures, listed by topic. There is no keyword index, but access to the quotes is provided by their topical arrangement and by subject and movie indexes. The quotation tracer will find this to be a useful and interesting book.

QUOTATIONS FROM NOVELS. David Powell's *Wisdom of the Novel* contains more than thirteen thousand quotable, though not necesarily quoted, passages from some nine hundred novels. Access to the quotations is made possible by their subject arrangement and by indexes to authors and novels and to keyword occurrences; however, the latter index does not repeat words from quotations. This book should prove to be helpful when the quotation you are tracing is already known to be from a certain novel or by a certain novelist.

Anthologies

Somewhat similar to the books of quotations examined in this chapter are the special anthologies of poems or of poems and prose pieces assembled around a certain subject or theme or made up of pieces belonging to a certain genre or classification of utterance. These may be used, though preferably only as a last resort, in a search for a quotation on a well-anthologized subject or a quotation whose source is representative of a well-anthologized category. I shall not mention any specific examples of such anthologies, but the tracer who must from time to time attempt to identify quotes on such popular but dissimilar subjects as animals, birds, books and reading, cats, childhood, dogs, drinking, fishing, flowers, holidays, hunting, motherhood, places, science, the sea, smoking, and trees should remember that collections of memorable poems and prose pieces on these and many other subjects do exist. References to such anthologies may be found fairly easily in the public catalog of most libraries under such subject headings as "Mothers—Poetry" and "Birds in Literature." Subject anthologies may be leafed through after more sensible measures have proved unsuccessful. Similarly, you should remember that anthologies of such genres as light verse, verse epigrams, nonsensical poems and prose, nursery rhymes, and parodies also exist. While I admit that, more often than not, my attempts to trace quotations by using subject and genre anthologies have gone unrewarded, I have occasionally succeeded in finding in one of these books the quotation I was seeking.

NOTE

1. Burton Stevenson, *The Home Book of Quotations*, 10th ed. (New York: Dodd, Mead and Co., 1967), 413.

4 | Single-Author Quotation Books

When called upon to trace a quotation that has been attributed to a certain author, the first and best thing to do is to look for it in the great and less great general dictionaries of quotations. When one of these does contain the passage, it usually supplies the correct wording and an adequate source citation. If the quotation is not found in any of these works, then you must turn to other resources.

A potentially helpful but usually overlooked reference tool is a book consisting of quotations from only one person. There is a strong possibility that two admirers of a writer or speaker—the quoter who has created the problem for the tracer and the compiler who has gone through the author's works and words and assembled a book of quotable passages—will have quoted the same passage. The compiler of a book of gems from the writings or speeches of one person usually provides either a precise and verifiable source reference for each quotation or at least the title of the work in which each memorable passage occurs. The persistent quote sleuth will be pleased just to learn that the passage occurs somewhere in a particular work and, in most cases, will gladly go to that source and turn pages until the passage is located. Indeed, even if the compiler of a one-author quotation book has provided no reference at all to the source of a passage included, a second attribution at least confirms the first and may even provide more accurate wording or a larger context—hence, a bigger target at which the searcher can aim.

Single-author quotation books vary a great deal in purpose, organization, content, and scope. A book may consist of quotations on one subject only, such as art or music, or it may consist of quotable passages on many subjects. It may contain long passages, or it may be made up of aphorisms. It may display examples of the author's beautiful style, or it may emphasize wit or wisdom—or, as is sometimes the case these days, the absence of such. Its contents may be arranged alphabetically by topic; or the quotations themselves may occur in alphabetical order; or separate sections of the book may each consist of quotations from one literary work; or the collection may contain one or two quotations for every day in the year with no other principle of organization. The book may have a good index or none at all. Source citations may be definitive or considerably less than definitive, but generally they are much more complete than are the citations found in the one-subject quotation books.

Whatever its strengths and deficiencies may be, a book of quotations from a single author represents an attempt to separate out the most memorable or the most quotable or the most beautiful or the most wise or the most characteristic or the most witty or the most ridiculous or the most uplifting expressions of one person. Consulting—or even scanning or reading—a book made up of such winnowed passages is infinitely easier than plowing through an author's complete works.

The number of one-author quotation books in existence probably runs into the thousands. A single author may be represented by several such collections compiled at different times and for different purposes by different individuals. If so, each book will contain some passages the others lack. My own experience has enabled me to become acquainted at various times with one or more collections of quotations from the following:

Spiro T. Agnew
Alfred Austin
Honoré de Balzac
Sir James Barrie
Henry Ward Beecher
Otto Eduard Leopold von
   Bismarck
Hugh Blair
Robert Blair
George Borrow
Lewis Brandeis
Phillips Brooks
Sir Thomas Browne
William F. Buckley, Jr.
Edmund Burke
George Bush
Thomas Carlyle
Miguel de Cervantes Saavedra
Lord Chesterfield
G. K. Chesterton
Sir Winston Churchill
Joseph Conrad
Marie Corelli
Richard J. Daley

Thomas De Quincey
John Dewey
Charles Dickens
Benjamin Disraeli
Norman Douglas
Dwight D. Eisenhower
George Eliot
Queen Elizabeth I
Ralph Waldo Emerson
W. C. Fields
Bernard Le Bovier de
   Fontenelle
Anatole France
Thomas Fuller
John Galsworthy
Mahatma Gandhi
Comtesse de Genlis
David Lloyd George
William Ewart Gladstone
Johann Wolfgang von Goethe
Billy Graham
Kenneth Grahame
Thomas Hardy
Heinrich Heine

Oliver Wendell Holmes
(both of them)
Laurence Housman
William Dean Howells
Hubert H. Humphrey
Thomas Huxley
Henrik Ibsen
William Ralph Inge
Robert Ingersoll
Henry James
William James
Thomas Jefferson
Douglas Jerrold
Jesus
Lyndon B. Johnson
Samuel Johnson
John Keble
John F. Kennedy
Robert F. Kennedy
Martin Luther King, Jr.
Charles Kingsley
Rudyard Kipling
Charles Lamb
Louis L'Amour
Walter Savage Landor
Abraham Lincoln
Henry Wadsworth
Longfellow
James Russell Lowell
E. V. Lucas
Martin Luther
Maurice Maeterlinck
Philip Massinger
George Meredith
Napoleon I
John Cardinal Newman
Friedrich Wilhelm Nietzsche
Richard M. Nixon
Sir William Osler
Ouida (Marie Louise
de la Ramée)

Adelaide Procter
Marcel Proust
Opie Read
Ronald Reagan
Samuel Richardson
Franklin D. Roosevelt
Theodore Roosevelt
Jean Jacques Rousseau
John Ruskin
Bertrand Russell
George Santayana
Albert Schweitzer
Sir Walter Scott
William Shakespeare
Bernard Shaw
Bishop Fulton J. Sheen
Sir Philip Sidney
Sydney Smith
Robert South
Herbert Spencer
Baruch Spinoza
C. H. Spurgeon
Adlai E. Stevenson
Robert Louis Stevenson
Sir Rabindranath Tagore
Jeremy Taylor
Alfred, Lord Tennyson
William Makepeace Thackeray
Henry David Thoreau
Archbishop John Tillotson
Harry S. Truman
Mark Twain
George Washington
H. G. Wells
Mae West
Alfred North Whitehead
John Greenleaf Whittier
Oscar Wilde
Harold Wilson
P. G. Wodehouse

Betty Jarboe, a colleague of mine at Indiana University, is compiling a book of quotations from John Wesley. Surely there are many, many more one-author compilations that I have not seen, though not nearly enough to meet the needs of quotation tracers.

To determine whether any such collection of quotations from a certain person has been compiled and whether a copy of such a compilation is available, you should begin by consulting the public catalog of the academic or local library to which you have easy access. The author of the quotations themselves, rather than the compiler of the collection, is almost always considered the author of a compilation of this sort. Such a book, if the library owns it, may or may not be represented under a subject subheading comparable to this one: "Chesterton, G. K. (Gilbert Keith), 1874–1936—Quotations"; and in the author section devoted to a certain writer's works, such a book may or may not be found under a group of "Selections." Libraries differ in how they present information of this kind. Indeed, even the same library varies from generation to generation in its cataloging practices, and changes in policy are not always retroactive. Thus, the only sure way to determine a library's holdings of books of this nature is to glance at every record of every book by a certain author. One-author quotation collections often have in their titles one of the following words or phrases: "wit and wisdom," "beauties," "the best of," "the quotable," "the pocket," "gems," "quotations," "wisdom," "thoughts," "sayings," "birthday book," "calendar," "day by day," "through the year with," "yearbook," "cyclopedia," "encyclopedia," "treasury," "aphorisms," "maxims," "epigrams," and "day book."

Sources other than the public catalog may provide references to additional titles of this sort. A bibliography of a writer, such as an author's entry in the *New Cambridge Bibliography of English Literature*, may mention one-author quotation compilations. The printed catalog of the British Library lists such books of selections at the end of an author's section, and the *National Union Catalog* includes a large number of these books, either interfiled with other titles or, if the author's entries are many, listed in a subsection of selections. A reference librarian may have other suggestions for identifying such collections and will certainly know how to help you gain access to them.

I have used one-author quotation collections numerous times in my work with reference questions and in my attempts to answer published queries. Once I took on the task of finding the text and source of Mark Twain's remark about school boards. I located it easily enough in Harnsberger's well-organized *Mark Twain at Your Fingertips*, and with its help I was able to quote this passage from *Following the Equator:* "In the first place God made idiots. This was for practice. Then He made School Boards."[1] Locating a quotation in a scholarly single-author compilation is easy enough, but I would also strongly recommend that you never shrink from leafing through author calendars and birthday books made up of quotes arranged haphazardly.

To indicate the varied nature of single-author quotation books and to provide a handy description of resources very likely to be needed when a passage to be traced has been attributed to a frequently quoted author, I shall describe briefly in the following pages and more fully in the bibliography one or more of the published collections of quotes from G. K. Chesterton, Sir Winston Churchill, Charles Dickens, Benjamin Disraeli, George Eliot, Ralph Waldo Emerson, Thomas Huxley, William James, Thomas Jefferson, Samuel Johnson, Abraham Lincoln, Theodore Roosevelt, William Shakespeare, Bernard Shaw, Robert Louis Stevenson, Mark Twain, and Oscar Wilde. No doubt there are other compilations of passages from some of these quotable persons, but those I shall mention are good examples of the genre. Indeed, some of these works are excellent—and even the least scholarly among them may lead you to the source of a quotation from one of these oft-quoted people. I should add also that persons *not* often quoted are frequently represented by compilations of this type.

George J. Marlin, Richard P. Rabatin, and John L. Swan have recently produced two excellent collections of quotes from G. K. Chesterton, *The Quotable Chesterton* and *More Quotable Chesterton.* Two older collections are less useful to the quote sleuth since they are based on early Chesterton works and were designed more for reading than for reference: *A Chesterton Calendar,* which was also published as *Chesterton Day by Day,* and Frances Chesterton's *Wit and Wisdom of G. K. Chesterton.* Incidentally, an index to Chesterton is mentioned in chapter 6.

Several collections of Churchill's quotations have been published. None of them satisfies the person in search of easily accessible and easily verifiable facts, but all do have some value. The best of these, though limited to quotations from speeches, is F. B. Czarnomski's *Wisdom of Winston Churchill.* Another major collection is Kay Halle's *Irrepressible Churchill.* Of less value but still useful are Leslie Frewin's *Immortal Jester* and Colin Coote's two collections, a book of Churchill's *Maxims and Reflections* and an enlargement of it, *A Churchill Reader.*

The best book of Dickens quotations is F. G. De Fontaine's well-organized and well-documented *Cyclopedia of the Best Thoughts of Charles Dickens,* also published as *The Fireside Dickens.* Religious quotations from Dickens are assembled and discussed in Charles H. McKenzie's *Religious Sentiments of Charles Dickens.* There are also a number of birthday books, yearbooks, and assorted slim compilations, including *The Dickens Birthday Book,* Lois E. Prentiss and Gertrude C. Spaulding's *Dickens Year Book,* Enid Dickens Hawksley's *Charles Dickens Birthday Book,* and a little book entitled *Maxims.* No doubt there are others.

Disraeli is represented by at least two collections, George Sampson's *Wit and Imagination of Benjamin Disraeli* and an earlier, more substantial compilation, *Wit and Wisdom of Benjamin Disraeli, Earl of Beaconsfield.* Anyone using the several collections of quotations from George Eliot must do much reading or scanning both before and after locating a passage being traced. The best such book is probably Alexander Main's *Wise, Witty, and Tender Sayings in Prose and Verse Selected from the Works of George Eliot,* or its almost identical twin, *Wit and Wisdom of George Eliot.* Others are *The George Eliot Birthday Book* and Alfred H. Hyatt's slim collection, *The Pocket George Eliot.*

The most useful compilation of Emerson quotations is H. H. Emmons's *Light of Emerson.* A smaller collection is Alfred H. Hyatt's *Pocket Emerson.* There are other resources also for the tracer of Emerson quotations to consult: the index in the last volume of most editions of his collected works, and concordances to the poetry and to some of the essays. Thomas Huxley is represented by an excellent little collection, Henrietta A. Huxley's *Aphorisms and Reflections from the Works of T. H. Huxley.* Elizabeth Aldrich's *As William James Said* is a good compilation of quotes from the philosopher, and John P. Foley's *Jeffersonian Cyclopedia* is the basic collection of quotations from our third president.

There are at least four collections of well-documented, topically arranged quotations from Samuel Johnson: *The Beauties of Samuel Johnson, LL.D.,* an old compilation; George Birkbeck Hill's *Wit and Wisdom of Samuel Johnson;* Constantia Maxwell's *Wisdom of Dr. Johnson;* and James Hay's *Johnson, His Characteristics and Aphorisms.* Another very useful work is Alexander Montgomerie Bell's compilation, *The Johnson Calendar.* Two collections lacking in documentation, W. A. Clouston's *Wisdom and Genius of Dr. Samuel Johnson,* which consists of passages from Johnson's writings, and H. C. Biron's " 'Sir,' Said Dr. Johnson—," a book of conversational quotes, are not without value. By confirming or correcting or enlarging the quotation being traced, and by indicating whether it has a written or spoken origin, these two works may add to what you already know about the quotation. Moreover, you should remember that there is a concordance to Johnson's poetry and that there are good indexes in scholarly editions of Johnson's writings and of Boswell's *Life of Samuel Johnson.*

A quotation attributed to Lincoln has not been adequately certified until it has been located in *The Collected Works of Abraham Lincoln,* edited by Roy Basler, or in some authoritative biographical or historical source. Any Lincoln quotation that cannot be so traced should be regarded with suspicion. The definitive Lincoln quotation collection or index has not yet appeared, but two excellent collections do exist, Archer H. Shaw's *Lincoln Encyclopedia* and Caroline Harnsberger's *Lincoln Treasury*. Both are well organized and well referenced, providing citations that refer to collected editions that were standard when the compilations were published. Using the information provided, it should be easy to locate the corresponding passages in Basler's edition of Lincoln's works. Smaller collections of some value are Fred Kerner's *Treasury of Lincoln Quotations* and Ralph B. Winn's *Concise Lincoln Dictionary*. Also worth consulting are collections of presidential quotations.

The basic resource for tracing Theodore Roosevelt quotations is Albert Bushnell Hart and Herbert Ronald Ferleger's *Theodore Roosevelt Cyclopedia*. Other collections are Alan Warner's *Real Roosevelt* and E. E. Garrison's *Roosevelt Doctrine*. Two books of presidential quotations discussed in chapter 3 should also be consulted.

A good collection of quotes from Shakespeare is Burton Stevenson's *Home Book of Shakespeare Quotations*. Once the passage is located, you should get its actual wording from a scholarly edition of the bard's works, not from a book of quotations based on the old Globe edition of 1911. Of course, you may prefer to use a Shakespeare concordance rather than a collection of Shakespeare quotations. I usually do.

The first collection of Shavian quotations you should consult is Caroline Harnsberger's *Bernard Shaw: Selections of His Wit and Wisdom*. Another large collection is S. Winsten's *Quintessence of G.B.S.: The Wit and Wisdom of Bernard Shaw*. Other compilations include Charlotte F. Shaw's *Selected Passages from the Works of Bernard Shaw*, whose value is somewhat limited by its early date, and N. H. Leigh-Taylor's *Bernard Shaw's Ready-Reckoner*. Still another resource for tracing Shaw quotations will be mentioned in chapter 6.

Although Robert Louis Stevenson is often quoted, the number of different passages attributed to him is not great. A good proportion of these may well turn up in one of three slim compilations: *The Pocket R.L.S.; Brave Words about Death from the Works of Robert Louis Stevenson;* and Florence L. Tucker's *Stevenson Day by Day*.

The task of tracing a quotation attributed to Mark Twain is complicated by the fact that he has been credited with saying a number of good things that he never said. Even tracing all the good things he *did* say is not yet possible because a definitive collection of his quotations or a series of concordances to his works, which would greatly benefit humanity, has not yet appeared. In the meantime, quote sleuths should consult any or all of these fine compilations of memorable quotations from the great humorist: the indefatigable Caroline Harnsberger's *Mark Twain at Your Fingertips;* her revision of that book, *Everyone's Mark Twain;* and Alex Ayres's *Wit and Wisdom of Mark Twain.*

Oscar Wilde is another writer and speaker to whom more good things have been attributed than can at present be authenticated. There is a great need for a definitive, well-indexed, well-referenced collection of his witticisms and other gems; another desideratum is a concordance to his plays, poems, and prose works. At present, however, we can manage fairly well by using the standard dictionaries of quotations and supplementing them with Alvin Redman's compilation of *The Epigrams of Oscar Wilde,* a collection entitled *Epigrams and Aphorisms,* and Stuart Mason's *Oscar Wilde Calendar.*

By now it should be fairly obvious that the one-author quotation book can and should be a major research tool to be employed when we attempt to identify the sources of quotations that have been attributed to specific persons. Of somewhat lesser value, although similar to the one-author quotation book, is the book of selected works from one author. Such an anthology may consist of representative selections of various sorts or on various subjects, or it may contain writing of one kind or on only one subject. A bit bothersome to use, the book of selections is nonetheless an important resource for the quotation tracer. If you are lucky, the editor who assembled the book of selections will have included a work containing the very passage you seek. I have successfully traced many a quotation by scanning likely parts of a book of selections from the author to whom a passage has been attributed.

NOTE

1. *Following the Equator,* 2 vols. in 1 (New York: Harper and Brothers, 1903), 2:295; *New York Times Book Review,* 3 May 1970, 47; ibid., 14 June 1970, 31; Mark Twain, *Mark Twain at Your Fingertips,* ed. Caroline Thomas Harnsberger (New York: Beechhurst Press, 1948), 425.

5 | Dictionaries of the English Language

> When first I collected these authorities, I was desirous that every quotation should be useful to some other end than the illustration of a word.
>
> Preface to Johnson's *Dictionary of the English Language*

You can identify the sources of many of the problem quotations you encounter by consulting dictionaries of the languages in which they are written. This is obvious, of course, but it is not obvious to everyone at all times. Indeed, the language dictionary is almost always overlooked by those who are trying to identify the sources of English and American quotations, just as it is overlooked by those who are trying to trace quotations in foreign languages.

Of the several dictionaries of the English language that can be used as dictionaries of quotations, the one whose name leads all the rest is *The Oxford English Dictionary* (*OED*). In addition to definitions, pronunciations, and etymological information, this monumental work contains an enormous number of quotations used to illustrate the history of words and their meanings. Until recently, the quotation tracer using the *OED* consulted the main set, which contains 1,827,306 quotations,[1] and, if it seemed appropriate, the four-volume supplement, which contains more than a half-million illustrative passages. The recently published second edition, which contains over 2.4 million quotations, integrates into one alphabetical sequence the contents of the first edition and the supplementary volumes; it also adds new word entries to bring the dictionary up to date.

Although the second edition, which is found in a growing number of libraries and even in personal collections, is preferred because of its completeness and its convenience of use, the first edition, with or without its supplements, will continue to be a major reference tool for the identification of quotation sources, as it will be for the accomplishment of primary lexicographical purposes. It is available in three formats: the original set of volumes, the two-volume compact edition, and a recent edition on compact disk. In any edition and in any format, the *OED* is a great dictionary of quotations.

The quotations and accompanying source citations appearing in chronological order following the definitions in the *OED* are of immense value to the student of the English language because they demonstrate representative instances of the uses of a word in its various forms and meanings over a period of time. However, the quote sleuth soon comes to believe that the principal function of the illustrative passages is not to provide information about meaning and usage but to identify the sources of quotations he or she is tracing. I can promise you that if you will routinely check this distinguished dictionary for practically all problem quotations in English that do not turn up in the general books of quotations, you are sure to succeed in an impressive number of cases.

In the discussion that follows, I shall assume that some version of the *OED* in book format is the only version that is easily accessible to you. I do want to encourage you to learn how to use the compact disk version as well, for searching on CD-ROM may lead to feats of retrieval that are not possible when you work with conventional formats. For now, however, I want to show you how to achieve miracles by opening a book and scanning illustrative quotations.

When trying to find the source of an unidentified passage by scanning quotations in the *OED*, you should begin with any obsolete or unusual words in the quotation, or words used figuratively or poetically rather than literally, or words used in unusual senses, or words that are verbal substantives or participial adjectives, or words that are used in special combinations with other words, as in idiomatic phrases and hyphenated compounds. In defining and illustrating an unusual word or unusual form or unusual sense, there is a good chance that the *OED* editors employed the very passage whose source you are trying to identify. Also, it is much easier to scan the relatively few successive quotations illustrating the use of such words or such meanings than to scan large numbers of examples of the use of ordinary words in ordinary senses. However, if this procedure is not possible or is not successful, then by all means plod through the quotations illustrating some of the ordinary words or ordinary meanings employed in the unidentified passage.

In scanning a succession of quotations used as examples, be sure to make use of what you already know about the quotation you are tracing. If you know from the vocabulary and the style or from a clue occurring in the quotation's context that it is not from an ancient source, then skip over the examples from the earliest periods. If you know the year in which the problem passage was quoted, then you can safely stop looking at a chronological sequence of passages after that date has been reached. And if, as sometimes happens, you already know the name of the author, then look at the dates and at the successive names of authors more than at the examples themselves, until you find what you are seeking or until you know that you cannot find it in the *OED*.

To save space in presenting the vast number of quotations, the *OED* editors have abbreviated the accompanying source citations. Ordinarily, these abbreviations can be understood without difficulty. If the compressed information is not immediately clear, however, help is available in the dictionary's bibliography volume.

Through more than a score of years as an active quotation tracer, I have made a significant proportion of my finds, including some very impressive ones, simply by consulting the *OED*. Since up to now I have not been one to talk about methods, those for whom I have traced quotations have credited me with considerably more erudition than I possess. An example or two of the queries I have answered with the silent help of the *OED* will give you some idea of how knowledgeable a not very knowledgeable quote sleuth can be made to look if he or she employs this obvious but neglected method of tracing.

In a query published years ago, someone asked for the source of this quotation: "God himself needs be traduced if there are no unicorns." When I consulted the *OED*, meaning 3.c. of "traduce" led me to a seventeenth-century work by Edward Topsell, *The Historie of Foure-footed Beastes*.[2] On another occasion a scholar working on a new edition of Hardy's novel *The Well-beloved* asked for the source of a quotation occurring in chapter 1 of part 2: ". . . the nation of every country dwells in the cottage." A similar quotation occurs, with a reference to a speech by John Bright, under meaning 4. of "nation."[3]

The *OED* exploit of mine that most amazed the person in need of information is related (as seen through a glass, darkly) by John S. Mayfield in his book *Swinburneiana*, in the chapter entitled "Swinburne's Disconsolate Widow."[4] At issue was the source of a passage in Swinburne's handwriting that occurred in single quotes:

> 'When a canary loses her mate she will often droop & die of a broken heart. The only hope of saving her life is to immerse the disconsolate widow in water. The occupation, always interesting to the female mind, of rearranging her plumage so diverts her thoughts that the once inconsolable bird recovers from her melancholy & joins once more in the feathery society.'

After a lengthy but unsuccessful search through Swinburne's writings, and after consulting every book of quotations in the Library of Congress and every book on canaries he could find anywhere, Mayfield sent a query to the *New York Times Book Review*, which I spotted and was able to answer with the *OED*'s help. In my reply, which the *Book Review* forwarded directly to the inquirer, I referred him to a certain page of a certain issue of the *Pall Mall Gazette*. I never told Mr. Mayfield how I pulled off this coup, and now, alas, it is too late to tell him that I found the reference by looking up the word "feathery."

The ten passages that follow are quotations, or include quotations, that anyone can trace by means of the *OED*. As the notes to the chapter indicate, all of the passages come from old periodicals. Needless to say, some of the quotations are actually misquotations. These mystery passages, which seem not to occur in Bartlett, the *ODQ2*, Stevenson, the *ODQ3*, Evans, *Benham's*, or *Hoyt's*, are followed by the five unsolved passages from our list of thirty-three, which may or may not prove to be traceable by means of the *OED*.

1.   "Like giants stand
To sentinel enchanted land."[5]

2. "Such resting found the soles of unblest feet!"[6]

3. ——"right glad to miss
The lumbering of the wheels."[7]

4. A great poet has told us that there are few things more delightful to a young matron, than to "bring her babe and make her boast" at her father's house;[8]

5. "——————————discharging foul
Her devilish glut, chained thunder-bolts and hail
Of iron globes——"[9]

6.   'Two winking Cupids
Of silver, each on one foot standing;'[10]

7.   "Ah! what avails it,
If the gulled conqueror receives the chain,
And flattery subdues when arms are vain."[11]

8.   'Between the span
Of clown unread and half-read gentleman,'[12]

9. "Closet long to quiet vowed
With mothed and dropping arras hung,"[13]

10. . . . a guest is, *ipso facto*, a "mush of concession."[14]

11. "The bellman writes better verses," said Mr. Osbaldistone, when he threw poor Frank's away.[15]

12. "Wherein the toga'd consuls can propose
As masterly,"[16]

13. The curse of growing factions and divisions
Still vex your councils!
Venice Preserved.[17]

    14.   Their personal experience would have led them to ratify the
           verdict of the Laureate—
           "Each man walks with his head in a cloud of poisonous flies."[18]

    15.   "Calm or convulsed, in breeze, or gale, or storm."[19]

Not wanting to do more scanning of *OED* quotations than necessary, I checked first for the one word in each of the first ten quotes that seemed most likely to have been illustrated by the use of the quotation in question. Usually I am not so lucky, but this time I was immediately led to the source of each quote. Had I failed the first time around, I would of course have gone on to another likely word, and another. In one or two cases, even though I had found what I was looking for, curiosity prevailed and I went on to discover which other words would have served me equally well.

In the first quotation, "sentinel," which I always think of as a noun, is used as a verb. Because this usage struck me as unusual, I elected to look at the quotations appearing under the verb "sentinel" in the *OED*. I identified the passage, which is from *The Lady of the Lake*, by scanning the examples in the first "trans." section of the definition. The second quotation, from *Paradise Lost*, was easily solved by scanning the illustrations following meaning 2.a. of the first verbal substantive "resting." (Looking at definition 3. of the participial adjective "unblessed, unblest" would also have led to the solution.) Part of the third quotation, which is from Cowper's "Diverting History of John Gilpin," illustrates the use of the first verbal substantive "lumbering." The fourth item on the list, from *In Memoriam*, can be found by looking up the phrase "to make (one's) boast," under definition 4. of the substantive "boast." The phrase is also listed under meaning 59.a. of "make," but the quotation in question is not used as an example.

The noun "hail" in the fifth quotation, from *Paradise Lost*, does not refer to ordinary hail but to something falling in the manner of hail. My recognizing this metaphor enabled me to find the solution quickly—under meaning 3. of the first substantive "hail," which has to do with transferred or figurative uses. In solving the sixth quotation, I chose the participial adjective "winking," though the noun "Cupid" would have worked just as well. The lines are from Shakespeare's *Cymbeline*. The seventh quotation, from Johnson's *London*, is used in the *OED* to illustrate the second participial adjective "gulled." The participial adjective "unread" led to the source of the eighth item on the list, Dryden's *Hind and the Panther*, and another one, "mothed," helped to trace the ninth to Browning's *Paracelsus*. To locate the source of the tenth quote, the metaphorical expression "mush of concession," I looked to meaning 3.c. ("transf. and fig.") of the substantive "mush." The source is Emerson's essay "Friendship."

At last, two of the problems left over from earlier chapters, beginning with the twelfth item on this list, can now be retired. Thanks to meaning 5. of the verb "propose," we discover that the quote is from *Othello*. ("Toga'd" or "togaed" would not have led us to it, though unbeknownst to us, "toged" would have.) The fourteenth passage, used to illustrate meaning 7. of the substantive "cloud," is from Tennyson's *Maud*. Of course, we could have solved the problem another way, by identifying "the Laureate" and then using a concordance.

Unfortunately, the eleventh, thirteenth, and fifteenth quotations on the list seem not to occur in the *OED*, nor do they appear in the dictionaries we are about to consider. We shall solve these in future chapters.

Another English dictionary helpful in the pursuit of quotation sources is *The Century Dictionary and Cyclopedia*, which first appeared as *The Century Dictionary*. For our purposes any edition of either title is an important collection of quotations, though the later editions are preferable, if available, since they contain more quotations. As a book of quotations, *The Century Dictionary* is much less useful to us than the *OED*. It has considerably fewer illustrative quotes—only two hundred thousand or so—and for the most part they are taken from literature earlier than about 1890. On the other hand, *The Century* is very easy to use. Since quotations are set off from the text and are printed in small type, since the words being illustrated are italicized in the quotations, and since there are not many quotations illustrating each word, scanning the quotations occurring under a particular word takes only a few seconds. In most cases source references are complete or nearly so. The tracker who routinely uses *The Century Dictionary and Cyclopedia* to supplement the standard dictionaries of quotations and the great *Oxford English Dictionary* for quotes thought to have been uttered before 1900 will occasionally be richly rewarded.

To get some experience using *The Century* and to confirm that it really does contain quotations that other sources do not, let us use it to trace several passages. So far as I can determine, these passages do not turn up in Bartlett, the *ODQ2*, Stevenson, the *ODQ3*, Evans, *Benham's*, *Hoyt's*, or the *OED*.

1. That all, as in some piece of art,
   Is toil cöoperant [*sic*] to an end—[20]

2. The owl is abroad,
   The bat and the toad,
   And so is the catamountain.[21]

3. What shook the stage, and made the people stare?
   Cato's long wig, flowered gown, and lacquered chair![22]

4. "Greatness of mind and nobleness their seat
   Build in her loveliest, and create an awe
   About her, as a guard angelic placed."[23]

5. 'Whatever clime the sun's bright circle warms'—[24]

6. "And darkness was the buryer of the dead."[25]

The adjective "coöperant" leads us to the source of the first quotation. The reference given is "*Tennyson*, In Memoriam, cxxviii." The second quote illustrates the use of the noun "catamountain." The source citation, "*B. Jonson*, Masque of Queens," is not as complete as we would prefer, but " 'tis enough, 'twill serve." The second line of the third quotation appears under the participial adjective "flowered." Though abbreviated, the source reference is sufficient: "*Pope*, Imit. of Horace, II.i.337." About half of the fourth passage occurs under the word "nobleness." The source citation reads, "*Milton*, P.L., viii.557." The fifth quote, which appears under "clime," can be traced to "*Milton*, Sonnets, iii." The sixth is an example of the use of "burier." The source is "*Shak.*, 2 Hen.IV., i.1." All of these, then, which seem not to occur in seven great dictionaries of quotations or in the *OED*, are traceable by means of *The Century Dictionary and Cyclopedia*.

Another English dictionary that contains many quotations of the sort we are often called on to trace is Samuel Johnson's *Dictionary of the English Language*, which first appeared in 1755. Of course, I do not recommend using a rare first or second edition of Johnson's *Dictionary* as a book of quotations; a facsimile reprint of the first edition is quite satisfactory, and if a copy is available, a very popular and frequently issued nineteenth-century one-volume reprint of the revision of 1773 is slightly better, since it contains some quotations not found in the 1755 edition.

According to Margaret Drabble, Johnson's *Dictionary* contains some one hundred fourteen thousand quotations from English writers.[26] Although there is a heavy concentration of passages from writings dating from the Elizabethan period to the Restoration, the work does include material from the eighteenth century as well. Since the wording of the quotations in this dictionary and the degree of completeness of the references to sources accompanying them do not meet the needs of most quote sleuths, and since many of the passages are to be found in the standard compilations or in the *OED* or *The Century*, you should use this work as a tracing tool only when the other resources fail you. Often, it too will fail you, but not always, and especially not when you consult it for English quotations that are thought to antedate the middle of the eighteenth century. Johnson's *Dictionary* came in very handy some years ago when I tried to identify two lines appearing without attribution in Chateaubriand's *Essai Historique sur les Révolutions:* "Thrice happy you, who look as from the shore / And have no venture in the wreck you see." After failing to locate the couplet elsewhere, I found it in Johnson's *Dictionary*, where it occurs under the noun "venture." The source given was merely "Daniel," but with that lead I was able to trace the lines to his *Civil Wars*.[27]

The quotations and misquotations that folllow seem not to occur in Bartlett, the *ODQ2*, Stevenson, the *ODQ3*, Evans, *Hoyt's, Benham's*, the *OED*, or *The Century Dictionary*. Some of them, we shall discover, do indeed occur in the *OED* as part of longer passages, but we cannot find them there until we look for those longer quotations. They do turn up in Johnson, however, although the source citations do not supply all of the information needed.

1.   'the pace
   Of some chaste footing near about this ground,'[28]

2. ————"billows roll ashore
   The beryl and the golden ore."[29]

3. "Alas! not dazzled by their noontide ray,
   Compute the morn and evening to the day."[30]

4. "Proper deformity seems not in the fiend
   So horrible as in woman;"[31]

5. Now like a maiden queen she will behold,
   From her high turrets, hourly suitors come—
   The East with incense, and the West with gold,
   Will stand like suppliants to receive her doom.[32]

The first quotation is part of a longer passage that illustrates the use of the word "footing." The source given is simply "Milton." To finish the search, it is best to start over with the expanded quotation:

Break off, break off; I feel the different sound
Of some chaste *footing* near about this ground:
Run to your shrouds, within these brakes and trees;
Our number may affright.

The expanded quotation, incidentally, is not worded correctly, but no matter. We may indeed find the source by looking for a Milton quotation among the passages illustrating meaning 3. of "shroud" in the *OED*. As suspected, the passage comes from Milton's *Comus*. Another easy way of proceeding, as will be seen in the next chapter, is to consult a concordance.

The second quotation, which occurs in Johnson's *Dictionary* under "beryl," with no significant enlargement, is also attributed to Milton.

This one is not so easily traced and will be saved for the chapter on concordances.

The third quote, we learn when we check Johnson's *Dictionary* under compute," is part of a longer passage attributed to Pope. The expanded passage reads:

> Alas! not dazzled with their noon-tide ray,
> *Compute* the morn and ev'ning to the day;
> The whole amount of that enormous fame,
> A tale that blends their glory with their shame.

The figurative use of "amount" tempts us to consult the *OED*, where we find the line containing it under meaning 2. of that substantive, along with a detailed reference to its location in Pope's *Essay on Man*. As will be seen, another method of tracing the quote is to use a concordance.

The fourth quotation, with "horrid" in place of the incorrect "horrible," is in Johnson's *Dictionary* under "deformity." The source given is *"Shakespeare's King Lear,"* which is an improvement over some of this dictionary's other source references. We can finish tracing the passage by using a book of Shakespeare quotations or by consulting a concordance to Shakespeare.

The fifth passage, most of which is found in Johnson under "suppliant," is attributed to Dryden. To locate it in Dryden's works, we must use the word index to Dryden, which we shall do in the next chapter. As you see, Johnson's *Dictionary* is, despite its deficiencies, a very useful dictionary of English quotations from the times of Shakespeare, Milton, Pope, and Dryden.

There are other general dictionaries of the English language that contain quotations, but more likely to be of help, I think, are quotation-filled dictionaries whose scope is limited to certain historical periods or to certain levels of usage or to certain geographical or national categories of expression. Do remember that such resources exist and consult them when conditions seem to warrant their use. Two outstanding examples are Sir William A. Craigie's *Dictionary of American English* and Mitford M. Mathews's *Dictionary of Americanisms*, both of which resemble the *OED*. An excellent resource for Scottish quotations and for quotations containing Scottish expressions is *The Scottish National Dictionary*.

English dialect and English and American slang are well covered also. Joseph Wright's *English Dialect Dictionary* includes, along with much else, numerous literary quotations containing dialect words and expressions. Of the many slang dictionaries that include quotations, I think the one most likely to help—and certainly the one most likely to entertain—is John S. Farmer and W. E. Henley's *Slang and Its Analogues*.

Although we all know that general and special dictionaries of the English language exist and that they contain illustrative passages, it is hard for the quote sleuth to remember to consult these works in the heat of the fray; and if we do remember that they exist, it is hard to bring ourselves to find them and use them. But use them we must, some of them routinely and others on likely occasions, if we are to achieve excellence in our noble calling. Let us here highly resolve that these dictionaries filled with quotations shall not have been compiled in vain!

NOTES

1. Eugene P. Sheehy, comp., *Guide to Reference Books*, 10th ed. (Chicago: American Library Association, 1986), 150.

2. *New York Times Book Review*, 21 May 1967, 55; ibid., 18 June 1967, 47.

3. *Notes and Queries* 220 (May 1975), 209; ibid., (October 1975), 450.

4. John S. Mayfield, *Swinburneiana* (Gaithersburg, Md.: Waring Press, 1974), 165–71; *New York Times Book Review*, 16 July 1967, 35.

5. *Cassell's Family Magazine*, (1877), 666.

6. *Atlantic Monthly* 15 (June 1865), 753.

7. *Fraser's Magazine* 8 (October 1833), 492.

8. *Belford's Monthly Magazine* 2 (July 1877), 338.

9. *Spectator* 8 (15 August 1835), 778.

10. *Blackwood's Edinburgh Magazine* 77 (June 1855), 689.

11. *National Anti-Slavery Standard* 27 (13 October 1866), 1.

12. *Atlantic Monthly* 24 (December 1869), 665.

13. *Bookman* 6 (September 1894), 175.

14. *Blackwood's Edinburgh Magazine* 85 (May 1859), 583.

15. *Fortnightly Review* 50 (1 July 1888), 33.

16. Ibid., (1 September 1888), 335.

17. Motto to chapter 30 of Sir Walter Scott's *Old Mortality*.

18. *Contemporary Review* 57 (February 1890), 180.

19. William Lloyd Garrison, *The Letters of William Lloyd Garrison*, ed. Walter M. Merrill and Louis Ruchames, 6 vols. (Cambridge: Belknap Press of Harvard University Press, 1973), 3:462.

20. *Saturday Review* 7 (16 April 1859), 472.

21. *Athenaeum*, no. 1127 (2 June 1849), 579.

22. Ibid., no. 594 (16 March 1839), 195.

23. *Christian Union* 6 (11 September 1872), 225.

24. *Edinburgh Review* 80 (October 1844), 213.

25. *Blackwood's Edinburgh Magazine* 54 (November 1843), 629.

26. Margaret Drabble, ed., *The Oxford Companion to English Literature*, 5th ed. (Oxford and New York: Oxford University Press, 1985), 514.

27. *American Notes & Queries* 10 (February 1972), 88; ibid., (April 1972), 121.

28. *Quarterly Review* 43 (May 1830), 211.

29. *Blackwood's Edinburgh Magazine* 58 (December 1845), 745.
30. *Spectator* 17 (4 May 1844), 421.
31. *Fraser's Magazine* 16 (July 1837), 14.
32. *Merchants' Magazine* 2 (March 1840), 218.

6 | Concordances and Word Indexes to Works in English and American Literature

Alexander Cruden, the compiler of the renowned
"Biblical Concordance" published in 1737, became
insane the following year.

T. H. Howard-Hill[1]

Two resources often overlooked by tracers of quotations are the concordance and the word index, which are alphabetical indexes to the occurrences of words in a text. The concordance records occurrences of words and their locations and also presents the words in their immediate contexts; the word index, or verbal index or *index verborum*, supplies references to the occurrences of words but does not show the words in their contexts. Occasionally, a word index or other index may call itself a concordance, or a concordance may call itself a word index, but in most instances the two terms are used as I have defined them.

The publication of concordances used to be made possible only by the laborious copying or pasting of passages on slips of paper and the time-consuming filing of these slips. As a result, not many concordances to English and American literature existed until fairly recently. Aided by computers, compilers of concordances have gone on a bender in the past three decades, adding scores of concordances and verbal indexes to the existing stock. There are now a great many concordances and word indexes to English and American literature and also to translations into English of works both literary and nonliterary. Almost all of them are published books, but a few are dissertations and several are microfiche publications.

There are one or more concordances or verbal indexes to one or some or all of the works of a large number of English and American authors, to anonymous classics written in early English, and to many works translated into English. Subjects of concordances and word indexes include:

Anglo-Saxon literature	Francis Bacon
Matthew Arnold	tbe Venerable Bede
W. H. Auden	*Beowulf*
Jane Austen	the Bible, in various versions

Elizabeth Bishop
William Blake
the Book of Common Prayer
the Book of Mormon
Charlotte Brontë
Emily Brontë
Elizabeth Barrett Browning
Robert Browning
Robert Burns
Lord Byron
Lewis Carroll
Geoffrey Chaucer
the Chester Mystery Plays
John Cleland
Samuel Taylor Coleridge
William Collins
William Congreve
Joseph Conrad
William Cowper
Hart Crane
Stephen Crane
Richard Crashaw
E. E. Cummings
Charles Darwin
Daniel Defoe
Thomas Dekker
Emily Dickinson
John Donne
John Dryden
Mary Baker Eddy
Ralph Waldo Emerson
the Episcopal Hymnal
Sir George Etherege
William Faulkner
Henry Fielding
Edward FitzGerald
F. Scott Fitzgerald
Ford Madox Ford
Benjamin Franklin
Robert Frost
W. S. Gilbert
Oliver Goldsmith
John Gower

Thomas Gray
Thomas Hardy
Nathaniel Hawthorne
George Herbert
Robert Herrick
John Heywood
Gerard Manley Hopkins
A. E. Housman
Langston Hughes
Henry James
Samuel Johnson
Ben Jonson
James Joyce
John Keats
John Keble
Thomas Kyd
Sidney Lanier
D. H. Lawrence
Edward Lear
C. S. Lewis
John Lyly
Sir Thomas Malory
Christopher Marlowe
Andrew Marvell
Herman Melville
George Meredith
the Methodist Hymnal
Middle English poems and
   metrical romances
John Milton
Marianne Moore
Sir Thomas More
Eugene O'Neill
Wilfred Owen
the Pilgrim Hymnal
Sylvia Plath
Edgar Allan Poe
Alexander Pope
Ezra Pound
Edwin Arlington Robinson
the Earl of Rochester
Theodore Roethke
William Shakespeare

the Shakespeare Apocrypha
Bernard Shaw
Percy Bysshe Shelley
Sir Philip Sidney
John Skelton
sonnet sequences
Edmund Spenser
Laurence Sterne
Wallace Stevens
Jonathan Swift
Edward Taylor
Alfred, Lord Tennyson

Dylan Thomas
Henry David Thoreau
the Towneley Plays
Thomas Traherne
Henry Vaughan
John Webster
Walt Whitman
Virginia Woolf
William Wordsworth
Sir Thomas Wyatt
William Butler Yeats
the York Plays

I have recorded in the relevant section of the bibliography a host of concordances and verbal indexes to the above authors and works. Except for the intentional omission of concordances to some of the translations of the Bible, the list is as full as I can make it; but even if it is complete as these words are being written (which is unlikely), it is surely not complete as these words are being read. One way to learn of additional concordances to these or other writers and works is to consult the public catalog of a research library under such a subject heading as "Congreve, William, 1670–1729—Concordances." If your library has an online catalog, you may easily check it for the keyword "concordance." Another means of locating recent concordances is to ask a computer expert at the reference desk to assist in checking the holdings of library networks such as RLIN and in searching various bibliographies on compact disk, such as the Modern Language Association's *International Bibliography* and *Dissertation Abstracts*, for references to concordances to certain authors or for references to concordances to any authors. Still another is to find the title indexes to *Books in Print* and *Forthcoming Books* and look at titles beginning with the word "concordance." You may also wish to keep up with what is being published by Garland Publishing and Cornell University Press.

Although the facilitation of quotation tracing has not been the chief aim of concordance compilers, it has certainly been an important by-product of their work. From the literary detective's point of view, there are both too many and too few concordances—too many that we seldom, if ever, have occasion to use and too few of the ones we want the most. Certain authors and certain sources indexed by excellent concordances have not been quoted much or at all, and some concordances duplicate the information already available in others. (The concordance section of the bibliography contains several pairs of contemporaneous concordances.) Some often-quoted English and American authors, on the other hand, are at this moment of writing apparently not represented by concordances, and others are not sufficiently or satisfactorily indexed. In the first group are, if I am not mistaken:

Francis Beaumont and John Fletcher
William Cullen Bryant
Edmund Burke
Thomas Campbell
Thomas Carlyle
Charles Churchill
Abraham Cowley
George Crabbe
Charles Dickens
George Eliot
T. S. Eliot[2]
John Gay
Felicia Hemans
Oliver Wendell Holmes (1809–94)
Thomas Hood
Charles Lamb
Letitia Landon
Abraham Lincoln
Henry Wadsworth Longfellow
James Russell Lowell
Thomas Middleton
Thomas Moore
Hannah More
Thomas Otway
Matthew Prior
Samuel Rogers
Will Rogers
Nicholas Rowe
Sir Walter Scott
Robert Louis Stevenson
James Thomson (1700–1748)
Martin Farquhar Tupper
Mark Twain
John Greenleaf Whittier
Oscar Wilde
Edward Young

In the group of authors in need of new or additional concordances are William Cowper, whose concordance does not include his minor poetry or his translations; John Dryden, whose concordance is only a word index to only his poetry; Ralph Waldo Emerson, whose concordances cover only his poetry and five essays; Ben Jonson and Samuel Johnson, whose concordances treat only their poetry; Alfred, Lord Tennyson, whose concordance has too few entries and too many parts; Elizabeth Barrett Browning, whose otherwise fine concordance contains too many alphabetical sequences; and Samuel Daniel and Michael Drayton, who are represented only in a concordance to sonnet sequences. In the opinion of this frustrated quotation tracer, the most badly needed new or additional concordances are to Beaumont and Fletcher, Cowley, Cowper, Crabbe, Dryden, George Eliot, Emerson, Lincoln, Lowell, Prior, Thomson, Twain, and Young.

Usually a concordance to an author covers all or a major part of that author's works, or, if the works are voluminous, it may index one of the author's major publications or all the examples of a major genre in the author's writings. Ideally, a concordance indexes authoritative texts and supplies accurate references to titles, line numbers, acts, scenes, and even pages, if needed; the contents are included in one alphabetical sequence; and all words except articles, conjunctions, prepositions, and some other very common words appear as entries. It should also be easy to read, easy to use, and easy to heft. Usually, the computer-made concordances are ideal in most of these respects. They are more complete and more authoritative than most of the hand-made, slip-generated ones, and they are based on good texts; but a few of them are less of a pleasure to use than the older ones because the printing is not attractive or easy to scan and because the phrases and lines that we seek are too well hidden in their contexts. On the other hand, an old slip-generated concordance that is falling apart affords little pleasure. If there is a choice of concordances, as with Pope, Milton, Keats, and Shakespeare, you should choose the computer-generated works; but if there is no choice, you can still manage very well with most of the older concordances if you are careful. No matter which concordance you use, however, you must be sure, after identifying the source of a passage, to quote and cite a standard edition of a literary work. Do not merely repeat the wording and the citation given in the concordance.

When should you use a concordance as a quotation-tracing tool? First of all, do not, as a rule, consult one unless the standard books of quotations have failed you, even if you already know the name of the author of the quote. I do not always follow this counsel myself, but the advice is sound. The citation in the dictionary of quotations is usually much more understandable than that given in the concordance, and both the citation and the wording in the former may well be more accurate also. If the authorship is known or strongly suspected, and if the standard compilations have not worked, then use the concordance if there is one; when the authorship of a passage is not known, consult several likely concordances in sequence.

Sometimes you can use a concordance imaginatively or creatively when you do not know the words of a quotation. For example, in the past year I have traced a quotation from A. E. Housman that had been translated into Chinese and later retranslated by a researcher into English; I have also located a passage from Whitman that had been translated into Spanish and later re-anglicized. Both problems—unusual but by no means unique—were solved in minutes using concordances to these poets. In such a tricky exercise, a number of words in the concordance may have to be consulted, but whenever possible the first word checked should be an English word that has no synonym or few synonyms.

I recall two instances of tracing Bible passages whose wording I did not know at all. In the first I used a concordance to one version to locate a verse in another version; in the second I used a concordance that was organized by subject rather than by words from the text. Once I needed to verify Samuel Johnson's statement in his edition of Shakespeare that the verb "file," meaning "defile," occurs in the Bishops' Bible.[3] There being no concordance to that translation, I consulted a concordance to the King James version for examples of "defile" and checked the corresponding passages in the Bishops' Bible until I found one that contained "fyle."[4] Not long ago, in the throes of writing this book, I tried to recall a certain Bible verse that I thought was somehow applicable, but I could not remember a single word of the passage. I knew, however, that it had to do with childbirth. Fortunately, I thought of Charles R. Joy's *Harper's Topical Concordance*, not made for the likes of me but designed to suggest texts for preachers. By looking under "birth," I easily located part of the verse I wanted, John 16:21: "A woman when she is in travail hath sorrow, because her hour is come: but as soon as she is delivered of the child, she remembereth no more the anguish, for joy that a man is born into the world." Such instances of creative tracking are not typical, however. Usually we employ concordances in a more straightforward fashion.

You would do well to remember certain factors when using concordances and word indexes to solve problems of source identification and citation. Often, perhaps usually, you will be dealing with misquotations or altered quotations; hence, one or more of the words in the quotation will not appear in the desired context in the concordance being consulted. For that reason alone the concordance may have to be checked at several points rather than only one; and there are still other reasons. Just as quotations are imperfect, so are the instruments we use in tracing them. We expect concordances to omit occurrences of articles, conjunctions, prepositions, and a few other very common words, and we are not at all inconvenienced by such omissions. However, many of the concordances made long ago fail to record every occurrence of even major words. For example, I finally located ". . . faintly trust the larger hope," one of the quotations from chapter 1, in Evans, with a reference to Tennyson. Not following my own advice to consult the basic dictionaries of quotations before trying other things, I had earlier consulted Baker's Tennyson concordance for the passage, because the words do sound Tennysonian. I failed to locate the quotation in it because I again failed to follow my own advice and chose to look only under "faintly." The passage is in Baker's Tennyson concordance but under "trust," "larger," and "hope." A third good reason to try several words if the first does not give you what you want is that we too are imperfect and may fail to see something even if it is there.

If there are several alphabetical sequences in the concordance, each must be checked, if need be, even if some sections are not large, as in Baker's concordance to Tennyson, Bartlett's concordance to Shakespeare, and Hudson's concordance to Elizabeth Barrett Browning. Begin with the section deemed most likely to contain the passage, but as a matter of course consult all the sections in turn until you find the passage or until you have consulted them all without success. The subject of a query published when I was inexperienced at using concordances was a slightly misquoted passage that sounded like Tennyson:

Who lights the faggot?
Not the full faith, but the lurking doubt.[5]

After consulting the main part of Baker's Tennyson concordance without finding the passage, I stupidly did not go on to the section covering the dramatic works. Thus I failed to learn from the concordance that the passage came from Tennyson's *Queen Mary* (3.4.79–80). Fortunately, I did succeed in finding the lines in an old dictionary of quotations and was thus able to answer the query, but the lesson was and still is a painful one. I hope you will learn from my mistakes.[6]

Although in extreme cases you must be prepared to check almost every word of a passage when using a concordance to the works of the author to whom a quotation has been attributed, you should always begin, if possible, with unusual words that are not likely to occur very often in the concordance. Obviously, it is much easier—and much less time-consuming—to scan a few lines listed under an uncommon word than to scan many lines listed under a common one. Looking at the choice of words from another direction and perhaps arriving at the same result, it is also helpful to begin with words that probably have survived any changes due to the quoter's faulty memory or the desire to make the passage fit its new context.

In using any concordance or verbal index, you should be aware of its limitations and its special characteristics. For example, Cruden's biblical concordance is not so exhaustive as Strong's; but, on the other hand, some editions of Cruden include the Apocrypha, whereas Strong and some other editions of Cruden do not. Montgomery and Hubbard's verbal index to Dryden includes the poems but not the plays, and it does not show words in their contexts. Reaver's concordance to O'Neill is based on an edition of O'Neill that omits some of the early plays. Neve's concordance to Cowper does not index the translations or the minor poems. Abbott's concordance to Pope does not index Pope's minor poems or his translation of Homer, but that of Bedford and Dilligan does. And several concordances, as I have noted already, contain more than one alphabet. An old concordance such as Reid's concordance to Burns may list singular and plural forms together under the singular. Also, using an *index verborum* is not the same as using a concordance. In using a word index such as Montgomery and Hubbard's index to Dryden or Pollin's word index to the fiction of Poe, you must compare the occurrences listed under two or more word entries until you find two or more words in the quotation that have the same location or contiguous locations in the indexed work. Then, by consulting an edition of the work indexed, you try to confirm that the precise source of the passage has been determined. There are, in addition, other special characteristics of particular concordances and word indexes, such as the manner in which sources are cited.

To learn how concordances and word indexes work, or to refresh your memory about them, and to see how this concordance differs from that one in coverage or in presentation of information, let us use a few of them to trace several quotations attributed to various authors. The first five passages, repeated from chapter 5, were originally unattributed quotations from my files but are now, with slightly different wording, illustrative quotations in Johnson's *Dictionary* attributed to Milton, Pope, Shakespeare, and Dryden. Two of them have already been located by tracing expanded quotations in the *OED*, but let us solve them again by consulting concordances; the second five are attributions in my own files that I have not, until now, taken the time to verify. I have not consulted books of quotations or English dictionaries for the latter group, since this is merely an exercise in concordance checking. I hope you will look at the concordances used and either anticipate or verify my statements:

1. Break off, break off; I feel the different sound
   Of some chaste *footing* near about this ground:
   Run to your shrouds, within these brakes and trees;
   Our number may affright.

   Milton.

2. May thy billows roul ashore
   The *beryl* and the golden ore.

   Milton.

3. Alas! not dazzled with their noon-tide ray,
   Compute the morn and ev'ning to the day;
   The whole amount of that enormous fame,
   A tale that blends their glory with their shame.

   Pope.

4. Proper *deformity* seems not in the fiend
   So horrid as in woman.

   Shakespeare's King Lear.

5.   Hourly suitors come:
The east with incense and the west with gold,
Will stand like *suppliants* to receive her doom.
                         Dryden.

6. . . . after quoting the famous expressions from Mrs. Browning,
as to our "little thinking if we work our *souls* as nobly as our
iron," . . .[7]

7. For this sentiment, he of the Excursion has called the author of
the Theory of Moral Sentiments a weed. If he be, then, to use an
expression which Wordsworth has borrowed from Spenser, 'tis
"a weed of glorious feature."[8]

8. . . . that whimpering, whinging, crying style of poetry which
Keats has well called,
"The shrill liquidity of dewy piping;"[9]

9. There are many Scotchmen who would go to great lengths to
gain, as Burn [*sic*] says, "the glorious privilege of being
independent,"[10]

10. I remember his saying to me that his ideal of a line of verse was
the line of Poe:
The viol, the violet, and the vine;[11]

As you may recall, we solved the first quotation by using the *OED*,
remarking that a concordance would have worked just as well. In
Bradshaw's *Concordance to the Poetical Works of John Milton*, we find
lines from this passage under "break," "feel," "different," "some,"
"chaste," "footing," "near," "ground," "run," "shrouds," "within,"
"brakes," "trees," "number," "affright," and, of course, "pace," which
in Johnson's *Dictionary* has been replaced by "sound." Under "chaste"
we find: "C. 146. some *c*. footing near about this ground." We are not
told what "C. 146" means, but we know it means "Comus," line 146.
In the more recent *Concordance to Milton's English Poetry* by Ingram
and Swaim, we find lines from the same passage under "break," "off,"
"feel," "I," "different," "pace," "some," "chaste," "footing," "near,"
"about," "this," "ground," "run," "your," "shrouds," "within,"
"these," "brakes," "trees," "number," "may," and "affright." Under
"chaste" we find: "Of som chast footing neer about this ground. Mask
146." The introduction explains that "Mask" is "A Mask (Comus)"
and that the base text used is the version in the 1645 edition of the
Poems.

    The second Milton quotation on the list is also, both concordances
tell us, from "Comus" or "A Mask" (ll. 932–33). In the Ingram and
Swaim concordance, the quotation can be traced by looking under the
words "may," "thy," "billows," "roll," "ashore," "beryl," "golden,"

and "ore." In Bradshaw the words to check are "billows," "roll," "ashore," "beryl," "golden," and "ore."

Edwin Abbott's *Concordance to the Works of Alexander Pope* locates the lines of the third quotation, which is ascribed to Pope in Johnson's *Dictionary*, under the words "dazzled," "noon," "ray," "compute," "morn," "ev'ning," "day," "whole," "amount," "enormous," "fame," "tale," "blends," "glory," and "shame." Under "compute" we find: "C. the morn and ev'ning to the day   E. M. iv.306." In a list of abbreviations, "E. M. iv." is expanded to "Essay on Man, Ep. IV." In Emmett G. Bedford and Robert J. Dilligan's excellent *Concordance to the Poems of Alexander Pope*, the quotation may be traced by checking the same words, except for "noon," and also by checking "alas" and "noon-tide." Under "compute" we find: "Compute the morn and ev'ning to the day; 3.EOM4.306.156." The citation means volume 3 of the Twickenham edition of Pope, "An Essay on Man, Epistle 4," line 306, page 156. Since the Twickenham edition is the edition that we should quote and cite, the details given us by Bedford and Dilligan save us much time; the user of Abbott's concordance would have to locate the poem in the Twickenham edition without such assistance. Incidentally, Bedford and Dilligan also refer users to a very similar, but not identical, passage that occurs elsewhere in Pope; Abbott does not.

The fourth quotation, ascribed to *King Lear*, is easily located in Bartlett's *New and Complete Concordance . . . to . . . Shakespeare*. Using a concordance is always easy if you know the title as well as the author, since passages from the same title are grouped together; simply look for the title and for the passage you seek. Under "deformity" we find: "Proper deformity seems not in the fiend So horrid as in woman   . *Lear* iv 2 60." We find the same passage under "horrid," with the citation "*Lear* iv 2 61." It may also be located under "proper," "seem" (under which we find occurrences of both "seem" and "seems"), "fiend," and "woman." The text and the citations are to the old Globe edition, which is not standard. Ordinarily, the user of Bartlett's concordance would have to find the same passage in the Riverside or some other good edition and quote and cite the text in it. In Marvin Spevack's *Harvard Concordance to Shakespeare*, which is based on the Riverside edition, we find the passage under "proper," "deformity," "shows," "fiend," "horrid," and "woman" but not under "seems," since in the Riverside edition the reading is "shows."

When we first encountered it in chapter 5, the fifth quotation was a quatrain attributed to no one. In Johnson's *Dictionary*, however, it is a three-line quotation attributed to Dryden ("Hourly suitors come . . ."). We can now locate it easily by means of a word index. In Guy Montgomery and Lester A. Hubbard's *Concordance to the Poetical Works of*

John Dryden, there are three references to "suitors," a word in the first line of the shortened quotation: "AM 1186," "M1 640," and "CAM 103." Each of these refers to a title and a line number. Under "hourly," a second word from the first line of the quotation, we find a dozen citations, one of which is "AM 1186," which matches one of the references given under "suitors." All that remains is to decipher the citation and find a reliable edition of Dryden. We learn that "AM" stands for "Annus Mirabilis, the Year of Wonders, 1666." Since there is no index or concordance to Dryden's plays, we must consider ourselves lucky to have found the passage in the index to Dryden's poetry.

The only difficult thing about solving the sixth quotation, which is ascribed to Elizabeth Barrett Browning, is determining which of the thirteen separate concordances constituting Gladys W. Hudson's *Elizabeth Barrett Browning Concordance* is most likely to help. Of course, we should be prepared to consult all thirteen, but in this instance that will not be necessary. After failing to find the passage in the concordance to *Aurora Leigh*, we proceed to the next most likely choice, the concordance to the *Poems, 1844*, and find the passage under every possible word: "little," "thinking," "if," "we," "work," "our," "souls," "as," "nobly," and "iron." We are referred to "Geraldin 203," or "Lady Geraldine's Courtship," line 203.

Tracing the seventh quotation, which is attributed both to Spenser and to Wordsworth, obviously requires the use of two concordances. In Charles Osgood's *Concordance to the Poems of Edmund Spenser*, we find the passage under "glorious," "feature," and, we learn later, "weeds." The line as given under "feature" is: "To feed on flowres and weeds of glorious *feature, ... Mui.* 213," or *Muiopotmos*, line 213. In Lane Cooper's *Concordance to the Poems of William Wordsworth*, we find Wordsworth's line under "weed," "glorious," and "feature": "Was beautiful to see—a weed of glorious feature. 191 *Beggars* 18," or line 18 of *Beggars*, which is on page 191 of the Oxford Wordsworth.

The eighth passage is a misquotation from Keats that I added to the list to remind us to check a concordance under more than one principal word of a quotation. The old concordance of Baldwin and the recent one of Becker, Dilligan, and Bender are equally useful in tracing the quotation. It is slightly easier to scan the succession of lines in Baldwin, but because of the authority of the newer work and of the text it indexes, I prefer Becker, Dilligan, and Bender. Of course, neither concordance locates the quotation under the word substituted by the quoter, "shrill," but both deal commendably with the words that are correctly quoted. Each concordance informs us in its own way that the passage is from "Sleep and Poetry," line 371.

The ninth quotation, a passage from "Burn," sends us to the century-old Burns concordance of J. B. Reid. By looking under "independent" or "glorious" or "priviledge [*sic*]," we find that the passage is from "Ep. to Young Friend. 7.," or "Epistle to a Young Friend," stanza 7.

The tenth quote, the line from Poe so much appreciated by Ernest Dowson, is easily located in Booth and Jones's concordance to Poe. Under "vine," "viol," and "violet," the source is given as "City 23," or line 23 of "The City in the Sea." In Wiley's recently published concordance to Poe, the line may be located under the same words, and the source given is "1   201   23   CITYH," or line 23 of "The City in the Sea," which may be found on page 201 of volume 1 of Mabbott's edition of Poe's works.

When the authorship of a quotation is known and there is a concordance, all you have to do to find a citation and a text is to get the location from the concordance and then base the text of the quotation and a source citation on a reliable edition of the author's work. If the authorship is not known, you must assume—or hope—that there is a concordance to the author's work and, if the general dictionaries of quotations have not helped, you should consult likely concordances in succession. This sequential checking takes time, but it should not be neglected, for many times it will be the only thing that enables you to succeed.

Which concordances to consult for a quotation of unknown authorship will depend upon a number of more or less obvious factors. As we shall see in chapter 8, clues in the quotation itself or in its context may suggest likely authors. The very subject of the passage and the date of the appearance of the quotation may also influence selection of possible parents of a foundling quotation. Even knowing for certain whether a passage is in verse or in prose will have some effect on the choice of concordances—in fact, if there is any doubt at all about this, always assume that the passage is probably poetical but possibly biblical. For example, to answer a query about quotations in Dana's *Two Years before the Mast*, I identified the source of "speedy gleams" by assuming that the phrase was poetical in origin and by consulting concordances to popular poets, including Burns;[12] to answer a query about quotations in Hardy's novel *A Pair of Blue Eyes*, I located "Beneath the shelter of an aged tree" by assuming that it was poetical and by consulting concordances to popular poets, including Burns.[13] This simple hint now enables us to solve one of the problem quotations from chapter 1, "Calm or convulsed, in breeze, or gale, or storm," an unattributed line used in the correspondence of William Lloyd Garrison. By consulting a series of concordances to poets who were popular in 1846, we come upon Ione Young's fine concordance to Byron, which tells us that the line comes from *Childe Harold's Pilgrimage.*

For the sleuth who has consulted without reward the standard quotation compilations and two or three English dictionaries in pursuit of a literary quotation in English and who has no clues or hunches to follow in choosing likely concordances to check, I can supply an all-purpose formula that will often lead to success and even glory. Following clues or hunches, of course, is preferable to using the formula, but the formula does have merit. I propose a basic group of thirteen concordances to be used in succession until the solution is found or until all of them have failed. My list consists of concordances to the King James Bible, Shakespeare, Spenser, Milton, Pope, Cowper, Burns, Byron, Wordsworth, Shelley, Keats, Browning, and Tennyson. You may wish to modify the formula by excluding certain authors because of their dates, and naturally there is no reason to use the formula at all to trace a prose passage unless it sounds Shakespearean or biblical. But for most of the quotations you will be called on to trace, there is a good chance that using the formula will lead you to the source—and possibly spare you some embarrassment. There are not many experiences in the life of a quotation tracer that are more disappointing and more humbling than to learn too late that a quotation could easily have been located in the concordance to a major writer.

In addition to using the concordances that exist, it is possible for the computer-wise quote sleuth to create his or her own concordance to an author's works by means of special programs, such as the Oxford Concordance Program and WordCruncher. An Electronic Text Corporation text retrieval program with an unlovely name, WordCruncher is both a source of pre-indexed texts such as the volumes in the Library of America series and a program by which you can index texts of your own choosing.[14]

When there is no concordance or verbal index to an author's works, there is often an alternative to scanning a writer's collected works in search of a particular quote—although the truly dedicated tracer will, on occasion, do just that. A subject index to the author's works may exist and may repeat words from the text, thus leading you right to the source of the quotation you are tracing. An index may be separately published as a book or, more commonly, may be included in an edition of the works either as an index volume or as part of the final volume of a set. A few of the many good examples of separately published author indexes are Joseph W. Sprug's *Index to G. K. Chesterton,* Lavonne B. Axford's *Index to the Poems of Ogden Nash,* Troy D. Reeves's *Annotated Index to the Sermons of John Donne,* and Augustus Ralli's *Guide to Carlyle,* which is both an outline and an index. William Wheeler's

Concordance to "The Spectator," which is not a concordance but an index, may be used by an ingenious tracer even if Morley's edition of *The Spectator,* to which it is keyed, is not available. Those in need of author indexes should check their library's public catalog under some such subject heading as "Chesterton, G. K. (Gilbert Keith)—1874–1936—Indexes."

Some multivolume works that include index volumes are Herbert Davis's edition of Swift's *Prose Works,* Robert Latham and William Matthews's edition of Pepys's *Diary,* P. P. Howe's edition of William Hazlitt, and E. T. Cook and Alexander Wedderburn's edition of Ruskin. Two standard editions that include indexes in their final volumes are Donald F. Bond's edition of *The Spectator* and Arthur Friedman's edition of Oliver Goldsmith. Various editions of Emerson also contain indexes. If you are trying to find the source of a passage attributed to a major prose writer, always assume that there is a scholarly edition of that writer's works and that this edition contains an index. Our assumptions, like our indiscretion, sometimes serve us well.

NOTES

1. T. H. Howard-Hill, "Foreword," in Andrew T. Crosland, *A Concordance to the Complete Poetry of Stephen Crane* (Detroit: Gale Research Co., 1975), ix.

2. A concordance to T. S. Eliot has appeared as a dissertation, but the important part of it, which is on microfiche, is not available from University Microfilms. See Charlotte Smith Pfeiffer, "A Concordance to 'The Complete Poems and Plays of T. S. Eliot' " (Ph.D. diss., Georgia State University, 1978; Ann Arbor, Mich.: University Microfilms, 1981).

3. *Notes and Queries* 210 (August 1965), 308.

4. My reference to *The songue of Solomon* 5:3 appeared in ibid. 219 (February 1974), 63.

5. Ibid. 212 (June 1967), 228.

6. Helena Swan, comp., *Dictionary of Contemporary Quotations (English)* (London: Swan Sonnenschein and Co., 1904), 119; *Notes and Queries* 213 (February 1968), 65.

7. *International Journal of Ethics* 9 (January 1899), 203.

8. *Blackwood's Edinburgh Magazine* 30 (July 1831), 93.

9. Ibid. 21 (June 1827), 834.

10. *Examiner,* no. 832 (11 January 1824), 26.

11. *Current Literature* 29 (September 1900), 274.

12. *Notes and Queries* 215 (June 1970), 223; ibid. 217 (April 1972), 138. The phrase is from "Tam o' Shanter," line 75.

13. *Notes and Queries* 220 (May 1975), 209; ibid., (October 1975), 450. The quotation is line 20 of "The Cotter's Saturday Night."

14. For a discussion of some recent developments, see Paula R. Feldman and Buford Norman, *The Wordworthy Computer: Classroom and Research Ap-*

plications in Language and Literature (New York: Random House, 1987), 87–91. The address and phone number of Electronic Text Corporation are 778 South 400 East, Orem, Utah 84058, (801)226–0616.

7 | Indexes to First Lines, Last Lines, Opening Words, and Keywords

The sources of some passages not readily traced by means of books of quotations may be identified by means of indexes to first lines, last lines, opening words, or keywords of poems, songs, recitations, or quotations. Some of these indexes are well known to reference librarians and to students of literature or music, but others are "things not generally known," as John Timbs would have called them, owing to their newness or their antiquity or their nonbook format or their limited subject area. Even the well-known ones are not used much in quotation tracing, because many of us do not usually think of them as quotation-tracing tools.

Sometimes we know from its context or from the inquirer's remarks that the passage we are tracing is the beginning of a poem or a song or a recitation. In such cases we should turn to some of the special tools that have been created to index such materials. Even in the absence of such information, however, when all else fails, consider the possibility that the first words of the quote are the first words of something larger and consult various first-line indexes or indexes to opening words to identify the work. Also, even a title index may function to some degree as a first-line index, since many songs and poems are known by their first lines.

It is natural not only to forget that a first-line index can sometimes be of use in tracing a line of verse not already known to be a first line but also to forget that opening-word indexes to prose passages even exist. After such indexes have miraculously solved a few problems for you, however, you are much more likely to remember to consider using them. I cannot promise large numbers of identifications to those who make use of indexes of first lines and opening words, but I can predict an occasional triumph. The really successful seeker of sources is ever willing to make use of tools that only occasionally produce positive results.

The basic first-line index is *Granger's Index to Poetry*, which is also the basic title index. *Granger's* indexes poems by title, first line, subject, and author, and it provides a bibliography of poetry collections containing the poems whose first lines and titles it indexes. Starting in

1904, when it was *An Index to Poetry and Recitations, Granger's Index to Poetry* has appeared in eight editions, two large supplements, and several lesser supplements. A ninth edition, now in press, is scheduled for 1990. Although there has been much duplication of contents in successive editions, much new information has been added in each one and much information from preceding editions has been dropped. Moreover, the scope of the work has changed over the years, as has the arrangement of material. Many people using *Granger's* content themselves with what they find or fail to find in the latest edition or two, but the determined quote sleuth should see the index steadily and see it whole. The eight editions and the major supplements constitute ten different indexes to poetry; the ninth will be another; the first three editions and the first supplement index the opening words of prose passages as well.

A few years ago I was one of several readers of a query who were able to identify a prose piece that was said to begin with these words: "Aunt Hettie Tarbox was as cheerful a person as you could find in a Sabbath day's journey."[1] I solved the problem by means of the first-line index in the second edition of *Granger's*, which includes this entry: "Aunt Hitty, otherwise Mrs. Silas Tarbox, was as cheery and loquacious a person. *See* Aunt Hitty Tarbox.—Wiggin." The title index informed me: "Aunt Hitty Tarbox. (*Sel. fr.* Timothy's Quest, Sc. X.)—Kate Douglas Wiggin.—MRS." I next learned that "MRS" stands for G. Riddle's *Modern Reader and Speaker*, but I did not have to consult it, for I was able to use the Wiggin book instead. As a rule, quotation tracers should not quote and cite an anthology unless they have no other choice. Use the anthology for the information it contains, but then find something more authoritative.

Granger's has been responsible for many of my finds. In one published query the inquirer asked for the identity of a poem that began with the words, "Went the day well?" The several numbered editions of *Granger's* did not help, but a supplement covering the years 1919–28 did. From this and from the anthology to which it referred me, Jean Broadhurst and Clara Lawton Rhodes's *Verse for Patriots,* I learned that "Went the day well?" was the beginning of the second of "Four Epitaphs" by J. M. Edmonds that had appeared in the *Times* (London). Fortunately, the indexer had considered the second epitaph a separate poem. By using *The Readers' Guide*, I found "Four Epitaphs" in an American periodical; and with an idea of the date of publication thus supplied, I was able to find the *Times* appearance by looking under the title in *Palmer's Index to the Times Newspapers.*[2] Another query asked for the source of "O wondrous power of words, by simple faith / Licensed to take the meaning that we love." This quote turned up in the eighth edition of *Granger's*. Not originally the beginning of a poem, it acquired that status when part of Wordsworth's *Prelude* was printed as a separate poem.[3]

Yes, *Granger's* is basic, but there are other useful first-line indexes also. An important work that I have used on occasion is the *Early American Periodicals Index to 1850*. This microform publication contains a first-line index to poems printed in the periodicals treated. An index to first lines of American poetry of the colonial period is found in J. A. Lemay's *Calendar of American Poetry in the Colonial Newspapers and Magazines and in the Major English Magazines through 1765*. A first-line index to individually published poems of the eighteenth century is given in D. F. Foxon's *English Verse, 1701–50: A Catalogue of Separately Printed Poems with Notes on Contemporary Collected Editions*. Other first-line indexes to poetry are found in Dorothy H. Chapman's *Index to Black Poetry*, Herbert H. Hoffman's *Index to Poetry: European and Latin American Poetry in Anthologies*, Herbert H. Hoffman and Rita Ludwig Hoffman's *International Index to Recorded Poetry*, and Jefferson D. Caskey's *Index to Poetry in Popular Periodicals, 1955–59* and its sequel, covering 1960–64.

Poems about childhood and poems written for children are represented in several indexes. First-line indexes to such poems include John E. Brewton and Sara W. Brewton's *Index to Children's Poetry* and its supplements, as well as the similar *Index to Poetry for Children and Young People, 1964–69*, with its continuations, by John E. Brewton and others. In John Mackay Shaw's *Childhood in Poetry*, poems are indexed not by first lines but by keywords taken from first lines, titles, or characteristic phrases.

First-line indexes to manuscript poems are also, to some extent, indexes to published poems. An excellent index to manuscripts is Margaret Crum's *First-Line Index of English Poetry, 1500–1800, in Manuscripts of the Bodleian Library, Oxford*, which lists the first lines of thousands of manuscript poems, with references to authors, if known. Several American libraries have microfilm copies of the unpublished, untitled, handwritten index of first lines of English poems in manuscript in the British Library, with names of authors supplied, if known. The fifth volume of the *Index of English Literary Manuscripts*, when it is published, is to contain an index of first lines.

It frequently will happen that the line you are trying to identify is not the first line but the concluding line of a poem; similarly, a passage of several lines may well be the concluding lines of a poem. Just as you should routinely check *Granger's* for a single line or for the first line of a verse passage you are tracing, you should routinely check Victoria Kline's *Last Lines: An Index to the Last Lines of Poetry* for a single line or for the last line of a verse passage you are trying to identify. Kline's book contains an alphabetical index of last lines and poem titles, interfiled, and a keyword index to last lines. Since some one hundred seventy-four thousand poems are indexed, *Last Lines*, which as I write these words is still in press, is sure to become a reference work that quotation tracers will find extremely useful.

A long since forgotten keyword and subject index to English poetry of the seventeenth and eighteenth centuries is the two-volume index to *The Works of the English Poets*, a collection chiefly important for inspiring Dr. Johnson's *Lives of the Poets*. This is essentially an index to memorable lines of poems included in the collection. Since many of these authors are often quoted in works of the eighteenth and nineteenth centuries, and since most of them have not been the subjects of concordances and are not well represented in books of quotations, the index can be helpful in tracing quotations of the period covered. It may be used to supplement Bysshe's collection and similar early works mentioned in chapter 2.

There are several first-line indexes, title indexes, and title and first-line indexes to songs and hymns. Most of these give references to collections in which the songs are located. Since many songs, like many poems, are known by their first lines, even title indexes may be used as first-line indexes. Some very useful indexes of this type are Minnie Earl Sears's *Song Index* and its supplement; Helen Grant Cushing's *Children's Song Index*; Patricia Pate Havlice's *Popular Song Index* and its supplements; Robert Leigh's *Index to Song Books*; Desiree de Charms and Paul F. Breed's *Songs in Collections*; Florence Brunnings's *Folk Song Index*; William Gargan and Sue Sharma's *Find That Tune*; Richard Lewine and Alfred Simon's *Songs of the Theater*; Ken Bloom's *American Song: The Complete Musical Theatre Companion*; and Roger Lax and Frederick Smith's *Great Song Thesaurus*. As you know, practically any hymn book includes a first-line index to its hymns, but hymn indexes of much larger scope also exist. First-line indexes to thousands of hymns are found in John Julian's *Dictionary of Hymnology* and in Katharine Smith Diehl's *Hymns and Tunes: An Index*. More than a half century ago, the Methodist Church in England published *Subject, Textual, and Lineal Indexes to the Methodist Hymn Book*, which contains an alphabetical index of every line in the hymns. I have already mentioned concordances to the Episcopal hymnal, the Pilgrim hymnal, and the Methodist hymnal of this country, and there may be indexes or concordances to other major hymnals as well.

Another kind of index of value to the quotation tracer is the index to quotations themselves. Such indexes occur as parts of larger indexes to journals that publish queries and replies. Charles R. Anderson's

Index to "The Exchange" is a keyword index to many years of that section of *RQ* entitled "The Exchange." Annual indexes to *American Notes & Queries* (now *ANQ*) are of occasional assistance, especially if you use them to help you recapture replies you remember reading. The most important index to queried quotes is the opening-word index to quotations that is included in the *General Index* to *Notes and Queries*. Since it began in 1849, *Notes and Queries* has been, among other valuable things, a clearinghouse for questions and answers about quotations, and its files are a treasure trove of information about quotes and their sources. There are, at this writing, fifteen volumes of the *General Index*, one for each of the first fifteen series of the journal. In these are cumulated the annual indexes of almost a century of the publication, 1849–1947. As for the four succeeding decades, the dedicated quote sleuth will have already read the queries and replies of all the volumes and will use the annual indexes to retrieve a reply he or she has already seen. The main heading for quotes in the many series of the *General Index* is, of course, "Quotations"; but there are also other headings of interest to the literary detective.

Although an index arranged by opening words has limitations, it can still be quite useful. Two quotations of the same passage, one being traced today and the other identified in series 7 of *Notes and Queries* and listed in the index, may not begin with the same words. If wordings do not mesh, you probably will not spot the quotation in the index; but they often do, enabling you to find what you are looking for in these indexes. Obviously, you should not begin a search for a source citation by consulting the fifteen *Notes and Queries* indexes, for you can often obtain easier access to information by using quotation compilations, English dictionaries, and concordances. But *Notes and Queries* does contain quotations and citations not to be found in those other materials. The *General Index* volumes are a major resource, even an essential resource, for scholarly searching.

The great strength of the accumulated knowledge of quotation sources to be found in *Notes and Queries* and the value of the *General Index* in solving quotation problems that arise today are illustrated by the following example. In 1875 someone wrote to *Notes and Queries* about an unidentified quotation appearing in a letter written in 1822 by Thomas Jefferson to John Adams:

> "When one by one our ties are torn,
>   And friend from friend is snatched forlorn;
>   When man is left alone to mourn,
>   Oh! then how sweet it is to die!
>
>   When trembling limbs refuse their weight,

And films slow gathering dim the sight;
When clouds obscure the mental light,
'Tis nature's kindest boon to die!"

In a reply published later in 1875, a reader identified the source as Mrs. Barbauld's poem "A Thought on Death."[4] The exchange was duly recorded in the index to the volume and in the index to series 5 of *Notes and Queries*, but apparently no one made a note of the information anywhere else; at any rate, the source is not identified in Lester J. Cappon's edition of *The Adams-Jefferson Letters*.[5] In 1983 the same passage from the same letter was the subject of a query published in an American magazine. Using the *General Index* to *Notes and Queries*, I was able to provide the source of the lines in question.[6] Although the *General Index* provides access to many kinds of information contained in the greatest of scholarly journals, in my opinion its most valuable function is to show where quotation sources have been "found and made a note of." The quote sleuth, like the researcher in other literary and historical fields, will benefit by consulting this important index. As a general rule, you should never concede failure in the search for the source of a literary quotation until you have consulted all the volumes in the *General Index* to *Notes and Queries* and failed to find it.

NOTES

1. *RQ* 15 (Winter 1975), 154; ibid., (Summer 1976), 332.

2. *Harvard Magazine* 88 (September-October 1985), 94; Jean Broadhurst and Clara Lawton Rhodes, *Verse for Patriots* (Philadelphia: J. B. Lippincott, 1919), 183; *Literary Digest* 57 (27 April 1918), 38; *Times* (London), 6 February 1918, 7; *Harvard Magazine* 88 (January-February 1986), 103.

3. *Harvard Magazine* 87 (July-August 1985), 12; ibid. 89 (November-December 1986), 80.

4. *Notes and Queries*, 5th ser., 4 (28 August 1875), 180; ibid., (16 October 1875), 320.

5. John Adams, *The Adams-Jefferson Letters: The Complete Correspondence between Thomas Jefferson and Abigail and John Adams*, ed. Lester J. Cappon, 2 vols. (Chapel Hill: University of North Carolina Press, 1959), 2:578.

6. *Harvard Magazine* 85 (July-August 1983), 8; ibid. 86 (March-April 1984), 22.

8 | Detective Work: Names, Titles, Clues

> "They say that genius is an infinite capacity for taking pains," he remarked with a smile. "It's a very bad definition, but it does apply to detective work."
>
> "A Study in Scarlet"

At the beginning of a search, methodical plodding through the indexes of the standard general dictionaries of quotations, unexciting though this may be, is usually a wiser course than the pursuit of clues, the following up of allusions, and the imaginative employment of special resources. If the text and the source citation you seek are in Bartlett or the *Oxford Dictionary of Quotations,* your goal is achieved in minutes and you can either accept what you have found or verify the information in a scholarly edition of the author's works. Solving the problem by more creative or more imaginative means and then locating the passage in an authoritative text require considerably more time and effort. If, however, the major compilations fail you, then a different tack must be taken.

What you do next depends on what you know or what you sense about the quotation and what you think the likelihood is that this tack or that one will be successful. Several types of reference works discussed in other chapters are available—single-author quotation books, single-subject quotation books and anthologies, concordances to the works of major authors, dictionaries of the English language or of foreign languages, and various collections of classical and foreign quotations. Some of these, such as the one-author quote book or the concordance to an author's works, can be used if you know the name of the author. Others, such as dictionaries of the language and one-subject quote books, can be used whether you have this information or not. If the authorship is not known, you may want to try a succession of likely concordances, or ask a knowledgeable friend, or make use of the information about the source that the quoter and the quoted passage have given you.

How to choose among all these options cannot be reduced to a formula. The decision, or a succession of decisions, must be made on the spot. When pressed for time, we tracers of quotations play what we think are the odds. Of course, factors other than time also influence our choices. We use whatever tools are at hand when a problem arises; and even when many resources are available, we naturally do what gives us mental pleasure and scholarly satisfaction. Thus, the quote sleuth often makes use of the clues that accompany the quotation even when another approach might work out just as well; on the other hand, the pursuit of clues and allusions is often the only available option.

The quotation's context or the passage itself may supply one or more of the following pieces of information: the name of the author of the quoted passage; a characterization or a description or an epithetical identification of the author; the title of the work quoted; the genre of the work; the subject treated by the work; the tone or mood of the work; the name of a literary character or a place associated with the passage or mentioned in it; the year in which the passage was quoted; the name of the quoter; the title of the work in which the passage appears as a quotation; the prevailing meter, the length of the lines, and the presence or absence of rhyme; the stanza form; and stylistic and typographical evidence suggesting possible authorship or probable period. If the author is named, you should proceed to a concordance or to a book made up of quotations from the author, if such books exist. Look at a book of selections from the author's works, or use the index to the author's collected works, or look at the works themselves. Look at biographical or critical works about the author of the quotation, starting with the indexes to them and then, if necessary, leafing through the materials themselves. If both the author and title are named, you should use an index to the works of the author or consult an index or a concordance to the work named as the source of the quotation. Or, you can scan or read the work until the passage turns up. Sooner or later, you will probably try all of these things.

Many quotes with which you may have to deal are introduced not by the name of the author but by some other indication of authorship. This may be an easily traceable phrase or some other fact or combination of facts that enables you to identify the author of the passage. Let us look at a few examples of this sort of thing, taken from old books and periodicals.

Here is an instance of what used to be a very common method of indicating authorship:

Not otherwise does the poet-laureate read it when he says:—
"All the past of time reveals
A bridal dawn of thunder-peals,
Wherever thought hath wedded fact."[1]

To solve this one, you need to know when the author of the lines was identified as the poet laureate and, after learning that the year was 1867, you need to know who the poet laureate was at that time. A list of the poets laureate and the dates of their appointments can be found anywhere—in an encyclopedia, in an almanac, in a literary handbook, or in a book about the poets laureate. You simply learn the name of the poet laureate, consult the Tennyson concordance, and verify what you found there by locating "Love thou thy land, with love far-brought" in an edition of the poet's works. An easy task.

British readers of 1733 had no trouble with this:

> . . . . and, as our *mad Poet* has it,
> ———*That wrath divine was hurl'd,*
> *Which might to atoms shake the solid world.*[2]

Today's readers, however, may need to consult a reference book to determine who the mad poets were or which poets have been referred to by the appellation "mad poet." Carl Sifakis's *Dictionary of Historic Nicknames* suggests two candidates, McDonald Clarke (1798–1842) and Nathaniel Lee (c. 1653–92). Jennifer Mossman's *Pseudonyms and Nicknames Dictionary* lists Clarke, Lee, and William Collins (1721–59). Clarke and Collins can be eliminated by their dates. Thus, I looked at rhyming couplets in Lee's works and found the passage at the end of act 4 of *Oedipus*, a play written by Lee and Dryden.

The use of the present tense in an 1888 description of the author of the next quotation made the solution less easy for me than it should have been:

> Or, to put the question in the words of him who is at once our greatest poet and our greatest moralist—
> "Shall we serve Heaven
> With less respect than we do minister
> To our gross selves?"[3]

Because Tennyson and Browning were great poets and great moralists, I began the search by consulting, in vain, the concordances to their works. Looking again at the quoter's characterization of the author, I decided that Shakespeare was the most likely candidate and used a concordance to locate the passage in *Measure for Measure* (2.2.85–87). No doubt the blank verse would eventually have suggested Shakespeare to me, but it was the description of the poet that actually did it.

The clue to the source of the next quotation is simply the word "Psalmist":

> He is like the good man described by the Psalmist,

"Who to his plighted vows and trust
    Hath ever firmly stood;
And though he promise to his loss,
    He makes his promise good."[4]

If "Psalmist" does not signify anything to you, then the first step is to consult a reference book, such as a dictionary or E. Cobham Brewer's *Reader's Handbook* or William Rose Benét's *Reader's Encyclopedia*. However, you will probably recognize it as a reference to the author or authors of the biblical Psalms. Moreover, since the quotation is in verse, the source has to be a metrical version of the Psalms. In 1839, when the lines were quoted (appropriately, I think) in *Merchants' Magazine*, Nahum Tate and Nicholas Brady's *New Version of the Psalms of David*, which was first published in 1696, was still very popular. Scanning the metrical version of Tate and Brady printed in a nineteenth-century edition of the Book of Common Prayer, I found the quote in Psalm 15. There are other metrical versions, but fortunately I happened to start with Tate and Brady.

An essentially similar problem was this puzzler:

An English public man, who was also a novelist and poet, wrote:
"Ne'er of the living can the living judge,
Too blind the affection or too fresh the grudge."[5]

This mystery was the subject of an unanswered query in the *New York Times Book Review* some years ago and the subject of a later query in *Notes and Queries*.[6] To trace the quote I tried to compile a list of English political figures who wrote novels and poems or of English novelists who were poets and political figures. In doing so I racked my memory and also turned pages in the old *Cambridge Bibliography of English Literature*. From my list of two I eliminated Disraeli, who I mistakenly thought had written no verse. I then scanned the poetry of the remaining candidate until the fine couplet turned up near the end of Bulwer-Lytton's *St. Stephen's*.

In each of the above cases I was able to locate the source by using the information about the author supplied by the quoter. In other cases, the information given is the title of the source. This may follow a quotation used as a motto or epigraph or it may be mentioned in the quotation's context. If you recognize the title immediately and recall the name of the author, use a concordance or an index to the author's works, if there is such a thing, or read or scan the work until the passage is located. If you do not recognize it, at least the title provides a clue to be followed until you can discover something about the work and learn the name of the author.

Titles can be identified by consulting a number of sources, beginning with the one that is handiest or with the one that seems most likely to provide the information. For poems, the title and first-line index in *Granger's Index to Poetry* is very useful, as are the title indexes in other works mentioned in chapter 7 in the discussion of indexes to poems and songs. Plays are indexed by title in G. William Bergquist's *Three Centuries of English and American Plays: A Checklist*, in H. J. Eldredge's *"The Stage" Cyclopaedia*, and in a number of other sources. Titles of plays and novels and other book-length publications can be traced by consulting various literary companions and handbooks, such as the *Reader's Encyclopedia* or the *Reader's Handbook* or the *Oxford Companion* to this literature or that; *The New Century Cyclopedia of Names*; a library's public catalog; computerized library networks; *Books in Print*; or persons likely to know. After you have traced the author and the nature of a work from its title, what remains is to locate a good text, find the passage in it, verify or correct the wording, and construct a source citation. If the source happens to be a work to which there is no concordance or index, you may have to scan or read your way to the passage.

Let us now look at a few examples of quotations accompanied by titles of works whose authors you may not know. A quotation that can be solved with the use of a handbook and, possibly, a concordance is this one from an old *Blackwood's*: " 'The heart of childhood is all mirth,' says the 'Christian Year,' and its generations of readers have echoed 'of course' without asking each of himself if it were indeed so in his individual case."[7] The title named can be identified in, among other places, *The New Century Cyclopedia of Names*, *Granger's*, and the *Oxford Companion to English Literature*. If you have access to the old concordance to John Keble's book, which is not very likely, you will discover almost immediately that the quotation is the first line of the poem for the second Sunday after Epiphany. It is also easily found in *The Christian Year* itself by using the first-line index or by scanning the text. As often happens, the tracer of this quotation not only accomplishes the goal of locating the passage in its original context but also learns a bit of literary history and becomes acquainted with a book that must be read later when time permits.

References to titles are often very helpful, but you need not make use of a clue merely because it is present. Another passage found in an old *Blackwood's* contains a misquoted couplet in praise of illiteracy:

> . . . and doubtless many *governors* would exclaim, as fervently as Lord Douglas in *Marmion*,
>> "Thanks to St Bothan, son of mine
>> Could never pen a written line![8]

If you choose to follow the clue, you would use a handbook to identify the author—Scott—and the nature of the work. Then, since there is no Scott concordance, you would have to leaf through the narrative poem until, in the fifteenth stanza of Canto Sixth, the couplet appears:

> Thanks to Saint Bothan, son of mine,
> Save Gawain, ne'er could pen a line;

An easier way to trace this particular couplet, however, is to disregard the clue and consult the *OED* under the verb "pen."

The quotation in the following passage can be traced by the use of handbooks:

> . . . still, according to the common-sense argument of the sage author
> of "Original Poems," remonstrating with an unwashed child,
> "If the water is cold, and the comb hurts your head,
>   What good will it do you to cry?"[9]

This misquotation from a book known by its shortened title is easy to trace by consulting the *Oxford Companion to Children's Literature*. From the article on "Original Poems, for Infant Minds" (pp. 388–89), we learn that the book was written by Ann Taylor, Jane Taylor, and others and that Ann Taylor's poem "Washing and Dressing" contains these lines:

> If the water is cold, and the comb hurts your head,
> And the soap has got into your eye;
> Will the water grow warmer for all that you've said?
> And what good will it do you to cry?

Two other resources that may be used to identify the book are an old edition of the *Oxford Companion to English Literature* and the public catalog of a research library. Of course, the quest does not end with either of these tools, for the book must still be examined and the poem must be located and identified.

Now, at last, we can deal with a passage that has hitherto resisted all our efforts:

> The curse of growing factions and divisions
> Still vex your councils!
>   *Venice Preserved.*[10]

Unlike many of Scott's chapter mottoes, this one is not a very notable or quotable passage, but it is an actual example of a quotation accompanied by the title of its source. Should you not recognize the title, you can find out something about it in almost any of the handbooks mentioned thus far. Some likely sources of information are *The New Century Cyclopedia of Names*, the *Reader's Encyclopedia*, and the *Oxford*

Companion to English Literature. Once you learn that *Venice Preserved* is a play by Otway and that there is no concordance to Otway, you must leaf through pages of the play until you find the passage in the fourth act.

Often, tracers are given not the name of the author of a quotation or the title of the work but the name of a literary character associated with the source. The character named may be the speaker of the quoted words or the person to whom they refer. If, as the quoter intended, you recognize the name of the character and immediately recall the author and title of the work quoted, then you usually encounter no real difficulty in locating the exact source of the quotation. When recognition fails, there are reference works that will identify the character for you. Sometimes a literary handbook or an *Oxford Companion* or *The New Century Cyclopedia of Names* will perform this function quite adequately; other times you must turn to more specialized works. The last-named book, incidentally, is an excellent resource when you do not know whether the character named is a real person or a fictitious one or when you do not know whether the name to be identified is a character or a title or a place or a real person.

William Freeman's *Everyman's Dictionary of Fictional Characters*, which is also published as the *Dictionary of Fictional Characters*, identifies characters from fiction, poetry, and drama. Characters from children's literature are found in Freeman, in the *Oxford Companion to Children's Literature*, and in Arthur D. Mortimore's *Index to Characters in Children's Literature*. Harold Sharp and Marjorie Sharp's invaluable *Index to Characters in the Performing Arts* identifies characters from plays, operas, musicals, and other dramatic or artistic productions. Another important resource is Thomas L. Berger and William C. Bradford's *Index of Characters in English Printed Drama to the Restoration*.

Let us now look at several examples I have run across of quotations or misquotations acompanied by names of characters, each of which can be traced with the help of some of the tools I have mentioned. The first one seems untraceable: "We all remember the words the Duke Aranza spoke to Juliana: 'She is best dressed who, in her husband's eyes, looks lovely—the fairest mirror that a virtuous wife can see her beauty in.' "[11] A good place to begin, especially when you do not know the genre, but also when you do, is Freeman or *The New Century Cyclopedia of Names*. This time, neither works. In Sharp and Sharp, however, Duke Aranza is identified as a character in John Tobin's play *The Honeymoon*; he is also identified in Brewer's *Reader's Handbook* and in the old *Century Cyclopedia of Names*. With that information in hand, we find the play and look at Aranza's speeches until we come to this passage near the end of act 3:

<blockquote>
She's adorn'd
Amply, that in her husband's eye looks lovely—
The truest mirror that an honest wife
Can see her beauty in![12]
</blockquote>

In an old volume of *Blackwood's* is a quotation that can be identified easily if you know who Ithuriel was:

<blockquote>
The wand of true genius is an Ithuriel's spear:—

"No falsehood can endure
Touch of celestial temper, but returns
Of force to its own likeness."[13]
</blockquote>

If you recognize the character Ithuriel, you would go directly to a Milton concordance; if you do not, he can be found in various handbooks for readers. Indeed, if you consult the unrevised edition of William Rose Benét's *Reader's Encyclopedia*, you will find a quotation that includes the above lines, along with a reference to *Paradise Lost*, 4.810.[14]

For anyone who does not know who the dickens Miss Pecksniff was, the following passage from *Every Saturday* seems at first to be a real challenge: "When Dr. Livingstone was sleeping out one night, in the course of his explorations, a lion seized and shook him, with a view to further proceedings. It is not many men who can say with Miss Pecksniff that they have 'lived to be shook' in such a style as this."[15] By consulting practically any of the literary handbooks or books of names or characters, we discover that two Misses Pecksniff appear in *Martin Chuzzlewit*—Charity (or Cherry) and Mercy (or Merry). Alas, the quotation is not so easily traced. Unaided by concordances or references to the passage, we must look through the novel until we find Cherry Pecksniff exclaiming in chapter 30, ". . . and oh, good gracious, that I should live to be shook!"

This indirect quotation from a real or fictional person appears in an old *Harper's Magazine*: "Will Honeycomb says he can tell the humor of a woman by the color of her hood."[16] To identify the speaker we first turn to *The New Century Cyclopedia of Names* or practically any of the handbooks that have been mentioned. We quickly learn that Honeycomb is a character in *The Spectator* of Addison and Steele. Consulting the index to Donald F. Bond's excellent edition of that work, under "Honeycomb, Will," we come to "on women's hoods, ii.532." At that location we find the answer: the quote is from Addison and appears in no. 265 of *The Spectator*, dated 3 January 1712.[17]

To solve the next problem we must first identify "the immortal Dr. Slop": ". . . . and in spite of the opinion of the immortal Dr. Slop, that 'virginity alone peoples paradise,' I at once threw up my ticket in that lottery, and resolved to take my chance for a prize on earth."[18] He is easily identified in Freeman or in *The New Century Cyclopedia of Names* or in one of the literary handbooks. Finding the passage in *Tristram Shandy*, however, is not easy unless you have access to a copy of Patricia Hogan Graves's dissertation, "A Computer-generated Concordance to Sterne's *Tristram Shandy*." I did and found that chapter 33 of volume 8 contains this line: "——'Tis Virginity, cried Slop, triumphantly, which fills paradise."

In an essay in *Small Press Review*, Laurel Speer quotes Blanche DuBois: "Here's Speer last October giving a four university reading tour in Connecticut and Long Island and, like Blanche DuBois, 'depending on the kindness of strangers.' "[19] In Freeman and in Sharp and Sharp we learn that Blanche DuBois is a character in Tennessee Williams's play *A Streetcar Named Desire*. With this information in hand, we scan her lines in the play until we come to the quote near the end of the final scene. But there is another way. Knowing now that the quotation is a fairly recent one, we can consult books of quotations in which modern quotes are strongly represented, such as the revised edition of J. M. Cohen and M. J. Cohen's *Penguin Dictionary of Modern Quotations*. We learn there that Blanche says in scene 11, "I have always depended on the kindness of strangers."

Now we have the tools to trace the last of the untraced quotations from the original list of thirty-three: " 'The bellman writes better verses,' said Mr. Osbaldistone, when he threw poor Frank's away."[20] In search of Mr. Osbaldistone, we find that Freeman and various other handbooks identify a number of characters bearing that surname, all of them appearing in Sir Walter Scott's novel *Rob Roy*. Leafing through the novel in search of the quotation, we naturally look very carefully at the second chapter of the first volume, for it has to do with Frank's poetic prowess. There we find Mr. Osbaldistone exclaiming, "Why, the bellman writes better lines."

If the quotation's context fails to give us the title of the work quoted or the name of a character or the name of the author or a clue leading directly to the identity of the author or of the work, it may yet provide us with other kinds of useful information. For one thing, it usually tells us the year in which the passage appeared as a quotation. Thus, we can exclude from consideration all authors not yet born by that year and all authors too young at that time to have written or uttered the quoted words. More positively, the date may help us think of likely candidates. What we know about the popularity of authors living and dead at that time, added to what we know about the quotation itself, will help us determine which concordance to consult or which author to investigate.

Still another kind of information may appear in the work in which a passage occurs as a quotation or in other works written by the person who quoted the passage. It often happens that a writer quotes from the same author more than once. Thus, if a quotation from Wordsworth appears in the article containing the passage you are trying to trace, then begin (and, with luck, end) the search by spending a few minutes with the Wordsworth concordance. If no such identified or identifiable quotation appears in the article, and you are a sufficiently persistent sleuth, you may want to scan other works written by the quoter and consider the author of every identifiable quote thus found to be the possible author of the quotation being traced. Now the amount of time and labor needed for going through the works of the quoter in search of quotations of known or traceable parentage and then determining whether the author of one of them is the author also of the quotation you are tracing may be more than you care to invest. Still, many quotation problems are important enough to justify such an expenditure. Studying the quoter's quoting habits after other methods of proceeding have been found wanting has much to recommend it, the chief thing being that it does work in many instances.

A simple example of the phenomenon of a quoter's returning to a favorite quotable author occurs in an article on thieves in an old *Atlantic*. To illustrate a point, the writer quotes Byron as follows:

"Your thief looks in the crowd," says Byron,
"Exactly like the rest, or rather better,"—
and this, not because physiognomy is false, but the thief's face true.

Later in the same article the writer describes a well-executed theft by a person resembling "the popular idea of a bank-president" and adds, "I know not whether the bank-president was or was not suspected;— 'All I can say is, that he had the money.' " The quote attributed to Byron is, we learn from his concordance, from the second act of *Werner*. The quote not attributed to anyone is, we also learn from the concordance, from Byron's *Don Juan* (1:1680).[21]

A variation of the phenomenon of repeated quoting of the same author within one article or book is likely to have occurred when an unattributed or misattributed or undocumented quote is found in a work hurriedly written or based on research characterized by insufficient note taking. To trace such a quotation, you should look first at various sources that have been named in the notes or in the bibliography, and especially at those named in notes identifying sources of statements occurring not far from the problem passage. Teachers expect to find occasional instances of such unattributed or mistakenly attributed or unreferenced quotes in research papers written by inexperienced writers, but these things also turn up in printed books. For example, William H. Whyte's popular book *The Organization Man* contains an undocumented quotation attributed to Laurence Sterne that is said to refer to Thomas Hobbes: "Thomas Hobbes worked out a complete set of algebraic equations to explain ethics. As Laurence Sterne remarked, his equations 'plussed or minussed you to heaven or hell . . . so that none but the expert mathematician would ever be able to settle his accounts with Saint Peter.'" A knowledgeable reader who could not find this in Sterne and who thought the comment would have been better applied to Francis Hutcheson than to Hobbes appealed first to Whyte, who could not supply the reference, and then to *Notes and Queries*. Beginning with a footnote occurring not far from the quote, I followed a trail of scholarly documentation from an article by Louis I. Bredvold in Richard F. Jones's *Seventeenth Century* to William R. Scott's *Francis Hutcheson* to a work entitled *The Koran*, which is included in some early editions of Sterne's works. I found that the undocumented passage was slightly misquoted in *The Organization Man*, that it did indeed apply to Hutcheson rather than to Hobbes, and that it ultimately came from a work once attributed to Sterne. Consulting Wilbur L. Cross's *Life and Times of Laurence Sterne*, I read that *The Koran* was "an imaginary autobiography" of Sterne written by Richard Griffith the elder.[22]

In tracing an unattributed quotation by looking for attributed or traceable quotations and investigating the possibility that the identified and the unidentified quotations have the same author, the tracer is not limited to information that can be found in the immediate vicinity of the untraced quotation or in the work in which the untraced quotation appears. I have, on a number of occasions, looked through a quoter's other works for identified or identifiable quotations or for clues likely to help me trace a particular passage. For example, William Gilpin's *Observations on the River Wye* contains an unidentified passage that almost defeated me:

> *Ah! happy thou,* if one superior rock
> Bear on its brow the shivered fragment huge
> Of some old Norman fortress: happier far,
> Ah! then most happy, if thy vale below
> Wash, with the crystal coolness of its rills,
> Some mould'ring abbey's ivy-vested wall.

To find its source, I leafed through several of Gilpin's works and tried to trace the quotations I found in them. In his *Observations on Several Parts of Great Britain, Particularly the High-lands of Scotland,* I came upon a long quotation that included these lines:

> Where'er she takes
> Her horizontal march, pursue her step
> With sweeping train of forest; hill to hill
> Unite with prodigality of shade.

Looking up the participial adjective "sweeping" in the *OED*, I learned that the source of this passage was William Mason's long poem *The English Garden*. I then looked through *The English Garden* in search of the untraced passage quoted in *Observations on the River Wye*—and found it.[23]

As you go through a writer's works looking for quotations of known or discoverable parentage that may lead you to the source of the quotation you are tracing, look also for references to authors and books, for these references may suggest likely sources. Similarly, a sale catalog or a list of the books in a writer's personal library or a book about a writer's reading will sometimes direct you to a work that may have been the source you are trying to identify. Even personal or literary associations of a writer with his or her contemporaries, which we can learn about from biographical or critical works, can suggest directions for research.

In 1794 Joseph Hucks and Samuel Taylor Coleridge took a walking tour through North Wales. In an account of the tour published the following year, Hucks speaks of seeing children who are "reckless that age and sorrow with icy hand hung over them." In 1975 this and three other quotations in the book appeared in a published query submitted by one of the preparers of a forthcoming edition of the account. Reading the quotation, I first of all suspected that it was verse and not prose. A short unattributed passage in single or double quotation marks is usually verse even if it is not printed as verse; and besides, this sounded like verse misremembered. After learning that the passage was not from Coleridge, Shakespeare, or a few other likely sources, I recalled that Coleridge had been much impressed with the poetry of William Lisle Bowles at about this time, and I reasoned that his companion must have been also. In search of this quote and the others given in the query, I read much of Bowles's poetry. In "Monody, Written at Matlock" I found the words, "Reck not how age, even thus, with icy hand, / Hangs o'er us."[24] Because I had made use of Hucks's actual association with Coleridge and of his likely familiarity with the works of a poet admired by Coleridge at the time of that association, I succeeded in finding the source of one of the passages. After tracing that one, I unselfishly left the remaining problems for others to solve.

It sometimes helps considerably to know whether the passage to be traced is in verse or in prose. The determination, however, is not always easy. Someone may take a memorable prose passage and print it as a poem, and this poetic version may be repeated by those who think the passage really is a poem. Poetry of the sort that closely resembles prose is itself rarely quoted without attribution, but a passage that in its original form is clearly verse may be altered by the quoter to look like prose; or, with little or no alteration in wording it may be printed to look like prose. However, it usually does not *sound* like prose. When I saw the following passage printed as prose, I knew from the rhyme and the recurring rhythm that it was verse: "The Ocean hath its chart and stars their map and Knowledge spreads them on her ample lap, but Rome is as a desert, where we steer. . . ." Checking poetical concordances in succession, I found it in Byron's *Childe Harold's Pilgrimage* (4.724–6).[25] On the other hand, a passage by Steinbeck that was said to be a poem and was printed as a poem was, I immediately suspected on reading it, prose. It began, "A Book Is Somehow Sacred. / A Dictator Can Kill And Maim People, / . . . ." Looking at likely prose works, I located the passage in Steinbeck's essay "Some Random and Randy Thoughts on Books."[26]

Mistaking verse for prose or prose for verse can be embarrassing to the quotation tracer. I once identified a passage from one of Mrs. Craik's novels as a poem by Mrs. Craik; fortunately, I discovered the gaffe before anyone else did.[27] On another occasion I failed to identify an easily identifiable passage attributed to John Donne: "Faces as frightful as theirs who whip Christ in old hangings." There is a concordance to Donne's poetry, but I did not consult it, for I was certain that this was a prose passage. I also failed to check the *OED* under the substantive "hanging." Either course would have led me to Donne's "Satyre 4," which contains the words, "And, though his face be as ill / As theirs which in old hangings whip Christ, still. . . ."[28] As it happened, several readers of the query in the *New York Times Book Review* either recognized the quotation or knew how to trace it.

Even knowing that a passage is in verse does not make the identification of the source of the passage inevitable or even probable. There are too few concordances to meet our needs—and, conversely, more of them than we are willing to consult for every poetical quotation that we try to trace. We must take the fact that a passage is in verse and combine that fact with every other fact or hint that we can glean. In addition to those that the quotation's context may provide, there may be still other clues in the quotation itself that suggest probable or possible sources. For example, you should know some basic stanza forms and know which poets have used them. You should immediately recognize the standard poetic feet and meters and know which poets are known for having used iambic or trochaic or other metrical lines of this length or that. These are mechanical matters that may be learned by studying books about literature or by reading much verse over many years.

Since they are so common in quotations, you should especially recognize blank verse and the heroic couplet on sight. Sometimes this is possible even if a quotation consists of one complete line and one or two incomplete ones. Many quotations in these forms can be located in a dictionary of quotations or in the *OED*, but if a quotation cannot be traced in one of these ways, then you should begin consulting concordances, taking into account the subject matter, the style, and what you can determine about the date of the passage.

Most blank verse has not yet been indexed by concordances, but two poets who used it and who are most often quoted without attribution, Shakespeare and Milton, are represented by fine concordances. Other poets who have employed it and are also indexed by concordances include Cowper, Wordsworth, Keats, and Browning. In choosing among the concordances to popular authors of blank verse, the tracer of quotations should try to determine the approximate date of the passage. This may be guessed at by considering the year the passage was quoted as the latest possible date and moving that back as the vocabulary, diction, subject of the passage, spelling, punctuation, and tone suggest. Some inexact but useful generalizations for the inexperienced tracer are: If the passage in blank verse is early and about the Creation and the Fall, it is almost certainly from Milton. If it is early and not about the Fall, it may be by Shakespeare or Milton. If it is early and not from either of these, some very old books of quotations mentioned in chapter 2 should be consulted, including one based on the drama. If it is later rather than early, then consult other concordances in turn, guessing at the odds with each choice.

When you see the heroic couplet, you should think first of Pope, who is much quoted and whose complete poetry is now represented by a concordance. Dryden, too, was a major writer of heroic couplets, and checking the word index to his poetry for words from couplets of unknown parentage is often worth the effort. Also, there are concordances to Johnson, Cowper, Goldsmith, and Byron, whose couplets are often quoted. That I am oversimplifying matters is made clear by the *Princeton Encyclopedia of Poetry and Poetics*.[29] This work mentions more than a dozen other writers of heroic couplets, including several for whom there are concordances—Chaucer, Donne, Jonson, Keats, Shelley, and Browning—and several for whom there are no concordances. Of the latter, the poet most frequently quoted is, I think, Crabbe.

Most readers of these words know very well that there is more to literary style than the employment of verse forms, just as there is more to tracing poetical quotations than the recognition of these forms. Make use of what you know about mechanical matters, but realize that what you really need is to have years of reading behind you. Literary interests and experience with literature imperceptibly and inexplicably prepare you to perceive the unique combination of form, content, diction, attitude, and purpose that make individual writers stand out as individual writers. Many of the most satisfying identifications come about because we immediately or gradually or eventually realize that a quotation sounds like or looks like the work of this author or that. Some writers, of course, are more recognizable than others, but most writers worth quoting have qualities that set them apart. The ability to recognize the work of individual writers is a rewarding by-product of the experience of reading and of the study of literature. The very act of reading good literature will make you a better quote sleuth.

Much of what I call detective work is not something that I can explain fully. It is usually a matter of combining knowledge that we already possess with a fact or a clue that we pick up from the quotation or its context at some time during the attempt at identification. We tracers of quotations benefit from whatever knowledge we already have on a world of subjects, particularly literary, historical, and bibliographical ones, but this knowledge must not keep us from being flexible in our approach and receptive to the ideas that are ready to occur to us. You no doubt recall the advice that Huxley gave to Kingsley: "Sit down before fact as a little child, be prepared to give up every preconceived notion, follow humbly wherever and to whatever abysses nature leads, or you shall learn nothing."[30] Good advice for the quotation tracer, too.

NOTES

1. *Contemporary Review* 5 (May-August 1867), 164.

2. *London Journal*, no. 712 (17 February 1733), reprinted in *London Magazine* 2 (February 1733), 83.

3. *Blackwood's Edinburgh Magazine* 143 (May 1888), 634.

4. *Merchants' Magazine* 1 (August 1839), 137.

5. J. W. Dafoe, *Laurier: A Study in Canadian Politics* (Toronto: Thomas Allen, 1922), 13.

6. *New York Times Book Review*, 29 March 1953, 31; *Notes and Queries* 202 (September 1957), 409; ibid. 212 (March 1967), 105.

7. *Blackwood's Edinburgh Magazine* 115 (June 1874), 678.

8. Ibid. 60 (August 1846), 140.

9. *Every Saturday* 1 (21 April 1866), 423.

10. Motto to chapter 30 of Sir Walter Scott's *Old Mortality*.

11. *Appletons' Journal* 6 (15 July 1871), 77.

12. John Tobin, *The Honey Moon* (London: Longman, Hurst, Rees, and Orme, 1805), 55.

13. *Blackwood's Edinburgh Magazine* 46 (September 1839), 369.

14. William Rose Benét, ed., *The Reader's Encyclopedia* (New York: Thomas Y. Crowell Co., 1948), 548.

15. *Every Saturday* 1 (17 February 1866), 178.

16. *Harper's New Monthly Magazine* 7 (September 1853), 547.

17. Donald F. Bond, ed., *The Spectator*, 5 vols. (Oxford: Clarendon Press, 1965), 2:530–32, 5:345.

18. Henry Augustus Wise [Harry Gringo, pseud.], *Tales for the Marines* (Boston: Phillips, Sampson, and Co., 1855), 109.

19. *Small Press Review* 19 (January 1987), 10.

20. *Fortnightly Review* 50 (1 July 1888), 33.

21. *Atlantic Monthly* 5 (April 1860), 412–13.

22. William H. Whyte, Jr., *The Organization Man* (New York: Simon and Schuster, 1956), 24–25; *Notes and Queries* 213 (May 1968), 188; ibid., (July 1968), 267.

23. William Gilpin, *Observations on the River Wye*, 5th ed. (London: T. Cadell and W. Davies, 1800), 48; William Mason, *The Works of William Mason, M.A.*, 4 vols. (London: T. Cadell and W. Davies, 1811), 1:225; William Gilpin, *Observations on Several Parts of Great Britain, Particularly the High-lands of Scotland*, 3d ed., 2 vols. (London: T. Cadell and W. Davies, 1808), 1:179; *Notes and Queries* 197 (8 November 1952), 502; ibid. 213 (June 1968), 226.

24. *Notes and Queries* 220 (March 1975), 121–22; ibid. 221 (November 1976), 510; Joseph Hucks, *A Pedestrian Tour through North Wales, in a Series of Letters, by J. Hucks, B.A. (1795)*, ed. Alun R. Jones and William Tydeman (Cardiff: University of Wales Press, 1979), 25, 79; William Lisle Bowles, *The Poetical Works of William Lisle Bowles*, ed. George Gilfillan, 2 vols. (Edinburgh: James Nichol, 1855), 1:66.

25. *Notes and Queries* 193 (1 May 1948), 194; ibid. 212 (August 1967), 310.

26. *American Notes & Queries* 9 (December 1970), 56; ibid., (June 1971), 155; John Steinbeck, "Some Random and Randy Thoughts on Books," in Ray Freiman, ed., *The Author Looks at Format* (New York: American Institute of Graphic Arts, 1951), 27–34.

27. *Notes and Queries* 210 (October 1965), 384; ibid. 211 (September 1966), 350; ibid. 213 (February 1968), 65.

28. *New York Times Book Review*, 23 March 1969, 47; ibid., 27 April 1969, 47.

29. *Princeton Encyclopedia of Poetry and Poetics*, rev. ed., ed. Alex Preminger (Princeton: Princeton University Press, 1974), 346.

30. Thomas Henry Huxley, *The Life and Letters of Thomas Henry Huxley*, ed. Leonard Huxley, 2 vols. (London: Macmillan and Co., 1900), 1:219.

9 | Tracing Classical and Foreign Quotations

In the writings in English of our contemporaries, we see hardly any quotations from classical or foreign sources; and the few that do occur are likely to be given in English. In the writings of past times, on the other hand, we see a great many classical and foreign quotations in their original languages. As independent scholars or as those who give scholarly assistance to others, we are called on from time to time to trace quotations from this legacy. Surprisingly, it is possible to trace a great many of them fairly easily. Indeed, it is easier to identify the source of an old Latin quotation than it is to trace a recent American aphorism. If you already have a good reading knowledge of the language of the quotation and some acquaintance with literature written in it, you have advantages that the monolingual tracer will envy. But such knowledge and such experience are not prerequisites. What is required is intelligence, interest, patience, and, of course, access to some good reference works.

Practically all of the non-English quotes we are likely ever to need to trace are from Latin, French, Italian, German, and Greek. In my discussion of ways of tracing quotations from these tongues, I shall devote a separate section to each. In addition to reading these sections, you should apply to the tracing of classical and foreign quotations the earlier discussions of special kinds of quotation books, of indexes of various sorts, and of methods of literary detection. Should you have occasion to trace a quotation from a foreign language and literature other than those treated in this chapter, you would be well advised to employ measures similar to the ones outlined here, to consult reference books suggested in Eugene Sheehy's *Guide to Reference Books* and *Walford's Guide to Reference Material*, and to consult some such subject heading as "Quotations—Russian" in your local or research library's public catalog.

Latin

In practically any sort of writing in English from centuries earlier than the twentieth, Latin quotations occur with greater frequency than do quotations in any of the other non-English languages mentioned. Resources of several kinds exist that can be used in tracing this major class of quotations. How you actually go about tracing a Latin passage depends on the availability of reference works, on the presence or absence of contextual indications of authorship or of stylistic or other clues in the quotation itself, on whether or not a translation of the passage is needed, and, naturally, on personal preference for this or that resource. However you begin, you must be willing to consult, if need be, a succession of reference materials.

At least ten general or specialized compilations of quotations may profitably be used in tracing Latin passages. General collections containing large numbers of Latin quotations are the *ODQ2*, Stevenson, and *Hoyt's*. Since their indexing of Latin quotations is not strong—Stevenson's is the weakest, with usually one index entry for every Latin quotation included—it is advisable to check their indexes under every possible Latin word before giving up. Bartlett's Latin stock is not large, but the book is easy to use and it may contain the quotation you are tracing. Two collections consisting of quotations from several non-English languages are King's *Classical and Foreign Quotations*, which is excellent, and Jones's *Dictionary of Foreign Phrases and Classical Quotations*, which is not. Some useful dictionaries of Latin or of Latin and Greek quotations are Ramage's *Familiar Quotations from Latin Authors*, Harbottle's *Dictionary of Quotations (Classical)*, Guterman's *Book of Latin Quotations*, and *Cree's Dictionary of Latin Quotations*. Of the several special collections of Latin, classical, or foreign and classical quotations, the most useful for tracing Latin passages are King, Ramage, and Harbottle, but all of them are of value, since even a weak collection may be the only compilation to include the quote you are trying to identify.

All ten compilations provide translations; and except for Jones, they provide detailed source citations as well. The quote sleuth can accept the text and translation as given or use the source reference in locating a more authoritative text and translation. Additionally, most of the collections include some passages of unknown origin—proverbs, legal maxims, and Latin phrases. Another place to look for Latin proverbs, incidentally, is Stevenson's *Home Book of Proverbs, Maxims, and Familiar Phrases*.

By consulting several books of quotations in succession (if necessary), you should be able to trace at least half of the Latin quotations that come your way. A good sequence to follow in tracking a passage in Latin is the *ODQ2*, King, Ramage, *Hoyt's*, the weakly indexed Stevenson, Harbottle, Guterman, *Cree's*, Bartlett, and the poorly documented Jones. Of course, if not all of these are available, then make do with what is.

Finding the source of a Latin quotation occurring in English translation is generally less easy than tracing a Latin passage given in its own language, but this feat can often be achieved. The tracer should employ a variety of methods until one of them is successful. One approach is to check the indexes of the *ODQ3*, Evans, and Bartlett under likely English words from the quotation. Another is to scan the subject sections in Stevenson, Mencken, and the *Dictionary of Foreign Quotations* of Collison and Collison, or to consult the English subject or keyword indexes in Harbottle, King, Guterman, and Ramage. If the anglicized quotation has been ascribed to a certain author, which is usually the case, an easy way to proceed is to look at that author's quotations in compilations organized by author—the *ODQ2*, the *ODQ3*, Ramage, Guterman, and Bartlett—and to scan Collison and Collison's author index with its accompanying subject references. Another is to translate a basic word or two back into Latin and consult a concordance or an index to the author's work.

Latin passages not found in the general or specialized compilations, like those that are found in them, are likely to turn up as illustrative quotations in dictionaries of the Latin language, several of which seem designed to help the quotation tracer. You should begin this stage of the search by consulting a hefty one-volume dictionary, either the *Oxford Latin Dictionary* or *Harpers' Latin Dictionary*, preferably the *Oxford*, though *de gustibus*. If this does not solve the problem, then go on to the other big single-volume dictionary. If the quote still eludes you, the multivolume sets should be consulted also—Forcellini's *Totius Latinitatis Lexicon* and the *Thesaurus Linguae Latinae*, a monumental work now about two-thirds complete. Check several words, if need be, in one dictionary and then, if unsuccessful, go on to another; or check the same word in several dictionaries, if necessary, and then start over with another word if the quote has not been identified. If you have easy access to only one of these Latin dictionaries, you should of course check that dictionary under every likely word.

If you do not understand the language of the quote you are tracing, then you may end up scanning some groups of illustrative quotations unnecessarily or you may fail to find other groups. Still, this partial inefficiency caused by ignorance should not deter you, for anyone can locate quotations by means of these dictionaries. Essentially, consulting Latin dictionaries in order to find quotations is like consulting *The Oxford English Dictionary* for the same purpose. As in checking the *OED*, you must be of good comfort and play the odds. Begin with words you consider uncommon and most likely to occur in the illustrations you are seeking, but be willing to go on to others. When you do find your quotation, decipher the source citation and then locate the quote in an authoritative text. A Loeb edition of the Latin writer provides both text and translation.

A quotation of known or suspected authorship should, if possible, be traced by means of the dictionaries of quotations used in identifying quotes of unknown authorship, for such resources are usually available, are easy to use, and supply all of the needed information—text, understandable source citation, and translation—in one place. If the compilations do not contain the answer, the next step is to consult the Latin dictionaries just as you would for quotations of unknown authorship, or to use a concordance or other index to the works of the author, or to examine a lexicon of the author's vocabulary. Concordances are also consulted in tracing Latin passages of unknown parentage.

The concordances used most frequently in tracing Latin quotations include those to Virgil, Horace, Ovid, and the Vulgate. The quote sleuth who routinely consults these for every Latin foundling that other methods have failed to trace will achieve many identifications that would otherwise be missed or that would have to be referred to a classicist. In addition to Virgil, Horace, and Ovid, many other Latin writers are represented by concordances or verbal indexes, or by lexicons that serve the same purpose, or by name indexes. Also, many scholarly editions of classical writers contain indexes to words or to names. References to concordances and to indexes of several kinds are found in Henri Quellet's *Bibliographia Indicum, Lexicorum, et Concordantiarum Auctorum Latinorum*.

Finally, I should mention a marvelous development, the machine-readable Latin corpus that is now being prepared. A preliminary and limited version of the database of Latin literature is being distributed by the Packard Humanities Institute. A quotation tracer with this disk and with access to the right computer, such as the Ibycus Scholarly Computer or a suitably programmed Macintosh, will be able to identify sources of many Latin quotations without doing the sequential checking of reference books that I have outlined.[1] For the present, however—and, for many of us, for the future also—tracing Latin quotations will continue to require the use of dictionaries of quotations, dictionaries of the language, and various concordances and indexes.

In deciding which concordance to consult or which author to investigate, you should make use of names and clues from the quotation's context or from the quotation itself. Some reference works useful in the pursuit of clues are *The New Century Cyclopedia of Names, Lemprière's Classical Dictionary*, and the *Oxford Companion to Classical Literature*.

The following quotations or misquotations I have come across can be traced by means of one or more of the many reference works mentioned in this section. In tracing them, I shall not use Latin dictionaries unless I fail to locate the quotes in one of the compilations; and in using the dictionaries, I shall usually not check every likely word in every dictionary.

1. Victrix causa Diis plausit, sed victa Catoni.[2]

2. "Impiger—iracundus—inexorabilis—acer,"[3]

3. Satis est equitem mihi plaudere.[4]

4. Ad nos vix tenuis famae perlabitur aura.[5]

5. "Non est, Tucca, satis, quod es gulosus:
Et dici cupis, et cupis videri."[6]

6. It is a rule given us by Horace, "if you wish to make me weep, you must first weep yourself."[7]

The first passage, which is misquoted with "plausit" for "placuit," is easily traceable. Its location in Lucan's works is found in the *ODQ2*, Stevenson, *Hoyt's*, King (where the quote appears in the supplementary index), Harbottle, Bartlett, Ramage, and Guterman; and the name of the author is given in Jones. The second, from Horace, is found in Harbottle; it turns up also in *Harpers'* under "impiger." The third, another passage from Horace, appears in the *ODQ2*. The fourth, from Virgil, does not occur in any of the compilations but can be found quite easily in both *Harpers' Latin Dictionary* and the *Oxford Latin Dictionary* under "perlabor." The fifth, from Martial, is not (or at least was not) found in any of the compilations or in *Harpers'*, the *Oxford*, or the main part of Forcellini's *Totius Latinitatis Lexicon;* however, I did find it under "Tucca" in the *Onomasticon*, bound with the *Lexicon*, and under "gulosus" in the *Thesaurus Linguae Latinae*.

The sixth passage is an example of an anglicized quotation attributed to a certain author. It can be traced via the English rendering, by looking at small groupings of the author's quotations in collections arranged by author, or by changing part of the quotation back into Latin and identifying it with a concordance or with various indexes to the Latin words. An easy way to locate this quotation is to look under "weep" in the index to Bartlett, where we find "if you wish me to w." and a reference to a page and an item number in the Horace section. In Bartlett the quotations from Horace are given in English, with Latin versions appearing in footnotes. Another way to find the passage is to turn to the Horace sections of the *ODQ2* or Bartlett and scan them until it turns up. Yet another, of course, is to check "flere" in the Horace concordance.

Obviously, many Latin quotation problems are much easier to solve than they first appear. If, however, a quotation does not yield to the measures just outlined, then it is altogether fitting and proper to consult a Latinist.

French

To trace a French quotation, I suggest that you begin by checking a succession (if necessary) of general dictionaries of quotations: the *ODQ2*, Stevenson, *Hoyt's*, and Bartlett. These do not contain great numbers of French quotations, but the collections themselves are readily available and are easy to use, and if they contain the passage, they usually provide all the information needed. If these compilations do not include the quotation, the next step is to start consulting dictionaries of foreign quotations and dictionaries of French quotations. Among the best known of these special collections are King's *Classical and Foreign Quotations*; Jones's poorly documented *Dictionary of Foreign Phrases and Classical Quotations*; Ramage's *Familiar Quotations from French and Italian Authors*; Harbottle and Dalbiac's *Dictionary of Quotations (French and Italian)*; Guterman's *Book of French Quotations*; Guerlac's *Citations Françaises*; Genest's *Dictionnaire des Citations*; Dupré's *Encyclopédie des Citations*; the *Larousse des Citations Françaises et Étrangères*; the *Dictionnaire de Citations Françaises*, or its clone, the *Nouveau Dictionnaire de Citations Françaises*; and the *Dictionary of Foreign Quotations* of Collison and Collison.

These collections are variously arranged and variously indexed, but each method of organization—quotations occurring in subject, author, or alphabetical arrangements—provides a different way of looking for the quotation, as does each method of indexing—by opening word, by French or English keyword, by French or English subject, or by author. Organized by authors are the *Dictionnaire de Citations Françaises*, Ramage, the *Nouveau Dictionnaire de Citations Françaises*, Dupré, Guerlac, Guterman, and the *Larousse*; by quotations in alphabetical order are Genest, Harbottle and Dalbiac, King, and Jones; and by subject is the *Dictionary of Foreign Quotations* by Collison and Collison. Good keyword indexes are found in Genest, Dupré, Guerlac, Harbottle and Dalbiac, and the *Larousse*. Other collections are indexed by subjects or authors or both. The most useful collections and the easiest to consult are Genest, Guerlac, Dupré, King, the *Larousse*, and Harbottle and Dalbiac.

If the authorship of a quotation is not known, then naturally you must use indexes and arrangements that do not depend on such knowledge: keyword indexes, indexes to opening words, subject indexes, and arrangements of quotations by opening word or by topic. If the authorship is known, then employ all the measures used in tracing a quotation of unknown parentage and also, if necessary, consult compilations that contain author sections or author indexes. A quotation known or thought to be from a certain author is sometimes traceable by means of a concordance to the works of the author or an index to the author's works. Here, of course, you must assume—or hope—that a scholarly edition of an author's works includes a good subject index to the set. There are not nearly enough concordances to French writers, but some important ones do exist, such as concordances to Montaigne and Racine, and the number of them is increasing slowly. Also, some French writers are represented by single-author quotation books. Scanning likely sections of an author's works is another measure that should be considered in tracing attributed quotations in French or in any other language.

To trace French quotations that you encounter only as translations into English is difficult, but fortunately these are often accompanied by author attributions or by helpful clues to their sources. English words from an anglicized French quotation may turn up in English keyword indexes to Bartlett, Evans, and the *ODQ3;* the quote can be sought under its English subject in Stevenson, Mencken, and Collison and Collison, which are all arranged by topic; and the English subject or keyword indexes in King, Harbottle and Dalbiac, and Ramage should be consulted as well. After some retranslating, you can also look for the quotation under French words in keyword indexes in the *ODQ2,* the *Larousse,* Dupré, Harbottle and Dalbiac, *Hoyt's,* and Guerlac. If an anglicized French quotation has been ascribed or traced to a certain author, then examine the author's quotations in the *ODQ2* or the *ODQ3,* Bartlett, Guterman, Ramage, Dupré, the *Dictionnaire de Citations Françaises,* or the *Larousse des Citations Françaises et Étrangères,* which are all arranged by author.

A French quotation you are trying to trace may well appear as an illustrative passage in a dictionary of the French language. The dictionary to consult first is Émile Littré's *Dictionnaire de la Langue Française.* Other dictionaries containing many quotations are Paul Robert's *Dictionnaire Alphabétique et Analogique de la Langue Française;* Paul Imbs's *Trésor de la Langue Française; Grand Larousse de la Langue Française;* and Edmond Huguet's *Dictionnaire de la Langue Française du Seizième Siècle.* Even if your knowledge of French is imperfect or nonexistent, using these dictionaries for the purpose of tracing quotations is no more difficult than using the *OED* for the same purpose.

Sometimes it is possible to make use of names and clues from the quotation's context or from the quotation itself in tracing a passage in

French. Reference works to be consulted in the identification of names and the pursuit of leads include *The New Century Cyclopedia of Names* and the *Oxford Companion to French Literature.*

I should also mention that a machine-readable corpus of French literature is becoming accessible. The ARTFL database (American and French Research on the Treasury of the French Language) includes the full text of some two thousand important French works of several centuries from literary and other fields. A French quotation that has defeated you may turn up among the 150 million words in the ARTFL retrieval system.[8]

The following French quotations and misquotations can be traced by means of reference works mentioned in this chapter:

1. "Qui ne sait se borner ne sait jamais écrire."[9]

2. "Le soleil ni la mort ne se peut regarder fixement."[10]

3. " 'Et cette alarme universelle
   Est l'ouvrage d'un moucheron.' "[11]

4. "Quoique vous écriviez, évitez la bassesse;
   Le style le moins noble a pourtant sa noblesse."[12]

5. . . . in the ancient city to which he loved to apply the line of Racine:—
   Et de Jérusalem l'herbe couvre les murs.[13]

6. There were bees, and there was an old stone well full of deep water, like Jocelyn's well,—
   "Dont la chaîne rouillée a poli la margelle,
   Et qu'une vigne étreint de sa verte dentelle."[14]

The first quotation, from Boileau, is found in Genest, Guerlac, the *Larousse*, Dupré, the *Dictionnaire de Citations Françaises*, and King (by way of the supplementary index). The second, from La Rochefoucauld, appears in King, Guerlac, the *Larousse*, Dupré, and the *Dictionnaire de Citations Françaises*. The third, from La Fontaine, is more difficult to identify. It occurs in one dictionary of quotations, Genest, which not everyone will have access to; also, it is used as an illustrative quotation in Littré, under "alarme." The fourth quote, from Boileau, seems not to occur in any of the collections, but it can be found in Littré as an example of the use of "bassesse." The fifth, which has been attributed to Racine, is easily solved by using Freeman's fine concordance to Racine.

The sixth passage looks as though it may defeat us. The quotation collections and the language dictionaries are of no help, but fortunately there is a clue in the quote's context that makes it possible to locate the source after some effort. The clue is "Jocelyn's well," which can

be traced through the *Oxford Companion to French Literature* to La-
martine's narrative poem *Jocelyn*. After much scanning of line endings
for the combination of "margelle" and "dentelle," we find the couplet
in "Suite de la Lettre à sa Soeur" of 3 mai 1798. Thus, we can say
with some confidence that tracing French quotations is no more difficult
than tracing English or Latin ones.

Italian

General dictionaries of quotations such as the *ODQ2*, Stevenson, *Hoyt's*, and Bartlett are often of little use in tracing Italian
quotations, but since they sometimes do provide a good text, a detailed
source citation, and a competent translation, it is wise to consult them
routinely at the beginning of a search. If they fail you, as they frequently
do, then turn to dictionaries of foreign quotations, dictionaries of Italian
quotations, and Italian dictionaries of quotations. Among the best
known of these are King's *Classical and Foreign Quotations*; Ramage's
Familiar Quotations from French and Italian Authors; Harbottle and Dalbiac's *Dictionary of Quotations (French and Italian)*; Fumagalli's *Chi l'ha
Detto?*; and Finzi's *Dizionario di Citazioni Latine ed Italiane*. These collections are organized by opening word (King, Harbottle and Dalbiac),
by subject (Fumagalli, Finzi), or by author (Ramage); and they are
indexed by keyword (Finzi, Harbottle and Dalbiac), by opening word
(Ramage, Fumagalli), or by subject (King, Harbottle and Dalbiac).
King's alphabetical listing, it should be noted, is supplemented by an
index to quotations and parts of quotations not findable in the main
listing. Documentation varies in completeness, from authors and titles
in Finzi to detailed source citations in King, Harbottle and Dalbiac, and
Ramage. The compilations may disappoint you because of the small
number of Italian quotes they contain, but they do help the cause often
enough to justify their use. All of them are fairly good, and any of
them may be the one compilation to include the quotation you seek.
As many of them as are available should be consulted, if necessary,
for an Italian quotation in need of tracing. If none of them leads to the
identification of the source, there are other measures available.

Anglicized Italian quotations ordinarily are accompanied by author
attributions. To trace such quotations, you should consult the author's
quotations in the *ODQ2*, Bartlett, and Ramage, which are arranged by
author; the English subject indexes in King and in Harbottle and Dalbiac; the English keyword indexes in Bartlett and in Evans; or the
subject sections of Collison and Collison's *Dictionary of Foreign Quotations*. Or, you can do some retranslating and consult a concordance

to the author's works, if there is one; or else scan an English translation of the author's works.

To trace an Italian quotation of known authorship, you have several options somewhat similar to the above, all of which may be needed. Begin as if the authorship were not already known and check the indexes of Bartlett, the *ODQ2, Hoyt's,* and Stevenson; or check the alphabetical arrangement of quotations in King and in Harbottle and Dalbiac; or look at the author's quotations in Bartlett, the *ODQ2,* and Ramage; or check the indexes to opening words in Ramage and Fumagalli and the keyword indexes in Finzi and in Harbottle and Dalbiac; or determine whether there are any published concordances or indexes to the author's works. Excellent concordances to Dante and Petrarch have been published. Indeed, these should be employed routinely in tracing passages of unknown authorship as well as passages that have been attributed to one or the other of these two major authors, since many unattributed Italian quotations do come from them.

As in tracing quotations from other languages, it is possible to locate the sources of Italian quotations by looking at illustrative passages occurring in language dictionaries. Three Italian dictionaries filled with quotations are Nicolò Tommaseo and Bernardo Bellini's *Dizionario della Lingua Italiana,* the *Vocabolario degli Accademici della Crusca,* and Salvatore Battaglia's *Grande Dizionario della Lingua Italiana.* These are very useful works indeed, but none of them is perfect. Citations in Tommaseo and Bellini are not sufficiently detailed; and although citations in Battaglia's *Grande Dizionario* and the *Vocabolario degli Accademici della Crusca* are complete, the dictionaries themselves are not. The *Vocabolario* stops after the letter *O;* and Battaglia's work, which will eventually serve as an excellent cornucopia of quotations, is at present only about half finished.

As in tracing quotations in other languages, you can sometimes trace an Italian quotation by means of clues that have been provided in the context of the quoted passage or in the quotation itself. A good reference book to consult for the purpose of identifying names is *The New Century Cyclopedia of Names.*

The following quotations and misquotations can be traced by means of one or more of the works mentioned in this section.

1. With regard to the water-colour drawings and miniatures, we think them best criticized by a free translation of a well-known half-line in Dante:—
   Don't look at them,—and pass on![15]

2. Non ragioniam di lor, ma guarda e passa.[16]

3. "Sotto l'usbergo del esser puro."[17]

4. "Perduto è tutto il tempo,
   Che in amor non si spende."[18]

5. Benedetto sia il giorno, e'l mese, e l'anno![19]

6. Nè greggi nè armenti
   Guida bifolco mai, guida pastore.[20]

To solve the first, we need to scan a small collection of well-known passages from Dante, preferably in English or accompanied by English translations. The modified quotation from the *Inferno* is easily found in Bartlett, the *ODQ2*, and the *ODQ3*, all of which are arranged by author; you may recognize it as well in Bartlett's index under "look." The second quotation, since it is in Italian, is easier to trace than was the first, which was an English version of half of the same line. It appears in the *ODQ2*, King, Harbottle and Dalbiac, Ramage, and Fumagalli. The third, which is yet another passage from the same work, is not included in most of the dictionaries of quotations, but it does appear in Fumagalli. Those who do not have access to Fumagalli can still find a source reference, though an incomplete one, in Tommaseo and Bellini's dictionary under "usbergo"; and someone without access to either of these can find it by routinely checking the concordances to Dante and Petrarch. The fourth quote, from Tasso, does not occur in most of the collections but is included in Harbottle and Dalbiac.

The fifth passage, which is from Petrarch, seems not to occur in any of the dictionaries of quotations, but it can be traced by looking at quotations used to illustrate "mese," in Tommaseo and Bellini and in the *Vocabolario degli Accademici della Crusca*. The sixth quote, again from Tasso, apparently is not included in any of the compilations but is easily identified by looking under "bifolco" in Battaglia's dictionary or in the *Vocabolario*.

German

In tracing a German quotation, you should usually begin by consulting a succession (if necessary) of general dictionaries of quotations: the *ODQ2*, Stevenson, *Hoyt's*, and Bartlett. These do not include large numbers of German quotations, but they have good texts, competent translations, and detailed source citations. If you do not locate your quotation in one of them, the next step is to consult dictionaries of foreign quotations, dictionaries of German quotations, and German dictionaries of quotations. Among those to consult are King's *Classical and Foreign Quotations*, Ramage's *Familiar Quotations from German and Spanish Authors*, Georg Büchmann's *Geflügelte Worte*, Lilian Dalbiac's

Dictionary of Quotations (German), Karl Peltzer's *Das Treffende Zitat*, and F. J. Lipperheide's *Spruchwörterbuch*.

These compilations of German quotations and of foreign quotations are organized and indexed in various ways: by author (Ramage, Büchmann), by keywords (Peltzer), by topics that are also keywords (Lipperheide), and by opening words (King, Dalbiac). King's alphabetical arrangement of quotations is supplemented by an index to quotations and parts of quotations not findable in that alphabetical arrangement. King also has a subject index in English that repeats many English words of the quotations. In Ramage, access to quotes is provided by a German index to opening words and an English index to subjects and keywords. Büchmann has a separate index to German quotations, arranged by catchword or by opening word. Documentation in Ramage's collection is less detailed than are the source references in King's work. In Dalbiac, there are good subject or keyword indexes in German and in English. Peltzer's excellent book has an author index in which words of the quotations are noted. Documentation in most of the collections is detailed. English translations, naturally, do not occur in some of them. All six compilations are strong collections, and if they are available, they should all be used in sequence until you have succeeded with one or failed with all.

When trying to trace a German quotation that occurs in English, several ways of proceeding present themselves. You can look under the English keywords in the indexes to Bartlett, the *ODQ2*, the *ODQ3*, Evans, Dalbiac, and Ramage; you can examine the subject sections of Stevenson, Mencken, and the *Dictionary of Foreign Quotations* of Collison and Collison; or you can consult the English subject indexes in King, Dalbiac, and Ramage. You can even retranslate some keywords and consult dictionaries of German or foreign quotations. If, as usually happens, the anglicized quotation is accompanied by an author attribution, then you should scan the author sections of compilations arranged by author, such as Bartlett, the *ODQ2*, or Ramage; or, after determining many or most of the likely German words of the quotation, you can employ special tools based on the author's works, just as you do when tracing an attributed quotation that occurs in German.

Whether you are working with an original or a reconstituted German quotation that has been ascribed to a certain author, remember that access to an author's works can often be facilitated by a concordance or an index to the works of the author, by a dictionary or a lexicon of the author's words or ideas, by a handbook to the author's works, or by a book made up of quotations from the author. Goethe, for example, is represented by reference works of several kinds. Heinrich Schmidt's old *Goethe-Lexikon* is in fact a book of Goethe quotations arranged under general catchwords and traced to titles of the author's works. Richard Dobel's *Lexikon der Goethe-Zitate* is an excellent collection of well-referenced Goethe quotations organized by keywords. Paul Fischer's *Goethe-Wortschatz* is a detailed glossary of words used by Goethe, with explanations, examples, and citations. The *Goethe Wörterbuch*, a work-in-progress, is for the early part of the alphabet the definitive Goethe dictionary and an invaluable collection of illustrative quotations from Goethe's works.

German authors other than Goethe have not inspired such a wealth of reference materials, but useful works do exist and should be looked at when the need arises. One of these is Heinz-Martin Dannhauer's *Wörterbuch zu Friedrich Hölderlin*. If you are working on a German quotation ascribed to a certain writer, you should check your local or research library's public catalog for such special materials, just in case. If time allows, go through the library's complete record of holdings of books by and about the author, looking especially for such subheadings as "concordances," "indexes," and "dictionaries." Also, single-author reference books can be used if you know or strongly suspect that the quotation is from a certain author.

Unfortunately, I do not always follow my own advice as quickly as I should. In 1980 this anglicized quotation attributed to Goethe was the subject of a published query: "This is the most difficult thing of all, though it would seem the easiest: to see that which is before one's eyes." I was unable to trace the passage at the time, but years later, as I was writing this very chapter, it occurred to me that I had left undone something I ought to have done. After consulting an English-German dictionary and listing the words "schwer," "leight," "sehen," "Auge," and "alle," I found the quote in Dobel's *Lexikon der Goethe-Zitate*, under "sehen": "Was ist das Schwerste von allem? Was dir das Leichteste dünket, / Mit den Augen zu sehn, was vor den Augen dir liegt." The source citation was *"Xenien aus dem Nachlass* 45," followed by the number 2,503; it refers to number 45 of some epigrams written by Goethe and Schiller, to be found on page 503 of the second volume of a recent edition of Goethe's works. Investigating further, I found the lines also printed in the works of Schiller.[21] My long delay in tracing the quotation certainly does illustrate the truth of the epigram.

Another approach in tracing German quotations is to consult the great dictionary of Jacob and Wilhelm Grimm. Their *Deutsches Wörterbuch* contains a large number of illustrative quotations from German literature. Like the *OED*, it is often overlooked as a compilation of quotations; but also like the *OED*, it can enable you to identify sources that would otherwise be missed. The *Deutsches Wörterbuch* should always be consulted when other measures have not succeeded in tracing a German quotation.

The quotations and misquotations that follow can be traced by the use of one or more of the reference works mentioned in this section:

1. "My house is my castle," says the Englishman, while the German asserts, "Ein' feste Burg ist unser Gott."[22]

2. "Wouldst thou a poet understand?
   Then visit first that poet's land,"
   Goethe has somewhere said. . . .[23]

3. *"Seid umschlungen, Millionen!"*[24]

4. Job felt what Schiller later wrote:
   "For, by the laws of spirit, in the right
   Is every individual character
   That acts in strict accordance with itself;
   Self-contradiction is the only wrong."[25]

5. "Die unbegreiflich hohen Werke
   Sind herrlich wie am ersten Tag."[26]

The first quotation, which is one from Martin Luther that most of us would recognize if it were in English, can be found by consulting Stevenson, the *ODQ2*, *Hoyt's*, or Dalbiac. In Bartlett it is given in English and is indexed under "fortress"; the German version occurs in a footnote. The second, an anglicized passage from Goethe, can be located by the persistent tracer who is willing to scan the Goethe quotations in Bartlett. The third passage, which turns out to be from Schiller, occurs in Peltzer, Lipperheide, Büchmann, Dalbiac, and, in English, in Bartlett; it appears also in the *Deutsches Wörterbuch* of the Brothers Grimm under "Million." The fourth, an English translation of a passage atttributed to Schiller, can be found by rummaging in Ramage among the Schiller passages or by consulting Dalbiac's English index under "self-contradiction." In Dalbiac we learn that the translation is by Coleridge. In search of the fifth quotation, which is from Goethe's *Faust*, I vainly consulted a number of compilations before looking under "unbegreiflich," which occurs under "unbegreifbar," in the great dictionary of the Brothers Grimm. As these examples show, tracing German quotations is not as difficult as it looks.

Greek

Many quotation tracers who are otherwise fearless and confident are intimidated by Greek quotations in need of identification, and when confronted by one of them they hasten to consult a classicist. Of course, if a problem does not yield to your best efforts, you can certainly ask a scholar of Greek for some assistance, but it is often not necessary to make a Grecian earn your gratitude. Tracing Greek quotations is something you can learn to do. In fact, you can reach a respectable level of Greek quotation tracing without even knowing the language, just as you can trace Latin and German quotations without knowing those languages. If you know the Greek alphabet or are willing to learn it, you can do very well at tracing Greek quotes provided you have access to a few basic reference materials and make careful use of them.

The quote sleuth does not often meet with Greek passages that need to be traced, but when they do appear, reference materials are available that should enable you to trace many of them fairly easily. Among these are the *ODQ2*, King's *Classical and Foreign Quotations*, Harbottle's *Dictionary of Quotations (Classical)*, and Ramage's *Familiar Quotations from Greek Authors*, which was also published as *Beautiful Thoughts from Greek Authors*. Bartlett, *Hoyt's*, and Collison and Collison's *Dictionary of Foreign Quotations* are of some value when the quotation is in English or when the authorship is already known; and Jones's *Dictionary of Foreign Phrases and Classical Quotations* provides helpful attributions of authorship. These collections are variously organized— two of them (Jones, Harbottle) by language and all of them by subject, author, or opening words—and most are indexed either by keywords, opening words, English subjects, authors, or a combination of these. Of the collections named, the *ODQ2*, King, and Harbottle are the most useful, but these should be supplemented by the others.

Tracing an English passage attributed to a certain Greek author is usually much more difficult than tracing a Greek passage of known authorship. A Greek quotation that occurs in an English rendering may be findable in the indexes to Bartlett, Stevenson, the *ODQ3*, *Hoyt's*, Evans, and Ramage; or among the author's quotations in Bartlett, the *ODQ2*, or Ramage; or under its subject in Stevenson, Mencken, or Collison and Collison. If, as often happens, the quotation is in English verse, you should look for it either as a Greek quotation or as an English quotation; and, if possible, you should find and supply references both to the Greek original and to the translation used by the quoter. If it is regarded as an English quotation, then look for it in practically any reference work used to trace English quotations, including dictionaries of the English language, old books of quotations, and concordances that include poetical translations. Thus, the Bedford and Dilligan concordance to Alexander Pope discussed elsewhere may provide the source of an iambic pentameter line attributed to Homer; working from this, you can easily find the corresponding passage in Homer, if it is needed.

Greek quotations of known authorship may be located in various collections under opening words (King, Harbottle), or under author (Bartlett, the *ODQ2*, Ramage), or under subject (Stevenson, Mencken, Collison and Collison); or they may be found in special reference materials based on the works of the author. When there is a choice, the general or special compilations are preferred over other reference tools because of the information they provide—text, understandable source citation, and translation. If these do not solve the problem, however, other approaches are possible. Chances are good that a concordance or index or author lexicon exists in which you will find your Greek passage of known or suspected parentage. A few of the many are James T. Allen and Gabriel Italie's *Concordance to Euripides*; Guy L. Prendergast's *Complete Concordance to the "Iliad" of Homer*; and H. Dunbar's *Complete Concordance to the "Odyssey" and Hymns of Homer*. Indeed, you will often be richly rewarded if you routinely consult the Homer concordances for all Greek quotations that have successfully resisted other measures of detection

Another important means of tracing Greek quotations of known or unknown authorship is to look at illustrative quotations in dictionaries of the language. Liddell and Scott's *Greek-English Lexicon* contains many quotations, most of which are relatively brief, and provides exact references to sources. Estienne's *Thesaurus Graecae Linguae* includes a much larger number of quotations, equally well referenced; these are often longer than the quotations in Liddell and Scott and thus easier to recognize. Source references in both works are abbreviated. As a rule, Liddell and Scott should be consulted first, since it is more readily available than Estienne and, being only one volume, is easier to use. Still another dictionary that the tracer of Greek quotations may find useful is Franz Passow's *Handwörterbuch der Griechischen Sprache*. Quotations in Passow are short, source references are abbreviated, and definitions and explanations are in German; but this resource should certainly be consulted if others fail. In using these dictionaries as quotation-finding tools, you should begin with the word deemed most likely to lead to victory, since the goal is to find the quotation without having to look under every word. If the words all seem equally likely, it is probably best to begin with the longest.

Finally, another reference tool that can be used in tracing quotations from ancient Greek literature is the Ibycus Scholarly Computer, which provides access to the Thesaurus Linguae Graecae (TLG) database of nearly sixty million words. If you take to a classicist a problem quotation that he or she does not recognize, it is likely that the Ibycus Scholarly Computer will be used in locating the source.[27]

Here are a few quotations and misquotations that can be traced by means of reference materials mentioned in this section. I shall point out one or two easy ways of finding the source of each quotation, starting with the general and special compilations; I shall not attempt to discover every possible way of tracing each passage.

1. ὄξος τ᾽ ἄλειφά τ᾽ ἐγχέας ταὐτῷ κύτει
   διχοστατοῦντ᾽ ἄν οὐ φίλοιν προσεννέποις.[28]

2. μαθοῦσιν αὐδῶ κ᾽ οὐ μαθοῦσι λήθομαι.
   .   .   .   .   .   .[29]

3. Πολλὰ δ᾽ ὕναντα, κάταντα, πάρυντά τε, δοχμιά τ᾽ ἦλθον.[30]

4. Ὕφεις μαγον τοιονδε μηχανορραφον
   δολιον αγυρτην, ὁστις εν ταις κερδεσιν
   μονον δεδορκε, την τεχνην δ᾽ εφυ τυφλος.[31]

5. It was a favourite saying with a crabbed old Greek, that—a Great Book is a Great Evil.[32]

6. The pure flame of patriotism burned ever in that heroic soul, and the sum of his religion might be expressed in Homer's line—
   The one best omen is to fight for fatherland.[33]

7. It is the step of Homer's ladies,
   "Of Troy's proud dames whose garments sweep the ground."[34]

The first passage, from Aeschylus' *Agamemnon*, is found in Harbottle in the main alphabetical arrangement of quotations. The second, which is from the same source, is found in King and in Harbottle, but in neither work is it findable in the main sequence of opening words. Rather, we find it by means of the Greek quotations index in King and by means of the Greek subject index in Harbottle. The third quote, from the *Iliad*, appears in Liddell and Scott under "katanta." The fourth, from Sophocles' *Oedipus Tyrannus*, is traced by means of Liddell and Scott or Estienne. It occurs under "tuphlos" in both and no doubt may be found under other entries as well. The fifth quotation, from the crabbed old Greek Callimachus, occurs in King and in Harbottle, where it can be traced by means of the English indexes, and in Collison and Collison, where it can be found among the quotations on the subject of books. The sixth, an English version of a passage from Homer, occurs in several compilations, where it can be found by scanning the quotations from Homer or by consulting the English subject or keyword indexes. Wording of the translation varies, but the quotation appears in Bartlett, the *ODQ2*, King, Harbottle, and Ramage. You probably recognize the seventh quote as a line of iambic pentameter and suspect that it comes from Alexander Pope's translation of Homer. The Bedford and Dilligan concordance to Pope reveals that the line is slightly misquoted from book 6 of Pope's translation of the *Iliad*.

Clearly, the prospect of tracing a Greek quotation should not intimidate any of us. It is quite possible to identify the sources of a goodly number of the Greek quotations we encounter.

NOTES

1. The address and phone number of the Packard Humanities Institute are 300 Second Street, Suite 201, Los Altos, CA 94022, (415)948–0150.

2. *National Review* 4 (October 1884), 260.

3. *Fraser's Magazine* 1 (June 1830), 588.

4. *Quarterly Review* 1 (February 1809), 103.

5. *Nineteenth Century* 1 (March 1877), 20.

6. *Fraser's Magazine* 2 (August 1830), 91.

7. *Tait's Edinburgh Magazine*, n.s., 1 (February 1834), 63.

8. The address and telephone number of the ARTFL database are ARTFL Project, Department of Romance Languages and Literatures, University of Chicago, 1050 East 59th Street, Chicago, IL 60637, (312)702–8488.

9. *Eclectic Magazine* 1 (April 1844), 523.

10. *Blackwood's Edinburgh Magazine* 157 (January 1895), 126.

11. Ibid. 162 (November 1897), 671.

12. *Eclectic Magazine* 1 (April 1844), 520.

13. *Nineteenth Century* 5 (February 1879), 235.

14. *Every Saturday* 2 (27 October 1866), 477.

15. *Athenaeum*, no. 1171 (6 April 1850), 377.

16. *Critic*, n.s., 5 (2 January 1886), 10.

17. *Blackwood's Edinburgh Magazine* 4 (December 1818), 354.

18. *Fraser's Magazine* 17 (April 1838), 443.

19. *Athenaeum*, no. 845 (6 January 1844), 15.

20. *Blackwood's Edinburgh Magazine* 8 (October 1820), 10.

21. *Harvard Magazine* 82 (January-February 1980), 12; ibid. 91 (September-October 1988), 79; Richard Dobel, ed., *Lexikon der Goethe-Zitate* (Zurich and Stuttgart: Artemis Verlag, 1968), 830; Johann Wolfgang Goethe, *Gedenkausgabe der Werke, Briefe und Gespräche*. 22 vols. (Zurich: Artemis-Verlag, 1949–), 2:503; Friedrich Schiller, *Sämtliche Werke*. 2 vols. (Berlin: Aufbau-Verlag, 1980), 1:230.

22. *International Journal of Ethics* 3 (January 1893), 231.

23. *Good Words* 32 (1891), 741.

24. *Nation* 2 (4 January 1866), 13.

25. *Monist* 9 (July 1899), 483.

26. *Saturday Review* 10 (4 August 1860), 150.

27. The address and phone number of Ibycus are P.O. Box 1330, Los Altos, CA 94022, (415)941–4553.

28. *Nineteenth Century* 3 (January 1878), 161.

29. Ibid. 10 (August 1881), 271.

30. *Quarterly Review* 1 (May 1809), 396.

31. *Fraser's Magazine* 1 (June 1830), 622.
32. *Saturday Magazine* 1 (7 July 1832), 1.
33. *Saturday Review* 8 (15 October 1859), 455.
34. *Ladies' Magazine and Literary Gazette* 3 (February 1830), 69.

10 | Some Axioms of a Quote Sleuth

A full year elapsed before I ventured to repeat the intrusion. Mrs. Routh met me in the street, and asked "why I did not go to see her dear man?" "I was afraid of being troublesome." "But he tells me that he wishes to see you." So I went. (It was Nov. 29th, 1847.) Would that I had preserved a record of what passed! But I believe it was then that I ventured to address him somewhat as follows: "Mr. President, give me leave to ask you a question I have sometimes asked of aged persons, but never of any so aged or so learned as yourself." He looked so kindly at me that I thought I might go on. "Every studious man, in the course of a long and thoughtful life, has had occasion to experience the special value of some one axiom or precept. Would you mind giving me the benefit of such a word of advice?" . . . He bade me explain,—evidently to gain time. I quoted an instance. He nodded and looked thoughtful. Presently he brightened up and said, "I think, sir, since you care for the advice of an old man, sir, you will find it a very good practice"—(here he looked me archly in the face),—"*always to verify your references, sir!*" . . . I can better recall the shrewdness of the speaker's manner than his exact words; but they were those, or very nearly those.

J. W. Burgon, *Lives of Twelve Good Men.*[1]

Time spent looking for quotations is never wasted.

The attribution of authorship is usually correct.

The attribution of authorship is not always correct. This is especially true of quotes ascribed to Twain, Lincoln, Wilde, Emerson, Voltaire, and Churchill.

The first line or the opening words of a quotation may also be the first line or the opening words of a poem, a song, or a recitation.

A one-line quotation may be the first line of a poem.

The opening words of a quotation may be the opening words of a quotation already identified in Notes and Queries.

Old editions of Granger's *contain information not to be found in recent editions.*

A one-line quotation may be the last line of a poem.

The last line of a poetical quotation may be the last line of a poem.

The Oxford English Dictionary *is a book of quotations.*

You should get ready for quotation problems long before they happen.

A long passage is usually easier to trace than a short one. It contains more words likely to be traceable, and if scanning is necessary, it becomes a bigger target. If you are given part of a passage to work with, make an effort to expand the quotation to include all known words of the passage.

If other methods are not successful in locating the source of a quotation attributed to a certain author, it is often a fairly easy matter to find it by scanning the author's works. You should start with the work deemed most likely to contain the passage or with a book of selections from the author's works.

Your capabilities will increase over time as you add to your knowledge and experience and as new reference works are published. Tomorrow you may be able to trace the quotation that defeated you today.

Even if correctly given, the quoted passage you are tracing may not mesh or coincide at all points with a corresponding quotation appearing in a dictionary of quotations. For example, the following quote from *Much Ado about Nothing* occurs in an old *Blackwood's:* "quips and sentences, and paper bullets of the brain."[2] In the *ODQ2*, the passage is shorter: "paper bullets of the brain." Only the words that the two versions have in common will enable you to trace the passage when you consult the index to the book of quotations. For that reason, every indexable word in any passage you are tracing must be checked in an index before you give up. In the above instance, the two quotations differed by only a few words. In many cases, however, the difference is a matter of several lines. If the two corresponding passages do not coincide in every respect, take care in citing line numbers: the numbers occurring in the source citation found in the dictionary of quotations may not accurately identify the line numbers you, as the tracer, must cite.

Inevitably, a competent tracer of quotations will be given credit for knowing a great deal that he or she does not know.

In identifying the source of a quotation, the sleuth is no match for the person who already knows the answer.

No matter how attractive it looks on the coffee table, and no matter how marvelous the quotations in it are, a book made up of undocumented quotations has no authority in wording of passages or in ascriptions to authors. Even so, although such books "cannot but make the judicious grieve," they sometimes contain information that can be verified elsewhere.

If still living, the person who attributed a quotation to a certain author may recall just where in the author's works the passage occurs and may be willing to impart that information to you. On at least two occasions, I have found the source of a quotation by writing to the quoter.[3]

Ideally, a library's concordances to major writers should be located where they can be found easily and consulted in sequence.

Solutions that you cannot find sometimes find you. As Pasteur said, however, chance favors only the prepared mind.

If at all possible, you should see the problem passage in its context. If the basic tracking techniques do not work, look at the context and glean from it whatever you can. For example, a quotation attributed to Balzac was the subject of a query that gave the name of the work containing the attribution. Finding the work and looking at the context, I learned that the quote was said to be from "the medieval Balzac." This phrase suggested that the quote was not from the nineteenth-century writer of that name but from an earlier one. The author, it turned out, was Jean-Louis Guez de Balzac, who died in 1654.[4]

Just as murderers are said to return to the scenes of their crimes, quoters often return to the authors they have quoted.

In working with another person's quotation problem, remember that the inquirer may have in his or her own head a clue to the solution.

Intense concentration will sometimes call to mind an idea that would not have come otherwise. It is good to worry continually about a problem, to keep going back to it, and to strain to reach the limits of your memory or your inventiveness.

Using your head can make solutions possible when tools and techniques fail to produce results. To verify the authorship of a prizewinning definition of success written in 1905, I made use of two weekly newspapers published in the putative author's hometown, reasoning that the award of $250 would have been big news in Lincoln, Kansas, in 1905. It was.[5]

It is good to keep and to review from time to time a file of untraced quotations and unanswered questions. In this file should be recorded all known details about each quotation and the steps already taken to trace it. If the problem did not originate in your own experience, you should record the details of the request for information so that when the answer eventually turns up, you do not discover that you have lost the name of the inquirer. Having had such an experience qualifies me, I think, to give such advice.

An unattributed quotation that is used to commemorate a person or that occurs in an article about that person may well have come from that person. To cite one example, a query asked for the source of this epigraph occurring on a brass plate set up in East Coker in memory of the explorer William Dampier: "The world is apt to judge of everything by the success and whosoever has ill fortune will hardly be allowed a good name." Using my principle, if I may call it that, I leafed through Dampier's works—and found the quote in *Voyage to New-Holland, &c. in the Year 1699.*[6]

Before undertaking any tedious and time-consuming measures in search of the source of a quotation attributed to a certain author, it is good to stop and determine whether someone else has already done the work for you. If the passage occurs as a quotation in a certain work, perhaps an editor of a different edition of that work or the compiler of a textbook containing that work or the author of a book or article about it has already identified the source of the passage. There may be a concordance or an index or a handbook to the works of the author to whom the quote has been ascribed. A critical study or a biography of the author may contain a documented version of the quotation, or there may be a bibliography that will suggest a place to look for the answer. Even if you do not know exactly what you are looking for, it is a good idea to spend some time going through your library's listing of books by and about the quoted author and of books by and about the author of the work in which the quotation appears as a quotation.

Quotations are often misquotations that, fortunately for the literary sleuth, contain some traceable words from the original passage. Keep this in mind as you consult quotation dictionaries, language dictionaries, and concordances—and do not give up until all likely words have been checked.

The wording of a quotation that has been successfully traced should, if needed for scholarly purposes, be taken not from the book of quotations in which it was located but from an authoritative text of the work cited. For most purposes of most people, however, the wording in Bartlett or in the *Oxford Dictionary of Quotations* is reliable enough.

A source citation needed for scholarly purposes should be taken not from the book of quotations in which the quote was located but from an authoritative text of the work cited. For most purposes of most people, however, the citation in Bartlett or the *Oxford Dictionary of Quotations* is reliable enough, provided that you remember to be careful in determining and citing line numbers.

Queries repeat themselves. To benefit from this phenomenon, you should make use of any index to queries and replies that exists. I have mentioned the general and annual indexes to *Notes and Queries*, the annual indexes to *American Notes & Queries*, and Charles Anderson's cumulated index to "The Exchange." Some reference departments keep a file of solutions to difficult problems that are likely to recur. Another way to make use of the fact that scholarly inquiry repeats itself, is, I confess, to read old questions and the answers to them. I have passed many enjoyable hours reading queries and replies, some of them quite ancient, in *Notes and Queries, American Notes & Queries,* the *New York Times Book Review, RQ, John o' London's Weekly, T.P.'s Weekly, Intermédiaire des Chercheurs et Curieux,* and one or two other publications. This pleasurable activity has on a few occasions led to my finding a fact that I already needed or that I would eventually need.

Persons interested in quotations should consider compiling reference works to be used in tracing them. There is a great need for concordances to works in several languages and literatures; for detailed indexes to the works of authors; for *scholarly* single-subject quotation books; for *scholarly* single-author quotation books; for first-line indexes to poems not represented in *Granger's*; for keyword indexes to quotations that have appeared in published queries and replies; for master indexes to the quotations in dozens of old books of quotations; for keyword indexes to first lines of poems; and for the creation of vast literary databases.

If you have not found the solution after doing all that you know to do on your own, you should appeal for help. Ask a fellow student, a teacher, a colleague, a reference librarian, or some other knowledgeable person for assistance. One of these may recognize the quote or be able to find the handle that has eluded you. If appeals to one or two individuals produce no results, then circulate or publish the problem locally. If even that brings no measure of success, the problem is indeed difficult and is worthy of notice in one of the journals that make scholarly assistance available to the needy.

•   •   •

RQ, a publication read by reference librarians, contains a section called "The Exchange" in which untraced quotations and other unanswered reference questions are printed. Librarians submit these queries on their own behalf or on behalf of library patrons they are trying to help. Usually, answers are received and published. *Notes and Queries* has been publishing queries and replies, among other useful things, since 1849, many of them having to do with quotations. This excellent journal is read by scholars all over the world. A query may deal with one problem or even with a list of untraced quotations and allusions. Another journal that the sleuth should make use of is *ANQ* (formerly *American Notes & Queries*), which publishes queries related to scholarly research. From time to time, the *Times Literary Supplement* publishes a little section of queries under the heading "Information, Please." Replies from readers are not published but are sent directly to the inquirers. And occasionally a quotation problem is the subject of a letter published in that journal. Except for the publications I have named and one that ordinarily only publishes queries from alumni of a certain major university, I know of no serial publication of large circulation that prints queries about quotations. There is a real need for the inauguration or restoration in an already widely circulated magazine of a regular feature resembling the late lamented "Queries and Answers" page of the *New York Times Book Review*.

Although it takes time to get a query printed and to have it answered, the published query is an effective tactic to add to the resources already discussed, for among a large number of knowledgeable readers there is likely to be at least one person who knows the answer or knows how to find it. If no one answers immediately, someone may still respond later. I have many times published an identification several years after the appearance of an inquiry but still in time to help the inquirer. On a few occasions I have even published a reply some decades after the publication of the query, partly, I must confess, to show off but mainly to get a source citation on record. In 1969 I responded to an item that had been published in *Notes and Queries* in 1912 along with this note from the editor or the inquirer: "asked for twice previously without identification of author." And in 1974 I replied to a query that had been published in 1910 about a quotation in Hazlitt.[7] If, as happened in these instances, an answer comes too late to help the inquirer, the world—or a small but important part of it—still benefits from the publication of the reply, for there is now a permanent record of the text and source of one more quotation.

Too often a person needing information is too proud or too timid or too busy to publish a request for assistance. As a consequence, many critical editions go to press with untraced but traceable quotations in them, and many persons spend years of their lives waiting in vain for a quotation to appear or reappear before them. If, as sometimes happens, a query is never answered, it still stands for all time as evidence that someone in need of the source of a quotation did all that was possible to find it.

NOTES

1. John William Burgon, *Lives of Twelve Good Men*, new ed. (London: John Murray, 1891), 38. An earlier version of this paragraph appeared in Burgon's "Memoir of Martin Joseph Routh," in *Quarterly Review* 146 (July 1878), 29–30. A still earlier rendering was used as an epigraph to Burgon's *Last Twelve Verses of the Gospel according to St. Mark Vindicated* (Oxford and London, 1871): " 'Advice to you,' sir, 'in studying divinity?' Did you say that you 'wished I would give you a few words of advice,' sir? . . . Then let me recommend to you the practice of always verifying your references, sir.—*Conversation of the late President Routh.*" See *Notes and Queries*, 5th ser., 4 (2 October 1875), 274. Routh, the president of Magdalen College, Oxford, was ninety-two at the time of Burgon's visit.

2. *Blackwood's Edinburgh Magazine* 122 (September 1877), 348.

3. *Notes and Queries* 220 (August 1975), 364; *Harvard Magazine* 86 (May-June 1984), 112.

4. *Notes and Queries* 229 (June 1984), 252; ibid. 230 (June 1985), 253.

5. Ibid. 221 (July 1976), 312.

6. Ibid. 217 (July 1972), 266; ibid. 231 (June 1986), 195–96.

7. Ibid., 11th ser., 5 (1 June 1912), 429; ibid. 214 (January 1969), 35; ibid., 11th ser., 1 (2 April 1910), 269; ibid. (16 April 1910), 317; ibid. 219 (September 1974), 343–44.

Bibliography

Recommended Reading

Boller, Paul F., Jr., and John George. *They Never Said It: A Book of Fake Quotes, Misquotes, and Misleading Attributions*. New York: Oxford University Press, 1989.

Kellett, Ernest Edward. *Literary Quotation and Allusion*. Cambridge: W. Heffer and Sons, 1933.

Merton, Robert K. *On the Shoulders of Giants: A Shandean Postscript*. New York: Free Press; London: Collier-Macmillan, 1965.

Pearson, Hesketh, ed. *Common Misquotations*. London: Hamish Hamilton, 1934; reprint, Folcroft Library Editions, 1973.

General Dictionaries of Quotations
Major Collections

Bartlett, John, comp. *Familiar Quotations: A Collection of Passages, Phrases, and Proverbs Traced to Their Sources in Ancient and Modern Literature*. 15th ed., ed. Emily Morison Beck and the editorial staff of Little, Brown and Co. Boston: Little, Brown and Co., 1980.

An excellent collection of some 22,500 well-chosen, well-documented quotations organized by authors appearing in chronological sequence. The author index must be consulted if all quotes by one author are to be scanned. Good twentieth-century coverage. Superbly indexed. Many classical and foreign quotations are given but are indexed only in English; others appear in English with original texts given in footnotes and with both versions occurring in the index.

The Oxford Dictionary of Quotations. 2d ed. London, New York, and Toronto: Oxford University Press, 1953.

An excellent collection of almost 20,000 well-chosen, well-documented quotations in many languages, organized by authors appearing in alphabetical sequence. Superbly indexed. Good twentieth-century coverage up to mid-century.

Stevenson, Burton, comp. *The Home Book of Quotations, Classical and Modern*. 10th ed. New York: Dodd, Mead and Co., 1967.

A collection of about 50,000 quotations in many languages. Any fairly recent edition will do, as there have been few changes in successive editions. Arrangement by subject is useful when exact wording is not remembered or when the quote cannot be located in the index. Weak index; typically, each entry is a noun that is the subject of the sentence. Source citations vary in completeness. Good classical and foreign coverage. Twentieth-century coverage is good only up to about 1930. Despite its defects and deficiencies, this is an important collection that should be consulted routinely.

Other Basic Collections

Adams, Franklin Pierce, comp. *FPA Book of Quotations*. New York: Funk and Wagnalls Co., 1952.

A collection of about 15,000 quotations appearing under more than 1,000 rubrics. No keyword index. Source citations are incomplete. Recommended only because of strong coverage of twentieth-century quotations.

Bartlett, John, comp. *Familiar Quotations*. 11th ed., ed. Christopher Morley. Boston: Little, Brown and Co., 1937.

———. *Familiar Quotations*. 12th ed., ed. Christopher Morley. Boston: Little, Brown and Co., 1948.

———. *Familiar Quotations*. 13th ed. Boston: Little, Brown and Co., 1955.

———. *Familiar Quotations*. 14th ed., ed. Emily Morison Beck. Boston: Little, Brown and Co., 1968.

Benham, Sir William Gurney, comp. *Benham's Book of Quotations, Proverbs, and Household Words*. Rev. ed. London: George G. Harrap and Co., 1948. Also published as *Putnam's Dictionary of Thoughts*.

A revision of the work first published in 1907, now said to contain 50,000 quotations, mostly in English. Arranged alphabetically by author, though classical and foreign quotations are in sections by language, arranged alphabetically by initial word. Source citations are only fairly complete. A one-chance index, with the phrase appearing once under a keyword or subject, refers the user to a page and column in the text.

Cohen, J. M., and M. J. Cohen, eds. *The Penguin Dictionary of Modern Quotations*. 2d ed. Harmondsworth: Penguin Books, 1980.

A very good collection of about 4,000 modern quotations, arranged by author. The quotes are well chosen, but documentation and indexing are not sufficiently detailed.

Evans, Bergen, comp. *Dictionary of Quotations*. New York: Delacorte Press, 1968.

An excellent collection of perhaps 13,500 well-chosen quotations, arranged by topic and, in the Delacorte edition, containing an index that is longer than the text. Includes quotations from many languages, but they are given only in English. Useful in tracing translated quotations. Best to consult this resource if you consider the quotation you are tracing wise, witty, urbane, or memorable. Source citations are scholarly but not always complete.

Hoyt, Jehiel Keeler, comp. *Hoyt's New Cyclopedia of Practical Quotations*. Rev. ed., ed. Kate Louise Roberts. New York and London: Funk and Wagnalls Co., 1922.

A good older collection with a fine index that may be consulted in seconds. Should be checked for any Latin quotation and any pre-1920 English quotation not in the major collections.

Mencken, H. L., ed. *A New Dictionary of Quotations on Historical Principles from Ancient and Modern Sources*. New York: Alfred A. Knopf, 1942.

Thousands of interesting quotations—but no old chestnuts—appear under hundreds of rubrics. No index. Hard to use, but an occasionally valuable supplement to other collections.

The Oxford Dictionary of Quotations. 3d ed. Oxford and New York: Oxford University Press, 1979.

A strong collection of about 17,000 quotations. Weaker than the *ODQ2* for a basic corpus of pre-1950 quotations but stronger for twentieth-century quotes and for quotes from women writers. Scholarly, with accurate texts and full source citations. Weak index, with fewer entries per quotation than in Bartlett or the *ODQ2*.

Platt, Suzy, ed. *Respectfully Quoted: A Dictionary of Quotations Requested from the Congressional Research Service*. Washington, D.C.: Library of Congress, 1989.

An important as well as an interesting and attractive recent collection of some 2,100 quotations that may be variously characterized as political, historical, literary, presidential, modern, or of interest to political leaders. Detailed source citations for most quotations; collection contains some anonymous or attributed quotations that the Congressional Research Service could not trace or verify. Includes interesting discussions of the quotations. Indexed by subjects (under which phrases from quotations appear) and authors.

The Reader's Digest Treasury of Modern Quotations. New York: Reader's Digest Press, 1975.

Some 6,000 modern quotations appear under about 70 broad headings. Source citations are to author and title or to author and issue of periodical, such as *Reader's Digest*. Sources named should be examined for better references. Author index and subject index;

the latter functions as keyword index. Useful for modern quotations if authorship is known or if you think the quote would have appealed to the editors of *Reader's Digest*.

Seldes, George, comp. *The Great Quotations*. New York: Lyle Stewart, 1960.

———. *The Great Quotations*. New York: Pocket Books, 1967.

A collection of ideas that appealed to the compiler, most of them in prose. The Lyle Stewart edition is arranged by author; the Pocket Books edition, by subject. Source citations are minimal. Subject index. Occasionally helpful in tracing sources of ideas of some significance.

Simpson, James B., comp. *Simpson's Contemporary Quotations*. Boston: Houghton Mifflin Co., 1988.

A very good collection of about 10,000 quotations, most not literary or bookish, from about 4,000 people. Based largely on media coverage of the years 1950–87. Documentation is uneven, from author, title, and page to "recalled at his death." Weak index of subjects and keywords must be used with care. Author index. A major reference tool for tracing quotations from the second half of the twentieth century, especially when authorship is known.

Stevenson, Burton, comp. *The Home Book of Proverbs, Maxims, and Familiar Phrases*. New York: Macmillan Co., 1948. Also published as *The Macmillan Book of Proverbs, Maxims, and Famous Phrases*.

A useful collection of proverbs, maxims, familiar phrases, and restatements of proverbs. Every quotation is indexed by at least one keyword.

Tripp, Rhoda Thomas, comp. *The International Thesaurus of Quotations*. New York: Thomas Y. Crowell Co., 1970.

Some 16,000 quotations, each of which makes a statement about some aspect of life, arranged by subject. Indexes to categories, authors, and keywords. Source citations vary in completeness. Strong in twentieth-century quotations.

Older Collections

Allibone, Samuel Austin, comp. *Poetical Quotations from Chaucer to Tennyson*. Philadelphia: J. B. Lippincott and Co., 1873.

Organized by subject. Source citations are undocumented author attributions. First-line index but no keyword index.

———. *Prose Quotations from Socrates to Macaulay*. Philadelphia: J. B. Lippincott and Co., 1875.

Organized by subject. Long passages with complete source citations; short ones with author attributions. Lacks a keyword index.

The Beauties of the English Stage. 3d ed., 3 vols. London: E. Withers and A. and C. Corbett, 1756. Also published as *The Beauties of the English Drama.* 4 vols. London: G. Robinson, 1777.

A revision of a work first published in 1737. Passages from Shakespeare's time up to the mid-eighteenth century are arranged by topics, from "absence" to "zeal." Citations refer to authors and titles, not to acts and scenes. Useful for early English quotes, particularly for tracing blank verse passages.

Bysshe, Edward. *The Art of English Poetry.* London: R. Knaplock, E. Castle, and B. Tooke, 1702; reprint, Menston: Scolar Press, 1968.

A collection of poetic and dramatic passages from English writers, largely from the seventeenth century. Arranged alphabetically by subject. Source citations are abbreviated and incomplete.

Day, Edward Parsons, comp. *Day's Collacon: An Encyclopaedia of Prose Quotations.* New York: International Printing and Publishing Office, 1884.

An old collection of maxims and words of wisdom that is still occasionally useful. Arranged by subject. Source citations are names of authors. Author index but no keyword index.

Douglas, Charles Noel, comp. *Forty Thousand Sublime and Beautiful Thoughts.* 2 vols. New York: Christian Herald/Bible House, 1904. Also published as *Forty Thousand Quotations: Prose and Poetical.* New York: A. L. Burt Co., 1917.

Quotations in prose and verse, arranged by subject and accompanied by undocumented author attributions. Lacks a keyword index.

Edwards, Tryon, comp. *The New Dictionary of Thoughts.* Rev. ed., ed. C. N. Catrevas. London and New York: Classic Publishing Co., 1931.

A revision of an old classic, Edwards's *Dictionary of Thoughts,* first published in 1891. Much like Day or Douglas. Quotations are arranged by subject and followed by names of authors. Lacks a keyword index.

Hale, Sarah Josepha, ed. *A Complete Dictionary of Poetical Quotations.* Philadelphia: Lippincott, Grambo and Co., 1855.

A once-popular collection of quotations from British and American poets, frequently published during the period 1849–83. Arranged by subject. Citations name authors or authors and titles. Lacks a keyword index.

Hayward, Thomas, ed. *The British Muse; or, A Collection of Thoughts Moral, Natural, and Sublime, of Our English Poets, Who Flourished in the Sixteenth and Seventeenth Centuries.* 3 vols. London: F. Cogan and J. Nourse, 1738. Also published as *The Quintessence of English*

Poetry. 3 vols. London: O. Payne, 1740.

A collection of sixteenth- and seventeenth-century quotations, much like Bysshe, arranged by subject. Source citations are incomplete.

A Poetical Dictionary; or, The Beauties of the English Poets, Alphabetically Displayed. 4 vols. London: J. Newbery [and others], 1761.

An old quotation collection arranged by subject. Contains long and short passages from poets and dramatists mainly of the seventeenth and eighteenth centuries. Worth consulting for old poetical or dramatic quotations that fit neatly under a subject.

Wood, James, comp. *Dictionary of Quotations from Ancient and Modern, English and Foreign Sources.* London: Frederick Warne, 1893. Also published as *The Nuttall Dictionary of Quotations.* Rev. ed., ed. A. L. Haydon. London and New York: Frederick Warne and Co., 1930.

Over 30,000 quotations, most of them complete sentences or complete thoughts, arranged alphabetically by initial word. Good keyword index for its time. Authors are named but works are not.

Single-Subject and Special-Category Quotation Books
Subject Collections
AMERICA

Edelhart, Mike, and James Tinen, comps. *America the Quotable.* New York: Facts on File, 1983.

Thousands of interesting quotations, old and new, about America, American life, and individual states and cities. Citations lack chapter and page references. Author index but no keyword index. Table of contents serves as subject index.

Fadiman, Clifton, ed. *The American Treasury, 1455–1955.* New York: Harper and Brothers, 1955.

A collection of materials about the United States—its government, history, and people—and of quotations by notable Americans about practically anything. Citations are incomplete, some woefully so. Indexes to subjects, authors, and familiar words and phrases.

AUTHORS

Moulton, Charles Wells, ed. *The Library of Literary Criticism of English and American Authors.* 8 vols. Buffalo, N.Y.: Moulton Publishing Co., 1901–5; reprint, New York: Peter Smith, 1935.

Useful in tracing or verifying quotations about English and American authors of the nineteenth century and earlier.

AUTHORSHIP

Charlton, James, ed. *The Writer's Quotation Book.* Rev. ed. Yonkers, N.Y.: Pushcart Press, 1985.

Some 600 sparkling statements on writing, mainly from twentieth-century writers. No index. Author attributions.

Winokur, Jon, comp. *Writers on Writing.* Philadelphia: Running Press, 1986.

About 1,500 remarkable quotations on nearly 50 topics. Subject index contains some keywords. Author attributions.

BOOKS AND READING

Jackson, Holbrook. *The Anatomy of Bibliomania.* 2 vols. New York: Charles Scribner's Sons, 1931.

Not a book of quotations, but it does contain many excellent, well-documented quotes. Author index is useful for tracing passages of known authorship. Subject approach is also possible by scanning appropriate chapters.

Langford, John Alfred, ed. *The Praise of Books, as Said and Sung by English Authors.* 2d ed. London: Cassell, Petter, Galpin and Co., 1898.

About 75 classic prose extracts. Author index.

Shaylor, Joseph, comp. *The Pleasures of Literature and the Solace of Books.* London: Wells Gardner, Darton and Co., 1898.

A small book of extracts in prose and verse. Includes a number of statements from important nineteenth-century English and American writers and statesmen. Author index.

BUSINESS AND ECONOMICS

Jackman, Michael, ed. *The Macmillan Book of Business and Economic Quotations.* New York: Macmillan Co., 1984.

Some 3,000 quotations occurring under about 60 topics. Citations consist of author attributions. Not all the quotations appear in the keyword index. Much space is filled by proverbs and anonymous quotations.

James, Simon, comp. *A Dictionary of Economic Quotations.* London: Croom Helm; Totawa, N.J.: Barnes and Noble Books, 1981.

An outstanding collection of about 2,000 quotes arranged by topic. Excellent source citations. Keyword and author indexes.

Kent, Robert W., ed. *Money Talks: The 2,500 Greatest Business Quotes from Aristotle to DeLorean.* New York: Facts on File, 1985.

Approximately 2,500 quotations, many of them proverbial or anonymous, appear under a dozen or so broad topics. Citations vary in degree of incompleteness. Author index but no subject or keyword index.

Kurian, George Thomas, comp. *Handbook of Business Quotations*. Englewood Cliffs, N.J.: Prentice-Hall, 1987.

Some 900 quotations occurring under about 350 topics. Author attributions but no documentation. Author index.

Rosenberg, Jerry Martin, ed. *Dictionary of Business and Management*. 2d ed. New York: John Wiley and Sons, 1983.

Contains an appendix of almost 400 "relevant quotations" arranged alphabetically by author. Citations are not complete but are better than in many other collections of this sort. Subject index.

COMMUNISM

Weeks, Albert L., comp. *Brassey's Soviet and Communist Quotations*. Washington, D.C.: Pergamon-Brassey's International Defense Publishers, 1987.

Over 2,000 quotations, all in English, from Communist leaders and theorists, past and present, gathered in 17 broad chapters. Subject and keyword indexes. Documentation is excellent.

EDUCATION

Farber, Bernard E., comp. *A Teacher's Treasury of Quotations*. Jefferson, N.C.: McFarland and Co., 1985.

A very good collection of about 5,000 quotations under 600 or so rubrics. Citations are relatively complete. Author and subject indexes but no keyword index.

Kerber, August, ed. *Quotable Quotes on Education*. Detroit: Wayne State University Press, 1968.

Some 2,500 quotations appearing under a broad range of topics. Citations are undocumented author ascriptions. Author and subject indexes.

Sen, N. B., ed. *Glorious Thoughts on Education*. 2d ed. New Delhi: New Book Society of India, 1967.

A collection of literary quotations, arranged first under broad subjects and then alphabetically by author. Source citations are minimal.

LAW

Cook, Paul C., comp. *A Treasury of Legal Quotations*. New York: Vantage Press, 1961.

Contains a small number of lengthy excerpts from judicial opinions, arranged by author. Excellent citations and a good subject index.

Gerhart, Eugene C., comp. *Quote It! Memorable Legal Quotations: Data, Epigrams, Wit, and Wisdom from Legal and Literary Sources*. New York:

Clark Boardman Co.; Albany, N.Y.: Sage Hill Publishers, 1969.

An excellent collection of about 4,000 quotations from legal and literary sources, arranged alphabetically by subject. Scholarly citations. Indexes to subjects, authors, and keywords.

Jackson, Percival E., ed. *The Wisdom of the Supreme Court.* Norman: University of Oklahoma Press, 1962.

A noteworthy collection of quotations from judicial and other writings of members of the Supreme Court, arranged alphabetically by subject. Excellent source citations.

James, Simon, and Chantal Stebbings, comps. *A Dictionary of Legal Quotations.* New York: Macmillan Co., 1987.

A scholarly collection of some 2,000 quotations from judicial, literary, historical, and political sources, arranged by subject. Author and keyword indexes.

McNamara, M. Frances, comp. *Ragbag of Legal Quotations.* Albany, N.Y.: M. Bender and Co., 1960. Also published as *2,000 Famous Legal Quotations.* Rochester, N.Y.: Aqueduct Books, 1967.

An excellent collection, arranged by subject, with complete source citations and an author index. Detailed subject index often includes wording from quotations.

Mead, Leon, and F. Newell Gilbert, comps. *Manual of Forensic Quotations.* New York: J. F. Taylor and Co., 1903; reprint, Detroit: Gale Research Co., 1968.

A small collection of quotations from trials and speeches of long ago. Level of documentation varies. Subject index.

Norton-Kyshe, James William, ed. *The Dictionary of Legal Quotations; or, Selected Dicta of English Chancellors and Judges from the Earliest Periods to the Present Time.* London: Sweet and Maxwell, 1904; reprint, Detroit: Gale Research, 1968.

An old but scholarly collection of quotations from English chancellors and judges, arranged by subject. Excellent citations. Even quotations occurring within quotations can be traced. Many quotes are listed in the index in letter-by-letter alphabetical order, under heading "words."

Shrager, David S., and Elizabeth Frost, comps. *The Quotable Lawyer.* New York: Facts on File, 1986.

Some 2,500 quotations arranged by subject. Source citations are incomplete but probably traceable; sometimes source cited is another collection of quotations. Subject and author indexes.

MEDICINE

Daintith, John, and Amanda Isaacs, eds. *Medical Quotes: A Thematic Dictionary.* Oxford and New York: Facts on File, 1989.

Contains some 2,000 interesting quotations, old and new, on about 200 topics having to do with medicine, disease, health, life, and death. Source citations range from author attributions to author-title and author-title-chapter references. Indexes to keywords and to names.

Strauss, Maurice B., ed. *Familiar Medical Quotations*. Boston: Little, Brown and Co., 1968.

An excellent collection of about 7,000 quotations, arranged by subject. Documentation is mostly good. Keyword index.

MILITARY MATTERS

Heinl, Robert Debs, Jr., comp. *Dictionary of Military and Naval Quotations*. Annapolis, Md.: United States Naval Institute, 1966.

Well-chosen quotations, taken from literary as well as political and military sources and given only in English, are arranged under hundreds of rubrics. Citations are less than complete but better than in most collections of this sort. Author index.

MUSIC

Crofton, Ian, and Donald Fraser, comps. *A Dictionary of Musical Quotations*. London: Croom Helm, 1985.

More than 3,000 first-rate quotations under about 150 headings on all aspects of traditional music. Documentation is fairly good. Indexes to authors and to subjects and keywords.

Shapiro, Nat, comp. *An Encyclopedia of Quotations about Music*. Garden City, N.Y.: Doubleday and Co., 1978; reprint, New York: Da Capo Press, 1981.

About 2,000 quotations arranged under some 45 broad headings. Documentation varies in thoroughness, from author attributions to author, title, and date. Indexes to names and keywords.

Slonimsky, Nicolas, ed. *Lexicon of Musical Invective: Critical Assaults on Composers since Beethoven's Time*. New York: Coleman-Ross Co., 1953.

An interesting anthology of critical comment on 43 composers. Quotations are arranged by composer. French and German passages are given in their original languages and also in translation. Documentation is very good. There is an index of "vituperative, pejorative and deprecatory words and phrases."

PERSONS

Kenin, Richard, and Justin Wintle, eds. *The Dictionary of Biographical Quotation of British and American Subjects*. New York: Alfred A. Knopf, 1978.

Quotations arranged by subject from a variety of materials about more than 1,000 famous or infamous British or American individuals no longer living. Citations are less than complete. Author index.

Ringo, Miriam, comp. *Nobody Said It Better: 2,700 Wise and Witty Quotations about Famous People.* Chicago: Rand McNally and Co., 1980.

A small collection of interesting quotations. Citations are adequate. Indexes to subjects, authors, and keywords.

PLACES

Clapp, James A., comp. *The City: A Dictionary of Quotable Thought on Cities and Urban Life.* New Brunswick, N.J.: Center for Urban Policy Research, Rutgers University, 1984.

A collection of 5,000 or so passages about specific cities and about urban living, from over 1,000 authors. Level of documentation varies. Lacks keyword index, but access to quotations is provided by author arrangement and by indexes to cities and subjects.

Yapp, Peter, comp. *The Travellers' Dictionary of Quotation: Who Said What, about Where?* London: Routledge and Kegan Paul, 1983.

A monumental collection of thousands of quotations about large and small places and about peoples, arranged alphabetically in sections and subsections. Citations are less than complete but are verifiable with some effort. Indexes to places and peoples and to authors.

POLITICS

Green, Jonathon, comp. *The Book of Political Quotes.* New York: McGraw-Hill Book Co., 1982.

Approximately 3,000 quotes arranged under about 20 broad topics. Useful if the name of the author is already known. Source citations are incomplete, but some are verifiable with a bit of effort. Author index.

Jackman, Michael, comp. *Crown's Book of Political Quotations: Over 2,500 Lively Quotes from Plato to Reagan.* New York: Crown Publishers, 1982.

About 2,500 short statements arranged alphabetically by topic. Citations are undocumented author attributions.

Montgomery, Hugh, and Philip G. Cambray, eds. *A Dictionary of Political Phrases and Allusions.* London: Swan Sonnenschein and Co., 1906; reprint, Detroit: Gale Research Co., 1968.

Gives sources of short phrases related to English politics before 1906.

Stewart, Robert MacKenzie, comp. *A Dictionary of Political Quotations.* London: Europa Publications, 1984.

A scholarly collection of 2,300 or so political statements, arranged alphabetically by author. Keyword index.

RELIGION

Mead, Frank S., ed. *The Encyclopedia of Religious Quotations*. Westwood, N.J.: Fleming H. Revell Co., 1965.

About 12,000 quotations arranged alphabetically by topic. Poetical and biblical citations are detailed; others are incomplete, some extremely so. Weak index of topics refers to page numbers. Not very useful.

Proctor, F. B., ed. *Classified Gems of Thought, from the Great Writers and Preachers of All Ages*. London: Hodder and Stoughton, 1887. Reprinted as the *Treasury of Quotations on Religious Subjects from the Great Writers and Preachers of All Ages*. Grand Rapids, Mich.: Kregel Publications, 1977.

A collection of old quotations arranged under some 3,000 topics. Citations are names of authors.

Stevenson, Burton, ed. *The Home Book of Bible Quotations*. New York: Harper and Brothers, 1949.

Not the only work to be consulted for a biblical quotation—Bartlett and the *ODQ2* contain many such quotations, and concordances are more complete—but a very good collection of passages from the King James version. Includes the Apocrypha. Well indexed and well referenced.

Woods, Ralph L., comp. *The World Treasury of Religious Quotations*. New York: Garland Books, 1966.

Some 15,000 quotations arranged by topic. Biblical and poetical quotes are excluded, and citations are incomplete. Author index. Not very useful.

SCIENCE

Mackay, Alan L., comp. *The Harvest of a Quiet Eye: A Selection of Scientific Quotations*. Bristol and London: Institute of Physics, 1977.

A charming collection of perhaps 1,500 passages in prose and verse on scientific subjects, arranged by author. Documentation is less than complete, though verifiable with a little effort. Keyword index.

SPORTS

Abel, Bob, and Michael Valenti, comps. *Sports Quotes: The Insiders' View of the Sports World*. New York: Facts on File, 1983.

Some 1,300 long passages on about 50 aspects of sport. Two source citations for each quote, one giving author and year of quotation and the other, in an easily overlooked chapter on sources, giving newspaper or journal reference. Index of persons. Difficult to use if the author of a quote is not known. One of the least unsatisfactory collections in this group.

Chieger, Bob, comp. *Voices of Baseball: Quotations on the Summer Game.* New York: Atheneum, 1983.

About 2,000 quotes appearing under some 40 baseball topics. Source citations are incomplete in varying degrees. Author index.

Chieger, Bob, and Pat Sullivan, comps. *Inside Golf: Quotations on the Royal and Ancient Game.* New York: Atheneum, 1985.

Perhaps 1,800 quotations under an assortment of golfing topics. Source citations vary in level of incompleteness. Index to persons but not keywords.

Green, Lee, comp. *Sportswit.* New York: Harper and Row, 1984.

Some 2,500 quotations occurring under 100 or so rubrics. Source citations are author attributions. Index to names but not to keywords.

Liddle, Barry, comp. *Dictionary of Sports Quotations.* London: Routledge and Kegan Paul, 1987.

A scholarly compilation of about 1,200 somewhat bookish, somewhat British quotes, arranged alphabetically by topic. Detailed citations. Indexes to authors and subjects but not to keywords.

Maikovich, Andrew J., comp. *Sports Quotations: Maxims, Quips, and Pronouncements for Writers and Fans.* Jefferson, N.C.: McFarland and Co., 1984.

Some 1,800 sparkling quotes on various sporty topics. Source citations are undocumented author ascriptions. Indexes to subjects and names but not to keywords.

Nelson, Kevin, comp. *Baseball's Greatest Quotes: The Wit, Wisdom, and Wisecracks of America's National Pastime.* New York: Simon and Schuster, 1982.

Perhaps 1,400 quotations occurring in 14 sections. Not documented but does contain acknowledgments of copyrighted material. Author index.

Genre Categories

Aphorisms

Auden, W. H., and Louis Kronenberger, comps. *The Viking Book of Aphorisms: A Personal Selection.* New York: Viking Press, 1962. Also published as *The Faber Book of Aphorisms: A Personal Selection.* London: Faber and Faber, 1964.

Some 3,000 pithy statements appearing under general topics. Undocumented author ascriptions. Indexes to authors and subjects but not keywords. May serve to lend support to an attribution of authorship or to confirm or improve the wording of an aphorism.

Gross, John, comp. *The Oxford Book of Aphorisms.* Oxford and New York: Oxford University Press, 1983.

About 3,500 aphorisms arranged by topic. Source citations usually supply author, title, and date. Index to authors but not to subjects or keywords. Useful if authorship is already known.

Smith, Logan Pearsall, ed. *A Treasury of English Aphorisms.* London: Constable and Co., 1943.

Excellent citations. Index to authors but not to subjects or keywords. Useful if authorship is already known.

LAST WORDS

Conrad, Barnaby, comp. *Famous Last Words.* Garden City, N.Y.: Doubleday, 1961.

A popular collection of about 850 dying pronouncements arranged by purported author. No references to sources and no indexes.

Le Comte, Edward Semple, comp. *Dictionary of Last Words.* New York: Philosophical Library, 1955.

The only scholarly collection in this group, with 1,664 ultimate utterances arranged by author. Printed sources for each quotation are indicated in a separate chapter.

Lockyer, Herbert, comp. *Last Words of Saints and Sinners.* Grand Rapids, Mich.: Kregel Publications, 1969.

Contains some 700 undocumented examples.

PROVERBS

Apperson, George Latimer, ed. *English Proverbs and Proverbial Phrases: A Historical Dictionary.* London: J. M. Dent and Sons; New York: E. P. Dutton and Co., 1929.

Provides many illustrative quotations from literature.

Hazlitt, William Carew, ed. *English Proverbs and Proverbial Phrases.* London: Reeves and Turner, 1907; reprint, Detroit: Gale Research Co., 1969.

An old classic in which many proverbs are traced to early appearances.

The Oxford Dictionary of English Proverbs. 3d ed., ed. F. P. Wilson. Oxford: Clarendon Press, 1970.

Provides many illustrative quotations from literature.

Stevenson, Burton, ed. *The Home Book of Proverbs, Maxims, and Familiar Phrases.* New York: Macmillan Co., 1948. Also published as *The Macmillan Book of Proverbs, Maxims, and Famous Phrases.* New York: Macmillan Co., n.d.

Probably the most useful compilation in this group. Many illustrative quotations. Each proverb appears in the index under at least one keyword.

Taylor, Archer, and Bartlett Jere Whiting, eds. *A Dictionary of American Proverbs and Proverbial Phrases, 1820–80.* Cambridge: Belknap Press of Harvard University Press, 1958.

A useful index to proverbs and proverbial phrases occurring in the works of nineteenth-century American writers.

SIMILES

Wilstach, Frank J., ed. *A Dictionary of Similes.* Rev. ed. Boston: Little, Brown and Co., 1924.

Contains about 19,000 similes quoted from 2,400 authors arranged under 4,600 subjects, in two alphabetical sequences. Each quote contains "like" or "as." Implicit comparisons are not included. Source citations are names of authors.

Author Categories

AUSTRALIANS

Murray-Smith, Stephen, comp. *The Dictionary of Australian Quotations.* Richmond, Victoria: Heinemann, 1984.

A scholarly collection, arranged by author, of perhaps 4,000 quotations by Australians or about Australia. Documentation is excellent. Subject and keyword indexes.

BLACKS

King, Anita, comp. *Quotations in Black.* Westport, Conn.: Greenwood Press, 1981.

A useful book of some 1,100 quotations by more than 200 black persons, arranged chronologically by author. Source citations are less than complete, though verifiable with some effort. Indexes to authors, subjects, and keywords.

CANADIANS

Hamilton, Robert M., and Dorothy Shields, comps. *The Dictionary of Canadian Quotations and Phrases.* Rev. ed. Toronto: McClelland and Stewart, 1979.

About 10,000 quotations appearing under almost 2,000 topics. Documentation is excellent. Author index and list of subjects but no keyword index.

CATHOLICS

Chapin, John, comp. *The Book of Catholic Quotations, Compiled from Approved Sources, Ancient, Medieval, and Modern.* New York: Farrar,

Straus and Cudahy, 1956.

More than 10,000 prose and verse quotations on many subjects from approved Catholic sources ranging from popes to poets. Latin quotations are given only in English. Scholarly citations. Index of sources and good keyword index.

THE IRISH

McMahon, Sean, comp. *A Book of Irish Quotations*. Dublin: O'Brien Press, 1984.

Perhaps 5,000 quotations arranged by author. Source citations are less than complete, though verifiable with some effort. Keyword index.

JEWS

Baron, Joseph L., comp. *A Treasury of Jewish Quotations*. Rev. ed. South Brunswick, New York, and London: Thomas Yoseloff, 1965.

A useful, lifelong collection of over 18,000 quotations classified under more than 1,000 subjects. Quotations are traced to individual authors and to the Talmud and the Bible. Indexes to subjects and authors.

Rosten, Leo, ed. *Leo Rosten's Treasury of Jewish Quotations*. New York: McGraw-Hill, 1972.

About 4,500 Jewish proverbs, folk sayings, and epigrams, arranged by topic. Most are not traced to individuals. Author index.

PRESIDENTS

Frost, Elizabeth, comp. *The Bully Pulpit: Quotations from America's Presidents*. New York: Facts on File, 1988.

A collection of about 3,000 interesting presidential quotes, from Washington to Reagan, appearing under some 200 subjects. Level of source citations varies, from undocumented ascriptions to references to dated letters and speeches. Since references to standard editions of letters and speeches and page references to any books named are lacking in the citations, verification of any quotation would require some effort. Indexes to subjects and authors but not keywords.

Harnsberger, Caroline Thomas, comp. *Treasury of Presidential Quotations*. Chicago: Follett Publishing Co., 1964.

A collection of 2,800 or so presidential quotes, from Washington to Lyndon Johnson, arranged alphabetically by topic. Documentation is excellent. Author index refers to quotations on specific subjects by each president. Index to subjects but not keywords.

Literary and Artistic Forms
MOVIES
Haun, Harry, ed. *The Movie Quote Book*. New York: Lippincott and Crowell, 1980; reprint, New York: Harper and Row, 1983.

Contains about 3,000 quotations from nearly 600 motion pictures, appearing under some 400 topics. Entries supply all the information likely to be needed. No keyword index.

NOVELS
Powell, David, comp. *The Wisdom of the Novel: A Dictionary of Quotations*. New York: Garland Publishing, 1985.

Contains perhaps 13,000 quotable passages from about 900 novels by some 300 novelists, arranged under 900 or so subjects. Very good source references. Wording from quotations is not repeated in the index.

Single-Author Quotation Books

CHESTERTON
Chesterton, G. K. *A Chesterton Calendar*. London: Kegan Paul, Trench, Trübner and Co., 1911. Also published as *Chesterton Day by Day*.

A long passage from an early Chesterton work for every day in the year. Source citations are book titles. Lacks topical arrangement and index.

———. *More Quotable Chesterton: A Topical Compilation of the Wit, Wisdom, and Satire of G. K. Chesterton*. Ed. George J. Marlin, Richard P. Rabatin, and John L. Swan. San Francisco: Ignatius Press, 1988.

An excellent collection to supplement *The Quotable Chesterton*.

———. *The Quotable Chesterton: A Topical Compilation of the Wit, Wisdom, and Satire of G. K. Chesterton*. Ed. George J. Marlin, Richard P. Rabatin, and John L. Swan. San Francisco: Ignatius Press, 1986.

An excellent collection of 1,200 passages arranged alphabetically by topic. Detailed source citations and a supplementary topic index, to be used if the quotation has not been located in the text.

———. *Wit and Wisdom of G. K. Chesterton*. Comp. Frances Alice Blogg Chesterton. New York: Dodd, Mead and Co., 1911.

Source citations are book titles. Lacks topical arrangement and index.

CHURCHILL
Churchill, Sir Winston. *A Churchill Reader: The Wit and Wisdom of Sir Winston Churchill*. Comp. Colin R. Coote. Boston: Houghton Mifflin Co., 1954.

An enlargement of *Maxims and Reflections.* Quotes appear under 18 main topics. Documentation lacks detail. No index.

———. *Immortal Jester: A Treasury of the Great Good Humour of Sir Winston Churchill, K.G., O.M., C.H., 1874–1965.* Comp. Leslie Frewin. London: Leslie Frewin, 1973.

Quotations, mostly undocumented, are grouped under 20 subjects. No index.

———. *Irrepressible Churchill: A Treasury of Winston Churchill's Wit.* Comp. Kay Halle. Cleveland: World Publishing Co., 1966.

Some 1,000 quotations arranged chronologically. Citations vary in quality; many of the quotes are undocumented. Index to subjects but not keywords.

———. *Maxims and Reflections of the Rt. Hon. Winston S. Churchill, C.H., M.P.* Comp. Colin Coote. London: Eyre and Spottiswoode, 1947.

Quotes are grouped under 10 main topics. Documentation lacks detail. No index.

———. *The Wisdom of Winston Churchill, Being a Selection of Aphorisms, Reflections, Precepts, Maxims, Epigrams, Paradoxes, and Opinions from His Parliamentary and Public Speeches, 1900–1955.* Ed. F. B. Czarnomski. London: George Allen and Unwin, 1956.

A very good collection of about 3,000 quotations from Churchill's speeches, arranged under headings that sometimes contain keywords from quotes. Source citations supply place and date but lack other details. No keyword index.

DICKENS

Dickens, Charles. *Charles Dickens Birthday Book.* Comp. Enid Dickens Hawksley. London: Faber and Faber, 1948.

A quote or two for each day. Source citations are titles. No index.

———. *A Cyclopedia of the Best Thoughts of Charles Dickens.* Comp. F. G. De Fontaine. New York: E. J. Hale and Son, 1873. Also published as *The Fireside Dickens: A Cyclopedia of the Best Thoughts of Charles Dickens.* New York: G. W. Dillingham, 1888.

A very good collection of quotations, arranged under subjects from "abbey—Nell in the old" to "youth—the depravity of." Citations supply title and chapter. Index to subjects but not keywords.

———. *The Dickens Birthday Book.* London: Raphael Tuck and Sons, n.d.

Contains 366 short quotations. Source references are book titles. No index.

———. *The Dickens Year Book.* Comp. Lois E. Prentiss and Gertrude C. Spaulding. Chicago: A. C. McClurg and Co., 1913.

One or two quotes for each day in the year. Source citations are names of characters.

————. *Maxims*. New York: A. L. Chatterton, n.d.

Perhaps 300 maxims. Source references are titles.

————. *The Religious Sentiments of Charles Dickens*. Comp. Charles H. McKenzie. London: Walter Scott, 1884; reprint, New York: Haskell House, 1973.

Quotations occur in discussions in 9 broad chapters. Source citations supply title and chapter. No index.

DISRAELI

Disraeli, Benjamin. *Wit and Imagination of Benjamin Disraeli*. Comp. George Sampson. London: Seeley and Co., 1908.

Quotations of varying length under general headings. Citations are book titles.

————. *Wit and Wisdom of Benjamin Disraeli, Earl of Beaconsfield, Collected from His Writings and Speeches*. London: Longmans, Green and Co., 1881.

A substantial collection of quotes from writings and speeches, arranged alphabetically by topic. Detailed references to speeches, but other source citations are book titles. Subject index.

ELIOT

Eliot, George. *The George Eliot Birthday Book*. Edinburgh: William Blackwood and Sons, n.d.

Provides a quotation or two for every day in the year. Speakers and book titles are given as sources.

————. *The Pocket George Eliot*. Comp. Alfred H. Hyatt. London: Chatto and Windus, 1907.

Some 400 passages indexed by opening words. Source references are titles of books.

————. *Wise, Witty, and Tender Sayings in Prose and Verse, Selected from the Works of George Eliot*. 6th ed., comp. Alexander Main. Edinburgh: William Blackwood and Sons, 1883.

Contains quotations arranged by book titles, followed by passages from Eliot's poems. Under each title quotations are organized by speaker. No index. Fourth or later edition is most complete.

————. *Wit and Wisdom of George Eliot*. Boston: Roberts Brothers, 1886.

A clone of Alexander Main's book. Fullest version is dated 1886 or later.

EMERSON

Emerson, Ralph Waldo. *Light of Emerson: A Complete Digest with Keyword Concordance, the Cream of All He Wrote*. Ed. H. H. Emmons. Cleveland: Rex Publishing Co., 1930.

Contains 1,745 passages grouped under titles of essays. Keyword index.

——. *The Pocket Emerson.* Comp. Alfred H. Hyatt. London: Chatto and Windus, 1906.

Some 500 quotations indexed by opening words. Source citations are titles of essays.

HUXLEY

Huxley, Thomas H. *Aphorisms and Reflections from the Works of T. H. Huxley.* Ed. Henrietta A. Huxley. London: Macmillan and Co., 1907.

An outstanding collection of 400 quotations. Documentation is excellent. Subject index.

JAMES

James, William. *As William James Said: Extracts from the Published Writings of William James.* Comp. Elizabeth Perkins Aldrich. New York: Vanguard Press, 1942.

Several hundred well-documented quotations under some two dozen headings. No index.

JEFFERSON

Jefferson, Thomas. *The Jeffersonian Cyclopedia: A Comprehensive Collection of the Views of Thomas Jefferson.* Ed. John P. Foley. New York: Funk and Wagnalls Co., 1900; reprint, 2 vols., New York: Russell and Russell, 1967.

A great collection of approximately 9,000 well-documented quotations of varying length, topically arranged.

JOHNSON

Hay, James. *Johnson: His Characteristics and Aphorisms.* London: Alexander Gardner, 1884.

Contains a large number of short sayings arranged by subject. Good documentation.

Johnson, Samuel. *The Beauties of Samuel Johnson, LL.D.* 9th ed. London: G. Kearsley, 1797.

A very good collection of quotations, topically arranged. Documentation is adequate or traceable with a little work.

——. *The Johnson Calendar; or, Samuel Johnson for Every Day in the Year.* Comp. Alexander Montgomerie Bell. Oxford: Clarendon Press, 1916.

No index, but quotations on similar subjects occur together. Documentation is good.

——. *" 'Sir,' Said Dr. Johnson—".* Comp. H. C. Biron. London: Duckworth and Co., 1911.

A collection of quotations from Johnson's conversations. Lacks documentation but may confirm or correct wording of the quote being traced or provide a bigger target for the tracer.

———. *Wisdom and Genius of Dr. Samuel Johnson, Selected from His Prose Writings.* Comp. W. A. Clouston. London: James Blackwood and Co., 1875.

Undocumented quotes from Johnson's prose writings. May be of some use.

———. *The Wisdom of Dr. Johnson, Being Comments on Life and Moral Precepts Chosen from His Writings.* Comp. Constantia Maxwell. London: George G. Harrap and Co., 1948.

Almost 1,000 well-chosen and well-referenced quotations under some 200 subjects. Index to subjects and keywords.

———. *Wit and Wisdom of Samuel Johnson.* Comp. George Birkbeck Hill. Oxford: Clarendon Press, 1888.

A well-selected, well-organized, and well-documented collection. Quotations arranged alphabetically by topic.

LINCOLN

Lincoln, Abraham. *The Lincoln Encyclopedia: The Spoken and Written Words of A. Lincoln, Arranged for Ready Reference.* Comp. Archer H. Shaw. New York: Macmillan Co., 1950.

A major collection of thousands of quotations, arranged alphabetically by subject. Documentation is very good. Most quotations are taken from the Gettysburg edition of *Lincoln's Complete Works,* published in 1905; others come from various printed sources.

———. *The Lincoln Treasury.* Comp. Caroline Thomas Harnsberger. Chicago: Wilcox and Follett Co., 1950.

A basic compilation of quotations, topically arranged. Scholarly source citations refer to the Lincoln Memorial University edition of the *Complete Works of Abraham Lincoln,* published in 1894, edited by Nicolay and Hay, and to other printed sources. Subject index.

———. *A Treasury of Lincoln Quotations.* Comp. Fred Kerner. Garden City, N.Y.: Doubleday and Co., 1965.

Contains about 1,500 quotations. Wording is based on Basler edition of Lincoln's *Collected Works,* now standard, but Kerner has made some alterations in spelling and punctuation.

Winn, Ralph Bubrich. *A Concise Lincoln Dictionary: Thoughts and Statements.* New York: Philosophical Library, 1959.

About 400 well-documented quotations, topically arranged.

ROOSEVELT

Roosevelt, Theodore. *The Real Roosevelt: His Forceful and Fearless Utterances on Various Subjects.* Ed. Alan Warner. New York: G. P. Putnam's Sons, 1910.

Relatively long quotations occurring under a dozen topics. Source references are less than complete. Good index.

————. *The Roosevelt Doctrine, Being the Personal Utterances of the President on Various Matters of Vital Interest.* Ed. E. E. Garrison. New York: Robert Grier Cooke, 1904.

A collection of quotations appearing under some 30 subjects. Well documented.

————. *Theodore Roosevelt Cyclopedia.* Ed. Albert Bushnell Hart and Herbert Ronald Ferleger. New York: Roosevelt Memorial Association, 1941.

The basic resource for tracing Theodore Roosevelt quotations. Contains thousands of quotations, topically arranged. Documentation is excellent.

Shakespeare

Stevenson, Burton, comp. *The Home Book of Shakespeare Quotations.* New York: Charles Scribner's Sons, 1937.

Some tracers find this collection, with its readily locatable entries and understandable source citations, easier to use than a Shakespeare concordance. Still, unlike a concordance, it does not contain all Shakespeare quotations. Based on the Globe edition of 1911.

Shaw

Shaw, Bernard. *Bernard Shaw: Selections of His Wit and Wisdom.* Comp. Caroline Thomas Harnsberger. Chicago: Follett Publishing Co., 1965.

Some 1,700 well-referenced quotations arranged alphabetically by topic. Index to subjects and concepts.

————. *Bernard Shaw's Ready-Reckoner: A Guide to Civilization.* Ed. N. H. Leigh-Taylor. New York: Random House, 1965.

Contains relatively long passages grouped under some 15 topics. Coded but detailed source references. Table of contents serves as index.

————. *The Quintessence of G.B.S.: The Wit and Wisdom of Bernard Shaw.* Comp. S. Winsten. London: Hutchinson and Co., 1949.

A large collection of quotes occurring under 30 or so topics. Source citations are titles of works. Lacks index, but there is a table of contents. Each quotation appears under a heading in the text.

————. *Selected Passages from the Works of Bernard Shaw.* Ed. Charlotte F. Shaw. London: Constable and Co., 1912.

Includes quotations from Shaw's early works, topically arranged. Table of contents serves as an index.

STEVENSON

Stevenson, Robert Louis. *Brave Words about Death from the Works of Robert Louis Stevenson.* London: Chatto and Windus, 1916.

A small collection of short and long passages. Source citations lack details. No index.

———. *The Pocket R.L.S., Being Favourite Passages from the Works of Stevenson.* London: Chatto and Windus, 1907.

Contains several hundred passages of varying length, indexed by opening words. Source references are titles of works.

———. *Stevenson Day by Day.* Ed. Florence L. Tucker. New York: T. Y. Crowell and Co., 1909.

A quotation for each day in the year. Source citations are titles. No index.

TWAIN

Twain, Mark. *Everyone's Mark Twain.* Ed. Caroline Thomas Harnsberger. South Brunswick: A. S. Barnes and Co., 1972.

Although it does not announce itself as such, this is a revision of Harnsberger's *Mark Twain at Your Fingertips.* Contains a goodly number of well-documented passages, arranged alphabetically by subject. Useful indexes and generous cross-references.

———. *Mark Twain at Your Fingertips.* Ed. Caroline Thomas Harnsberger. New York: Beechhurst Press, 1948.

Very similar to Harnsberger's *Everyone's Mark Twain.*

———. *The Wit and Wisdom of Mark Twain.* Ed. Alex Ayres. New York: Harper and Row, 1987.

Contains perhaps 1,000 quotations organized by subject. Source citations provide title and chapter references.

WILDE

Wilde, Oscar. *Epigrams and Aphorisms.* London: John W. Luce, 1905.

Quotations grouped under titles of works in which they occur.

———. *The Epigrams of Oscar Wilde: An Anthology.* Ed. Alvin Redman. London: Alvin Redman, 1952.

A collection of sparkling quotations appearing under about 50 topics. Citations consist of titles of works. No index.

———. *The Oscar Wilde Calendar: A Quotation from the Works of Oscar Wilde for Every Day in the Year, with Some Unrecorded Sayings.* Ed. Stuart Mason. London: Frank Palmer, 1910.

Quotations from Wilde's works and from his unrecorded conversations. No documentation, but useful in confirming attributions or verifying or correcting wording.

Dictionaries of the English Language

THE CENTURY DICTIONARY AND CYCLOPEDIA
The Century Dictionary and Cyclopedia. 10 vols. New York: Century Co., 1906.

Contains some 200,000 illustrative quotations, most of them from works published before 1890. Source citations are complete or almost so.

JOHNSON'S DICTIONARY OF THE ENGLISH LANGUAGE
Johnson, Samuel, ed. *A Dictionary of the English Language.* 2 vols. London: W. Strahan, 1755; reprint, 2 vols., New York: AMS Press, 1967; 2 vols. in 1, New York: Arno Press, 1979.

According to Drabble's *Oxford Companion to English Literature,* 5th ed., Johnson's *Dictionary* contains some 114,000 quotations from English writers. Most source citations are names of authors.

———. *A Dictionary of the English Language.* London: H. G. Bohn, 1852; reprint, London: Reeves and Turner, 1877.

A reissue in one volume of the 1773 edition. Contains some quotations not included in the 1755 edition.

THE OXFORD ENGLISH DICTIONARY
A New English Dictionary on Historical Principles. Ed. James A. H. Murray, Henry Bradley, William A. Craigie, and C. T. Onions. 10 vols. Oxford: Clarendon Press, 1888–1928.

Introduction, Supplement, and Bibliography to A New English Dictionary on Historical Principles. Oxford: Clarendon Press, 1933.

The Oxford English Dictionary, Being a Corrected Reissue with an Introduction, Supplement, and Bibliography of "A New English Dictionary on Historical Principles." Ed. James A. H. Murray, Henry Bradley, William A. Craigie, and C. T. Onions. 13 vols. Oxford: Clarendon Press, 1933.

According to Sheehy's *Guide to Reference Books,* the *OED* contains 1,827,306 quotations. Source citations are abbreviated but detailed.

The Compact Edition of the Oxford English Dictionary, Complete Text Reproduced Micrographically. 13 vols. in 2. New York: Oxford University Press, 1971.

A complete though compact version of the original set.

A Supplement to the Oxford English Dictionary. Ed. R. W. Burchfield. 4 vols. Oxford: Clarendon Press, 1972–86.

Contains some 500,000 quotations with abbreviated but detailed source citations.

The Oxford English Dictionary: The Original Oxford English Dictionary on Compact Disk. New York: Oxford University Press/Tri Star Publishing, 1987.

A CD-ROM version of the original set.

The Oxford English Dictionary. 2d ed., prepared by J. A. Simpson and E. S. C. Weiner. 20 vols. Oxford: Clarendon Press, 1989.

Combines the original dictionary, the four-volume supplement, and thousands of new words and meanings in one alphabetical sequence. More than 2,400,000 quotations. Abbreviated but detailed source citations.

Other English Language Dictionaries

Craigie, Sir William A., and James R. Hulbert, eds. *A Dictionary of American English on Historical Principles.* 4 vols. Chicago: University of Chicago Press, 1938–44.

Contains thousands of quotations illustrating the uses of words that are of American origin or of great American currency or that are connected with the history and development of the United States.

Farmer, John S., and W. E. Henley, eds. *Slang and Its Analogues, Past and Present.* 7 vols. London: Printed for subscribers only, 1890–1904; reprint, 7 vols. in 3, New York: Kraus, 1965.

A collection of quotations illustrating slang words and expressions, many of them bawdy. Probably the most useful repository of slang quotations; certainly the most entertaining.

Mathews, Mitford M., ed. *A Dictionary of Americanisms on Historical Principles.* Chicago: University of Chicago Press, 1951.

Contains a large number of quotations illustrating the uses of words that originated in the United States.

The Scottish National Dictionary. Ed. William Grant and David D. Murison. 10 vols. Edinburgh: Scottish National Dictionary Association, 1931–76.

Contains many Scottish quotations and quotations containing Scottish expressions.

Wright, Joseph, ed. *The English Dialect Dictionary.* 6 vols. London: Henry Frowde, 1898–1905.

Incorporates many literary quotations containing dialectical words and expressions.

Concordances and Word Indexes to Works in English and American Literature

In making this list, some degree of overkill has been deemed advisable: to increase your chances of locating one concordance to a writer, I have sometimes listed two or more.

ANGLO-SAXON LITERATURE

Bessinger, Jess B., Jr., comp. *A Concordance to the Anglo-Saxon Poetic Records.* Ithaca: Cornell University Press, 1978.

Healey, Antonette diPaolo, and Richard L. Venezky, eds. *A Microfiche Concordance to Old English: The List of Texts and Index of Editions.* Toronto: Dictionary of Old English Project, Centre for Medieval Studies, University of Toronto, 1980.

Venezky, Richard L., and Antonette diPaolo Healey, comps. *A Microfiche Concordance to Old English.* Newark: University of Delaware, 1980.

ARNOLD

Parrish, Stephen Maxfield, comp. *A Concordance to the Poems of Matthew Arnold.* Ithaca: Cornell University Press, 1959.

AUDEN

Dowling, Dean Edward, comp. "A Concordance to the Poetry of W. H. Auden." Ph.D. diss., Columbia University, 1972; Ann Arbor, Mich.: University Microfilms International, 1981.

AUSTEN

De Rose, Peter L., and S. W. McGuire, comps. *A Concordance to the Works of Jane Austen.* 3 vols. New York: Garland Publishing, 1982.

BACON

Davies, David W., and Elizabeth S. Wrigley, comps. *A Concordance to the Essays of Francis Bacon.* Detroit: Gale Research Co., 1973.

BEDE

Jones, Putnam Fennell, comp. *A Concordance to the "Historia Ecclesiastica" of Bede.* Cambridge, Mass.: Mediaeval Academy of America, for the Concordance Society, 1929.

BEOWULF

Bessinger, Jess B., Jr., comp. *A Concordance to "Beowulf."* Ithaca: Cornell University Press, 1969.

——. *A Concordance to the Anglo-Saxon Poetic Records.* Ithaca: Cornell University Press, 1978.

Cook, Albert S., comp. *A Concordance to "Beowulf."* Halle: Max Niemeyer, 1911; reprint, New York: Haskell House, 1968.

BIBLE (KING JAMES VERSION)

Practically all biblical quotations in English are from the King James or Authorized version. Some of these are from the apocryphal books formerly included in the Authorized version. For references to concordances to other major translations, see Sheehy's *Guide to Reference Books.*

Cruden, Alexander, ed. *A Complete Concordance to the Old and New Testament . . . with . . . a Concordance to the "Apocrypha."* . . . London and New York: Frederick Warne and Co., n.d.

First published in 1737, Cruden's concordance has appeared in numerous editions, not all of which contain a concordance to the Apocrypha, the source of many biblical quotations.

Joy, Charles R., comp. *Harper's Topical Concordance.* New York: Harper and Brothers, 1940.

Some 25,000 verses from the King James version, occurring under more than 2,000 alphabetically arranged topics.

Strong, James, ed. *The Exhaustive Concordance of the Bible.* London: Hodder and Stoughton, 1894; reprint, New York: Abingdon-Cokesbury Press, 1955.

An excellent concordance to the King James version. Much more complete than Cruden in its treatment of the material indexed and much easier to use. The Apocrypha is not included.

Bishop

Greenhalgh, Anne Merrill, comp. *A Concordance to Elizabeth Bishop's Poetry.* New York: Garland Publishing, 1985.

Blake

Erdman, David V., comp. *A Concordance to the Writings of William Blake.* 2 vols. Ithaca: Cornell University Press, 1967.

This concordance indexes prose works as well as verse.

The Book of Common Prayer

Green, John, ed. *A Concordance to the Liturgy, or Book of Common Prayer, &c.* London: Hope and Co., 1851.

Huggett, Milton, ed. *A Concordance to the American Book of Common Prayer.* New York: Church Hymnal Corp., 1970.

The Book of Mormon

Reynolds, George, comp. *A Complete Concordance of the Book of Mormon.* Ed. Philip C. Reynolds. Salt Lake City: Deseret Book Co., 1976.

Charlotte Brontë

Sabol, C. Ruth, and Todd K. Bender, comps. *A Concordance to Brontë's "Jane Eyre."* New York: Garland Publishing, 1981.

Emily Brontë

Sabol, C. Ruth, and Todd K. Bender, comps. *A Concordance to Brontë's "Wuthering Heights."* New York: Garland Publishing, 1984.

Elizabeth Barrett Browning

Hudson, Gladys W., comp. *An Elizabeth Barrett Browning Concordance.* 4 vols. Detroit: Gale Research Co., 1973.
Thorough, with 13 alphabetical sequences.

Robert Browning

Broughton, Leslie Nathan, and Benjamin F. Stelter, comps. *A Concordance to the Poems of Robert Browning.* 2 vols. New York: G. E. Stechert and Co., 1924–25; reprint, 4 vols., New York: Haskell House, 1970.

Burns

Reid, J. B., comp. *A Complete Word and Phrase Concordance to the Poems and Songs of Robert Burns.* Glasgow: Kerr and Richardson, 1889; reprint, New York: Russell and Russell, 1967.

Byron

Hagelman, Charles W., Jr., and Robert J. Barnes, comps. *A Concordance to Byron's "Don Juan."* Ithaca: Cornell University Press, 1967.
Young, Ione Dodson, comp. *A Concordance to the Poetry of Byron.* 4 vols. Austin, Tex.: Pemberton Press, 1965.
The last of the slip-generated concordances.

Carroll

Preston, Michael J., comp. *A Concordance to the Verse of Lewis Carroll.* New York: Garland Publishing, 1985.
———. *A KWIC Concordance to Lewis Carroll's "Alice's Adventures in Wonderland" and "Through the Looking-glass."* New York: Garland Publishing, 1986.

Chaucer

Tatlock, John S. P., and Arthur G. Kennedy, comps. *A Concordance to the Complete Works of Geoffrey Chaucer and to "The Romaunt of the Rose."* Washington, D.C.: Carnegie Institution of Washington, 1927.

The Chester Mystery Plays

Pfleiderer, Jean D., and Michael J. Preston, comps. *A Complete Concordance to "The Chester Mystery Plays."* New York: Garland Publishing, 1981.

CLELAND

Coleman, Samuel S., and Michael J. Preston, comps. *A KWIC Concordance to John Cleland's "Memoirs of a Woman of Pleasure."* New York: Garland Publishing, 1988.

COLERIDGE

Logan, Sister Eugenia, comp. *A Concordance to the Poetry of Samuel Taylor Coleridge.* Saint Mary-of-the-Woods, Ind.: privately printed, 1940.

McEahern, Patricia A., and Thomas F. Beckwith, comps. *A Complete Concordance to the "Lyrical Ballads" of Samuel Taylor Coleridge and William Wordsworth, 1798 and 1800 Editions.* New York: Garland Publishing, 1987.

COLLINS

Booth, Bradford Allen, and Claude E. Jones, comps. *A Concordance of the Poetical Works of William Collins.* Berkeley: University of California Press, 1939.

CONGREVE

Mann, David, comp. *A Concordance to the Plays of William Congreve.* Ithaca: Cornell University Press, 1973.

CONRAD

Bender, Todd K., comp. *A Concordance to Conrad's "Heart of Darkness."* New York: Garland Publishing, 1979.

———. *A Concordance to Conrad's "An Outcast of the Islands."* New York: Garland Publishing, 1984.

———. *A Concordance to Conrad's "The Rescue."* New York: Garland Publishing, 1985.

———. *A Concordance to Conrad's "The Secret Agent."* New York: Garland Publishing, 1979.

———. *A Concordance to Conrad's "A Set of Six."* New York: Garland Publishing, 1981.

———. *Concordances to Conrad's "The Mirror of the Sea" and "The Inheritors."* New York: Garland Publishing, 1983.

———. *Concordances to Conrad's "The Shadow Line" and "Youth: A Narrative."* New York: Garland Publishing, 1980.

———. *Concordances to Conrad's "Tales of Unrest" and "Tales of Hearsay."* New York: Garland Publishing, 1982.

Bender, Todd K., and Kirsten A. Bender, comps. *Concordances to Conrad's "Typhoon and Other Stories" and "Within the Tides."* New York: Garland Publishing, 1982.

Bender, Todd K., and James W. Parins, comps. *A Concordance to Conrad's "Romance."* New York: Garland Publishing, 1985.

Briggum, Sue M., and Todd K. Bender, comps. *A Concordance to Conrad's "Almayer's Folly."* New York: Garland Publishing, 1978.

Gaston, Paul L., and Todd K. Bender, comps. *A Concordance to Conrad's "The Arrow of Gold."* New York: Garland Publishing, 1981.

Higdon, David Leon, and Todd K. Bender, comps. *A Concordance to Conrad's "The Rover."* New York: Garland Publishing, 1985.

——. *A Concordance to Conrad's "Under Western Eyes."* New York: Garland Publishing, 1983.

Parins, James W., and Todd K. Bender, comps. *A Concordance to Conrad's "The Nigger of the Narcissus."* New York: Garland Publishing, 1981.

Parins, James W., Robert J. Dilligan, and Todd K. Bender, comps. *A Concordance to Conrad's "Lord Jim."* New York: Garland Publishing, 1976.

——. *A Concordance to Conrad's "Nostromo."* New York: Garland Publishing, 1984.

——. *A Concordance to Conrad's "Victory."* New York: Garland Publishing, 1979.

COWPER

Neve, John, comp. *A Concordance to the Poetical Works of William Cowper.* London: Sampson Low, Marston, Searle, and Rivington, 1887; reprint, New York: Greenwood Press, 1969.

Does not index Cowper's minor poems or his translations.

HART CRANE

Landry, Hilton, and Elaine Landry, comps. *A Concordance to the Poems of Hart Crane.* Metuchen, N.J.: Scarecrow Press, 1973.

Lane, Gary, comp. *A Concordance to the Poems of Hart Crane.* New York: Haskell House, 1972.

STEPHEN CRANE

Baron, Herman, comp. *A Concordance to the Poems of Stephen Crane.* Ed. Joseph Katz. Boston: G. K. Hall, 1974.

Crosland, Andrew T., comp. *A Concordance to the Complete Poetry of Stephen Crane.* Detroit: Gale Research Co., 1975.

CRASHAW

Cooper, Robert M., comp. *A Concordance to the English Poetry of Richard Crashaw.* Troy, N.Y.: Whitston Publishing Co., 1981.

CUMMINGS

McBride, Katharine Winters, comp. *A Concordance to the Complete Poems of E. E. Cummings.* Ithaca: Cornell University Press, 1989.

DARWIN

Barrett, Paul H., Donald J. Weinshank, and Timothy T. Gottleber, comps. *A Concordance to Darwin's "Origin of Species," First Edition.* Ithaca: Cornell University Press, 1981.

Barrett, Paul H., Donald J. Weinshank, Paul Ruhlen, and Stephan J. Ozminski, comps. *A Concordance to Darwin's "The Descent of Man, and Selection in Relation to Sex."* Ithaca: Cornell University Press, 1987.

Barrett, Paul H., Donald J. Weinshank, Paul Ruhlen, Stephan J. Ozminski, and Barbara N. Berghage, comps. *A Concordance to Darwin's "The Expression of the Emotions in Man and Animals."* Ithaca: Cornell University Press, 1986.

DEFOE

Owens, W. R., and P. N. Furbank, comps. *A KWIC Concordance to Daniel Defoe's "Moll Flanders."* New York: Garland Publishing, 1985.

Spackman, I. J., W. R. Owens, and P. N. Furbank, comps. *A KWIC Concordance to Daniel Defoe's "Robinson Crusoe."* New York: Garland Publishing, 1987.

DEKKER

Small, V. A., R. P. Corballis, and J. M. Harding, comps. *A Concordance to the Dramatic Works of Thomas Dekker.* 5 vols. Salzburg: Institut für Anglistik und Amerikanistik, Universität Salzburg, 1984.

DICKINSON

Rosenbaum, Stanford Patrick, comp. *A Concordance to the Poems of Emily Dickinson.* Ithaca: Cornell University Press, 1964.

DONNE

Combs, Homer Carroll, and Zay Rusk Sullens, comps. *A Concordance to the English Poems of John Donne.* Chicago: Packard and Co., 1940.

DRYDEN

Montgomery, Guy, and Lester A. Hubbard, comps. *Concordance to the Poetical Works of John Dryden.* Berkeley: University of California Press, 1957.

The name of the second compiler comes from a corrected title page. Does not supply the contexts of the words indexed. Dramatic works and prose works are not treated.

EDDY

Conant, Albert Francis, comp. *Complete Concordance to Miscellaneous Writings . . . [of] Mary Baker Eddy.* Boston: By the trustees under the will of Mary Baker G. Eddy, 1934.

———. *A Complete Concordance to Science and Health with Key to the Scriptures.* Boston: By the trustees under the will of Mary Baker G. Eddy, 1933.

EMERSON

Hubbell, George Shelton, comp. *A Concordance to the Poems of Ralph Waldo Emerson.* New York: H. W. Wilson, 1932.

Ihrig, Mary Alice, ed. *Emerson's Transcendental Vocabulary: A Concordance.* New York: Garland Publishing, 1982.

A concordance to occurrences of certain word clusters in the published prose: "beauty," "culture," "fate," "genius," "greatness-heroism," "nature," "prudence," "soul-spirit," and "wealth-riches."

Irey, Eugene F., comp. *A Concordance to Five Essays of Ralph Waldo Emerson: "Nature," "The American Scholar," "The Divinity School Address," "Self-Reliance," "Fate."* New York: Garland Publishing, 1981.

THE EPISCOPAL HYMNAL

Klepper, Robert F., comp. *A Concordance of "The Hymnal 1982" according to the Use of the Episcopal Church.* Metuchen, N.J.: Scarecrow Press, 1989.

ETHEREGE

Mann, David D., comp. *A Concordance to the Plays and Poems of Sir George Etherege.* Westport, Conn.: Greenwood Press, 1985.

FAULKNER

Capps, Jack L., comp. *"As I Lay Dying": A Concordance to the Novel.* West Point, N.Y.: Faulkner Concordance Advisory Board; Ann Arbor, Mich.: University Microfilms International, 1977.

———. *"Go Down, Moses": A Concordance to the Novel.* 2 vols. West Point, N.Y.: Faulkner Concordance Advisory Board; Ann Arbor, Mich.: University Microfilms International, 1977.

———. *"Light in August": A Concordance to the Novel.* 2 vols. West Point, N.Y.: Faulkner Concordance Advisory Board; Ann Arbor, Mich.: University Microfilms International, 1979.

Polk, Noel, comp. *"Intruder in the Dust"*: *A Concordance to the Novel.* West Point, N.Y.: Faulkner Concordance Advisory Board; Ann Arbor, Mich.: University Microfilms International, 1983.

———. *"Requiem for a Nun"*: *A Concordance to the Novel.* West Point, N.Y.: Faulkner Concordance Advisory Board; Ann Arbor, Mich.: University Microfilms International, 1979.

Polk, Noel, and John D. Hart, comps. *"Absalom, Absalom!"*: *A Concordance to the Novel.* 2 vols. West Point, N.Y.: Faulkner Concordance Advisory Board; Ann Arbor, Mich.: University Microfilms International, 1989.

———. *"The Mansion"*: *A Concordance to the Novel.* 2 vols. West Point, N.Y.: Faulkner Concordance Advisory Board; Ann Arbor, Mich.: University Microfilms International, 1988.

———. *"Pylon"*: *A Concordance to the Novel.* West Point, N.Y.: Faulkner Concordance Advisory Board; Ann Arbor, Mich.: University Microfilms International, 1989.

Polk, Noel, and Lawrence Z. Pizzi, comps. *"The Town"*: *A Concordance to the Novel.* 2 vols. West Point, N.Y.: Faulkner Concordance Advisory Board; Ann Arbor, Mich.: University Microfilms International, 1985.

Polk, Noel, and Kenneth L. Privratsky, comps. *"A Fable"*: *A Concordance to the Novel.* 2 vols. West Point, N.Y.: Faulkner Concordance Advisory Board; Ann Arbor, Mich.: University Microfilms International, 1981.

———. *"The Sound and the Fury"*: *A Concordance to the Novel.* 2 vols. West Point, N.Y.: Faulkner Concordance Advisory Board; Ann Arbor, Mich.: University Microfilms International, 1980.

Privratsky, Kenneth L., comp. *"The Wild Palms"*: *A Concordance to the Novel.* West Point, N.Y.: Faulkner Concordance Advisory Board; Ann Arbor, Mich.: University Microfilms International, 1983.

FIELDING

Farringdon, Michael G., comp. *A Concordance and Word-Lists to Henry Fielding's "Joseph Andrews."* Swansea, Wales: Ariel House Publications, 1984. Text-fiche.

———. *A Concordance and Word-Lists to Henry Fielding's "Shamela."* Swansea, Wales: Ariel House Publications, 1982. Text-fiche.

EDWARD FITZGERALD

Tutin, John Ramsden, comp. *A Concordance to FitzGerald's Translation of the "Rubáiyát" of Omar Khayyám.* London: Macmillan and Co.; New York: Macmillan Co., 1900; New York: Johnson Reprint, 1967; reprint, New York: B. Franklin, 1968.

F. SCOTT FITZGERALD

Crosland, Andrew T., comp. *A Concordance to F. Scott Fitzgerald's "The Great Gatsby."* Detroit: Gale Research Co., 1975.

FORD MADOX FORD

Sabol, C. Ruth, and Todd K. Bender, comps. *A Concordance to Ford Madox Ford's "The Good Soldier."* New York: Garland Publishing, 1981.

FRANKLIN

Barbour, Frances M., comp. *A Concordance to the Sayings in Franklin's "Poor Richard."* Detroit: Gale Research Co., 1974.

FROST

Lathem, Edward Connery, comp. *A Concordance to the Poetry of Robert Frost.* New York: Holt Information Systems, 1971.

GILBERT

Dixon, Geoffrey, comp. *The Gilbert and Sullivan Concordance: A Word Index to W. S. Gilbert's Libretti for the Fourteen Savoy Operas.* 2 vols. New York: Garland Publishing, 1987.

GOLDSMITH

Paden, William Doremus, and Clyde Kenneth Hyder, comps. *A Concordance to the Poems of Oliver Goldsmith.* Lawrence, Kans., 1940.

GOWER

Pickles, J. D., and J. L. Dawson, comps. *A Concordance to John Gower's "Confessio Amantis."* Cambridge: D. S. Brewer, 1987.

GRAY

Cook, Albert S., comp. *A Concordance to the English Poems of Thomas Gray.* Boston: Houghton Mifflin Co., 1908.

HARDY

Preston, Cathy Lynn, comp. *A KWIC Concordance to Thomas Hardy's "Tess of the D'Urbervilles."* New York: Garland Publishing, 1989.

HAWTHORNE

Byers, John R., Jr., and James J. Owen, comps. *A Concordance to the Five Novels of Nathaniel Hawthorne.* 2 vols. New York: Garland Publishing, 1979.

HERBERT

Di Cesare, Mario A., and Rigo Mignani, comps. *A Concordance to the Complete Writings of George Herbert.* Ithaca: Cornell University Press, 1977.

Mann, Cameron, comp. *A Concordance to the English Poems of George Herbert.* Boston: Houghton Mifflin Co., 1927.

HERRICK

MacLeod, Malcolm Lorimer, comp. *A Concordance to the Poems of Robert Herrick.* New York: Oxford University Press, 1936.

HEYWOOD

Canzler, David George, comp. "A Concordance to the Dramatic Works of John Heywood." Ph.D. diss., University of Oregon, 1961; Ann Arbor, Mich.: University Microfilms International, 1981.

HOPKINS

Borrello, Alfred, comp. *A Concordance of the Poetry in English of Gerard Manley Hopkins.* Metuchen, N.J.: Scarecrow Press, 1969.

An error appears on the title page of early copies: *Manly.*

Dilligan, Robert J., and Todd K. Bender, comps. *A Concordance to the English Poetry of Gerard Manley Hopkins.* Madison: University of Wisconsin Press, 1970.

HOUSMAN

Hyder, Clyde Kenneth, comp. *A Concordance to the Poems of A. E. Housman.* Lawrence, Kans., 1940.

Takeuchi, Yutaka, comp. *The Exhaustive Concordance to the Poems of A. E. Housman.* Tokyo: Shohakusha Publishing Co., 1971.

HUGHES

Mandelik, Peter, and Stanley Schatt, comps. *A Concordance to the Poetry of Langston Hughes.* Detroit: Gale Research Co., 1975.

JAMES

Bender, Claire E., and Todd K. Bender, comps. *A Concordance to Henry James's "The Turn of the Screw."* New York: Garland Publishing, 1988.

Bender, Todd K., comp. *A Concordance to Henry James's "Daisy Miller."* New York: Garland Publishing, 1987.

———. *A Concordance to Henry James's "The Awkward Age."* New York: Garland Publishing, 1989.

Bender, Todd K., and D. Leon Higdon, comps. *A Concordance to Henry James's "The Spoils of Poynton."* New York: Garland Publishing, 1988.

Higdon, David Leon, and Todd K. Bender, comps. *A Concordance to Henry James's "The American."* New York: Garland Publishing, 1985.

Hulpke, Erika, and Todd K. Bender, comps. *A Concordance to Henry James's "What Maisie Knew."* New York: Garland Publishing, 1989.

JOHNSON

Naugle, Helen Harrold, comp. *A Concordance to the Poems of Samuel Johnson.* Ithaca: Cornell University Press, 1973.

JONSON

Bates, Steven L., and Sidney D. Orr, comps. *A Concordance to the Poems of Ben Jonson.* Athens: Ohio University Press, 1978.

Di Cesare, Mario A., and Ephim Fogel, comps. *A Concordance to the Poems of Ben Jonson.* Ithaca: Cornell University Press, 1978.

JOYCE

Anderson, Chester G., comp. *Word Index to James Joyce's "Stephen Hero."* Ridgefield, Conn.: Ridgebury Press, 1958; reprint, Norwood, Pa.: Norwood Editions, 1977.

Bauerle, Ruth, comp. *A Word List to James Joyce's "Exiles."* New York: Garland Publishing, 1981.

Doyle, Paul A., comp. *A Concordance to the Collected Poems of James Joyce.* New York: Scarecrow Press, 1966.

Füger, Wilhelm, comp. *Concordance to James Joyce's "Dubliners."* Hildesheim and New York: Georg Olms, 1980.

Hancock, Leslie, comp. *Word Index to James Joyce's "Portrait of the Artist."* Carbondale: Southern Illinois University Press, 1967.

Hanley, Miles Lawrence, comp. *Word Index to James Joyce's "Ulysses."* Madison: University of Wisconsin Press, 1951.

Hart, Clive, comp. *A Concordance to "Finnegans Wake."* Minneapolis: University of Minnesota Press, 1963.

Lane, Gary, comp. *A Word Index to James Joyce's "Dubliners."* New York: Haskell House, 1972.

Steppe, Wolfhard, comp., with Hans Walter Gabler. *A Handlist to James Joyce's "Ulysses": A Complete Alphabetical Index to the Critical Reading Text.* New York: Garland Publishing, 1985.

KEATS

Baldwin, Dane Lewis, Leslie Nathan Broughton, Laura Cooper Evans, John William Hebel, Benjamin F. Stelter, and Mary Rebecca Thayer, comps. *A Concordance to the Poems of John Keats.* Washington, D.C.: Carnegie Institution of Washington, 1917.

Becker, Michael G., Robert J. Dilligan, and Todd K. Bender, comps. *A Concordance to the Poems of John Keats.* New York: Garland Publishing, 1981.

KEBLE

A Concordance to "The Christian Year." New York: Pott and Amery, 1871.

KYD

Crawford, Charles, comp. *A Concordance to the Works of Thomas Kyd.* Louvain: A. Uystpruyst, 1906–10; Vaduz: Kraus Reprint, 1963.

LANIER

Graham, Philip, and Joseph Jones, comps. *A Concordance to the Poems of Sidney Lanier.* Austin: University of Texas Press, 1939.

LAWRENCE

Garcia, Reloy, and James Karabatsos, comps. *A Concordance to the Poetry of D. H. Lawrence.* Lincoln: University of Nebraska Press, 1970.

———. *A Concordance to the Short Fiction of D. H. Lawrence.* Lincoln: University of Nebraska Press, 1972.

LEAR

Lyons, Anne Kearns, Thomas R. Lyons, and Michael J. Preston, comps. *A Concordance to the Complete Nonsense of Edward Lear.* Norwood, Pa.: Norwood Editions and University of Colorado at Boulder, 1980.

LEWIS

McLaughlin, Sara Park, and Mark O. Webb, comps. *A Word Index to the Poetry of C. S. Lewis.* West Cornwall, Conn.: Locust Hill Press, 1988.

LYLY

Mittermann, Harald, and Herbert Schendl, comps. *A Complete Concordance to the Novels of John Lyly.* Hildesheim and New York: Georg Olms, 1986.

MALORY

Kato, Tomomi, comp. *A Concordance to the Works of Sir Thomas Malory.* Tokyo: University of Tokyo Press, 1974.

MARLOWE

Crawford, Charles, comp. *The Marlowe Concordance.* 7 pts. in 3 vols. Louvain: A. Uystpruyst, 1911–32.

Fehrenbach, Robert J., Lea Ann Boone, and Mario A. Di Cesare, comps. *A Concordance to the Plays, Poems, and Translations of Christopher Marlowe.* Ithaca: Cornell University Press, 1982.

Ule, Louis, comp. *A Concordance to the Works of Christopher Marlowe.* Hildesheim and New York: Georg Olms, 1979.

MARVELL

Guffey, George Robert, comp. *A Concordance to the English Poems of Andrew Marvell.* Chapel Hill: University of North Carolina Press, 1974.

MELVILLE

Cohen, Hennig, and James Cahalan, comps. *A Concordance to Melville's "Moby-Dick."* 3 vols. Glassboro, N.J.: Melville Society; Ann Arbor, Mich.: University Microfilms International, 1979.

Irey, Eugene F., comp. *A Concordance to Herman Melville's "Moby-Dick."* 2 vols. New York: Garland Publishing, 1982.

Wegener, Larry Edward, comp. *A Concordance to Herman Melville's "Clarel: A Poem and Pilgrimage in the Holy Land."* 3 vols. Glassboro, N.J.: Melville Society; Ann Arbor: University Microfilms International, 1979.

———. *A Concordance to Herman Melville's "The Confidence-Man: His Masquerade."* New York: Garland Publishing, 1987.

———. *A Concordance to Herman Melville's "Pierre; or, The Ambiguities."* 2 vols. New York: Garland Publishing, 1985.

MEREDITH

Hogan, Rebecca S., Lewis Sawin, and Lynn L. Merrill, comps. *A Concordance to the Poetry of George Meredith.* 2 vols. New York: Garland Publishing, 1982.

THE METHODIST HYMNAL

Klepper, Robert F., comp. *Methodist Hymnal Concordance.* Metuchen, N.J.: Scarecrow Press, 1987.

MIDDLE ENGLISH POEMS AND METRICAL ROMANCES

Kottler, Barnet, and Alan M. Markman, comps. *A Concordance to Five Middle English Poems: "Cleanness," "St. Erkenwald," "Sir Gawain and the Green Knight," "Patience," "Pearl."* Pittsburgh: University of Pittsburgh Press, 1966.

Preston, Michael J., comp. *A Concordance to the Middle English Shorter Poem*. 2 vols. Leeds: W. S. Maney and Son, 1975.

Saito, Toshio, and Mitsunori Imai, comps. *A Concordance to Middle English Metrical Romances*. 2 vols. Frankfurt am Main: Verlag Peter Lang, 1988.

MILTON

Bradshaw, John, comp. *A Concordance to the Poetical Works of John Milton*. London: Swan Sonnenschein and Co.; New York: Macmillan and Co., 1894.

Cooper, Lane, comp. *A Concordance of the Latin, Greek, and Italian Poems of John Milton*. Halle: Max Niemeyer, 1923.

Hudson, Gladys W., comp. *"Paradise Lost": A Concordance*. Detroit: Gale Research Co., 1970.

Ingram, William, and Kathleen Swaim, comps. *A Concordance to Milton's English Poetry*. Oxford: Clarendon Press, 1972.

Misek, Linda D., comp. *Context Concordance to John Milton's "Paradise Lost."* Cleveland: Andrew R. Jennings Computing Center, Case Western Reserve University, 1971.

Sterne, Laurence, and Harold H. Kollmeier, comps. *A Concordance to the English Prose of John Milton*. Binghamton, N.Y.: Medieval and Renaissance Texts and Studies, 1985.

MOORE

Lane, Gary, comp. *A Concordance to the Poems of Marianne Moore*. New York: Haskell House, 1972.

MORE

Bolchazy, Ladislaus J., comp. *A Concordance to the "Utopia" of St. Thomas More and a Frequency Word List*. Hildesheim and New York: Georg Olms, 1978.

O'NEILL

Reaver, J. Russell, comp. *An O'Neill Concordance*. 3 vols. Detroit: Gale Research Co., 1969.

The text used does not include certain early plays.

OWEN

Heneghan, Donald A., comp. *A Concordance to the Poems and Fragments of Wilfred Owen*. Boston: G. K. Hall, 1979.

THE PILGRIM HYMNAL

Klepper, Robert F., comp. *A Concordance of the "Pilgrim Hymnal."* Metuchen, N.J.: Scarecrow Press, 1989.

PLATH

Matovich, Richard M., comp. *A Concordance to the Collected Poems of Sylvia Plath*. New York: Garland Publishing, 1986.

POE

Booth, Bradford Allen, and Claude E. Jones, comps. *A Concordance of the Poetical Works of Edgar Allan Poe*. Baltimore: Johns Hopkins Press, 1941.

Dameron, J. Lasley, and Louis Charles Stagg, comps. *An Index to Poe's Critical Vocabulary*. Hartford, Conn.: Transcendental Books, 1966.
 An index to words of critical significance from Poe's letters, reviews, and essays.

Pollin, Burton R., ed. *Word Index to Poe's Fiction*. New York: Gordian Press, 1982.

Wiley, Elizabeth, comp. *Concordance to the Poetry of Edgar Allan Poe*. Selinsgrove, Pa.: Susquehanna University Press, 1989.

POPE

Abbott, Edwin, comp. *A Concordance to the Works of Alexander Pope*. New York: D. Appleton and Co., 1875; New York: Kraus Reprint, 1965.
 Minor poems and the translations are omitted.

Bedford, Emmett G., and Robert J. Dilligan, comps. *A Concordance to the Poems of Alexander Pope*. 2 vols. Detroit: Gale Research Co., 1974.
 An excellent concordance to Pope's complete poetical works, including the translations.

POUND

Dilligan, Robert J., James W. Parins, and Todd K. Bender, comps. *A Concordance to Ezra Pound's "Cantos."* New York: Garland Publishing, 1981.

Lane, Gary, comp. *A Concordance to "Personae": The Shorter Poems of Ezra Pound*. New York: Haskell House, 1972.

ROBINSON

Sundermeier, Michael W., comp. "A Concordance to the Poetry of Edwin Arlington Robinson." Ph.D. diss., University of Nebraska, 1972; Ann Arbor, Mich.: University Microfilms International, 1981.

EARL OF ROCHESTER

Moehlmann, John F., comp. *A Concordance to the Complete Poems of John Wilmot, Earl of Rochester*. Troy, N.Y.: Whitston Publishing Co., 1979.

ROETHKE

Lane, Gary, comp. *A Concordance to the Poems of Theodore Roethke.* Metuchen, N.J.: Scarecrow Press, 1972.

SHAKESPEARE

Bartlett, John, comp. *A New and Complete Concordance or Verbal Index to Words, Phrases, and Passages in the Dramatic Works of Shakespeare, with a Supplementary Concordance to the Poems.* London: Macmillan and Co., 1894. Also published as *A Complete Concordance or Verbal Index to Words, Phrases, and Passages in the Dramatic Works of Shakespeare, with a Supplementary Concordance to the Poems.* London: Macmillan; New York: St. Martin's Press, 1966.
   Based on the old Globe edition. Contains two alphabetical sequences.

Spevack, Marvin, comp. *A Complete and Systematic Concordance to the Works of Shakespeare.* 8 vols. Hildesheim: Georg Olms, 1968–75.
———. *The Harvard Concordance to Shakespeare.* Cambridge: Belknap Press of Harvard University Press, 1973.
   An excellent one-volume concordance to the text of *The Riverside Shakespeare.*

THE SHAKESPEARE APOCRYPHA

Ule, Louis, comp. *A Concordance to the Shakespeare Apocrypha.* 3 vols. Hildesheim, Zurich, and New York: Georg Olms Verlag, 1987.

SHAW

Bevan, E. Dean, comp. *A Concordance to the Plays and Prefaces of Bernard Shaw.* 10 vols. Detroit: Gale Research Co., 1971.

SHELLEY

Ellis, Frederick Startridge, comp. *A Lexical Concordance to the Poetical Works of Percy Bysshe Shelley.* London: B. Quaritch, 1892.

SIDNEY

Donow, Herbert S., comp. *A Concordance to the Poems of Sir Philip Sidney.* Ithaca: Cornell University Press, 1975.

SKELTON

Fox, Alistair, and Gregory Waite, comps. *A Concordance to the Complete English Poems of John Skelton.* Ithaca: Cornell University Press, 1987.

THE SONNET SEQUENCES

Donow, Herbert S., comp. *A Concordance to the Sonnet Sequences of Daniel, Drayton, Shakespeare, Sidney, and Spenser.* Carbondale: Southern Illinois University Press, 1969.

SPENSER

Osgood, Charles Grosvenor, comp. *A Concordance to the Poems of Edmund Spenser.* Washington, D.C.: Carnegie Institution of Washington, 1915.

STERNE

Graves, Patricia Hogan, comp. "A Computer-generated Concordance to Sterne's *Tristram Shandy.*" Ph.D. diss., Emory University, 1974; Ann Arbor, Mich.: University Microfilms International, 1981.

STEVENS

Walsh, Thomas F., comp. *Concordance to the Poetry of Wallace Stevens.* University Park: Pennsylvania State University Press, 1963.

SWIFT

Kelling, Harold D., and Cathy Lynn Preston, comps. *A KWIC Concordance to Jonathan Swift's "A Tale of a Tub," "The Battle of the Books," and "A Discourse concerning the Mechanical Operation of the Spirit, a Fragment."* New York: Garland Publishing, 1984.

Shinagel, Michael, comp. *A Concordance to the Poems of Jonathan Swift.* Ithaca: Cornell University Press, 1972.

TAYLOR

Russell, Gene, comp. *A Concordance to the Poems of Edward Taylor.* Washington, D.C.: Microcard Editions, 1973.

TENNYSON

Baker, Arthur Ernest, comp. *A Concordance to the Poetical and Dramatic Works of Alfred, Lord Tennyson.* London: Kegan Paul, Trench, Trübner and Co., 1914; reprint, London: Routledge and Kegan Paul, 1965.

Contains several alphabetical sequences. Some significant words are not indexed.

THOMAS

Farringdon, Michael G., comp. *A Concordance and Word-Lists to Dylan Thomas's "Under Milk Wood."* Swansea, Wales: Ariel House Publications, 1982. Text-fiche.

Lane, Gary, comp. *A Concordance to the Poems of Dylan Thomas.* Metuchen, N.J.: Scarecrow Press, 1976.

Williams, Robert Coleman, comp. *A Concordance to the Collected Poems of Dylan Thomas.* Lincoln: University of Nebraska Press, 1967.

THOREAU

Karabatsos, James, comp. *A Word-Index to "A Week on the Concord and Merrimack Rivers."* Hartford, Conn.: Transcendental Books, 1971.

Ogden, Marlene A., and Clifton Keller, comps. *"Walden": A Concordance.* New York: Garland Publishing, 1985.
A word index to the Princeton edition.

Sherwin, J. Stephen, and Richard C. Reynolds, comps. *A Word Index to "Walden," with Textual Notes.* Charlottesville: University of Virginia Press, 1960.

——. *A Word Index to "Walden," with Textual Notes.* Corrected ed. Hartford, Conn.: Emerson Society, 1969.
A word index to the Modern Library edition.

THE TOWNELEY PLAYS

Preston, Michael J., and Jean D. Pfleiderer, comps. *A KWIC Concordance to the Plays of the Wakefield Master.* New York: Garland Publishing, 1982.

TRAHERNE

Guffey, George Robert, comp. *A Concordance to the Poetry of Thomas Traherne.* Berkeley: University of California Press, 1974.

VAUGHAN

Tuttle, Imilda, comp. *Concordance to Vaughan's "Silex Scintillans."* University Park: Pennsylvania State University Press, 1969.

WEBSTER

Corballis, Richard, and J. M. Harding, comps. *A Concordance to the Works of John Webster.* 3 vols. in 11. Salzburg: Institut für Englische Sprache und Literatur, Universität Salzburg, 1979–81.

WHITMAN

Eby, Edwin Harold, comp. *A Concordance of Walt Whitman's "Leaves of Grass" and Selected Prose Writings.* Seattle: University of Washington Press, 1949–54.
Contains two alphabetical sequences. The compiler is incorrectly identified on the title page as Harold Edwin Eby.

WOOLF

Haule, James M., and Philip H. Smith, Jr., comps. *A Concordance to "Between the Acts" by Virginia Woolf.* Oxford: Oxford Microform Publications, 1982.

——. *A Concordance to "Mrs. Dalloway" by Virginia Woolf.* London and New York: Oxford Microform Publications, 1984.

——. *A Concordance to "Night and Day" by Virginia Woolf.* Oxford and New York: Oxford Microform Publications, 1986.

——. *A Concordance to "Orlando" by Virginia Woolf.* London and New York: Oxford Microform Publications, 1985.

——. *A Concordance to "The Waves" by Virginia Woolf.* Oxford and New York: Oxford Microform Publications, 1981.

——. *A Concordance to "The Years" by Virginia Woolf.* London and New York: Oxford Microform Publications, 1984.

——. *A Concordance to "To the Lighthouse" by Virginia Woolf.* Oxford: Oxford Microform Publications, 1983.

WORDSWORTH

Cooper, Lane, comp. *A Concordance to the Poems of William Wordsworth.* New York: E. P. Dutton, 1911.

McEahern, Patricia A., and Thomas F. Beckwith, comps. *A Complete Concordance to the "Lyrical Ballads" of Samuel Taylor Coleridge and William Wordsworth, 1798 and 1800 Editions.* New York: Garland Publishing, 1987.

WYATT

Hangen, Eva Catherine, comp. *A Concordance to the Complete Poetical Works of Sir Thomas Wyatt.* Chicago: University of Chicago Press, 1941.

YEATS

Domville, Eric, comp. *A Concordance to the Plays of W. B. Yeats.* 2 vols. Ithaca: Cornell University Press, 1972.

Parrish, Stephen Maxfield, comp. *A Concordance to the Poems of W. B. Yeats.* Ithaca: Cornell University Press, 1963.

THE YORK PLAYS

Kinneavy, Gerald Byron, comp. *A Concordance to "The York Plays."* New York: Garland Publishing, 1986.

Some Useful Author Indexes

ADDISON AND STEELE

The Spectator. Ed. Donald F. Bond. Vol. 5. Oxford: Clarendon Press, 1965.

Contains a detailed index.

Wheeler, William, ed. *A Concordance to "The Spectator."* London: George Routledge and Sons, 1895.

An index, not a concordance, to Henry Morley's one-volume edition. The artful searcher may use this as an index to other editions.

CARLYLE

Ralli, Augustus. *Guide to Carlyle.* 2 vols. London: George Allen and Unwin, 1920.
Both an outline and an index.

CHESTERTON

Sprug, Joseph W., ed. *An Index to G. K. Chesterton.* Washington, D.C.: Catholic University of America Press, 1966.

DONNE

Reeves, Troy D., comp. *An Annotated Index to the Sermons of John Donne.* 3 vols. Salzburg: Institut für Anglistik und Amerikanistik, Universität Salzburg, 1979–81.

GOLDSMITH

Goldsmith, Oliver. *Collected Works of Oliver Goldsmith.* Ed. Arthur Friedman. Vol. 5. Oxford: Clarendon Press, 1966.
Contains an index to Goldsmith's works.

HAZLITT

Hazlitt, William. *The Complete Works of William Hazlitt.* Ed. P. P. Howe. Vol. 21. London: J. M. Dent and Sons, 1934.
Contains a general index to Hazlitt's works.

NASH

Axford, Lavonne B., ed. *An Index to the Poems of Ogden Nash.* Metuchen, N.J.: Scarecrow Press, 1972.

PEPYS

Pepys, Samuel. *The Diary of Samuel Pepys.* Ed. Robert Latham and William Matthews. Vol. 11, *Index.* Comp. Robert Latham. Berkeley: University of California Press, 1983.

RUSKIN

Ruskin, John. *The Works of John Ruskin.* Ed. E. T. Cook and Alexander Wedderburn. Vol. 39, *General Index.* London: George Allen, 1912.
An excellent index to Ruskin's works and words.

SWIFT

Swift, Jonathan. *The Prose Works of Jonathan Swift.* Ed. Herbert Davis. Vol. 14, *Index.* Comp. William J. Kunz, Steven Hollander, and Susan

Staves, under the supervision of Irvin Ehrenpreis. Oxford: Basil Blackwell, 1968.

An excellent index to Swift's prose writings.

Indexes to First Lines, Last Lines, Opening Words, and Keywords

Poetry Indexes

Brewton, John E., and Sara W. Brewton, comps. *Index to Children's Poetry*. New York: H. W. Wilson Co., 1942.[1]

An interfiled author, subject, title, and first-line index to more than 15,000 poems in 130 collections.

———. *Index to Children's Poetry, First Supplement*. New York: H. W. Wilson Co., 1954.

———. *Index to Children's Poetry, Second Supplement*. New York: H. W. Wilson Co., 1965.

Brewton, John E., Sara W. Brewton, and G. Meredith Blackburn III, comps. *Index to Poetry for Children and Young People, 1964–69*. New York: H. W. Wilson Co., 1972.

An interfiled author, subject, title, and first-line index to more than 11,000 poems in 117 collections.

Brewton, John E., G. Meredith Blackburn III, and Lorraine A. Blackburn, comps. *Index to Poetry for Children and Young People, 1970–75*. New York: H. W. Wilson Co., 1978.

———. *Index to Poetry for Children and Young People, 1976–81*. New York: H. W. Wilson Co., 1984.

British Library. [*Index of First Lines of English Poetry*.] 6 reels, n.d. Microfilm. See the *National Union Catalog, Pre-1956 Imprints*, 76:445.

A handwritten index of some 17,000 first lines of English poems in manuscript form in the British Library. Supplies names of authors if known. May on occasion serve as an index to published poetry.

Caskey, Jefferson D., comp. *Index to Poetry in Popular Periodicals, 1955–59*. Westport, Conn.: Greenwood Press, 1984.

Contains title, first-line, author, and subject indexes to over 7,000 poems. Indexes many poems not included in *Granger's*.

———. *Index to Poetry in Popular Periodicals, 1960–64*. Westport, Conn.: Greenwood Press, 1988.

Chapman, Dorothy H., comp. *Index to Black Poetry*. Boston: G. K. Hall, 1974.

Contains author, subject, and title and first-line indexes to poems by black authors and to poems on the black experience. Covers 94 works by individual poets and 33 anthologies.

Crum, Margaret, ed. *First-Line Index of English Poetry, 1500–1800, in Manuscripts of the Bodleian Library, Oxford.* 2 vols. Oxford: Clarendon Press, 1969.

Indexes thousands of manuscript poems, with references to authors if known. May on occasion also serve as an index to first lines of published poetry.

Early American Periodicals Index to 1850. 8 boxes. New York: Readex Microprint Corp., 1964.

This resource, originally prepared by WPA workers and subsequently readied for publication by Nelson F. Adkins, includes a largely handwritten index of some 80,000 first lines of poems. Source citations are references to American journals.

Foxon, David Fairweather, comp. *English Verse, 1701–50: A Catalogue of Separately Printed Poems with Notes on Contemporary Collected Editions.* 2 vols. London: Cambridge University Press, 1975.

Contains an index to first lines of thousands of poems published in the eighteenth century.

Granger, Edith, ed. *An Index to Poetry and Recitations.* Chicago: A. C. McClurg and Co., 1904.

Includes title, author, and first-line or opening-word indexes to over 30,000 poems and recitations in 369 collections and supplies references to these collections. Alphabetizing of first lines is old-fashioned: to find "The boy stood on the burning deck," look under *T* in the first-line index. In the title index, initial articles are disregarded. This edition and other old editions of *Granger's* contain some material not found in later ones.

——. *An Index to Poetry and Recitations.* Rev. ed. Chicago: A. C. McClurg and Co., 1918.

Contains indexes to titles, authors, and first lines of over 50,000 poems and recitations in 450 collections. Alphabetizing practice follows that of the earlier edition.

——. *A Supplement to Granger's Index (1919–28).* Chicago: A. C. McClurg and Co., 1929.

A major supplement, with indexing and alphabetizing practices following those of earlier editions.

——. *Granger's Index to Poetry and Recitations.* 3d ed., ed. Helen Humphrey Bessey. Chicago: A. C. McClurg and Co., 1940.

Covers 75,000 titles in 592 books, with indexing and alphabetizing practices following those of earlier editions.

——. *Granger's Index to Poetry.* 4th ed., ed. Raymond J. Dixon. Morningside Heights, N.Y.: Columbia University Press, 1953.

No longer an index to prose pieces. Title and first-line indexes of earlier editions have been combined and interfiled, and a subject index has been added. Initial articles are now ignored when alphabetizing index entries.

———. *Granger's Index to Poetry*. 5th ed., ed. William F. Bernhardt. Morningside Heights, N.Y.: Columbia University Press, 1962.

Follows the pattern of the fourth edition.

———. *Granger's Index to Poetry*. 6th ed., ed. William James Smith. New York: Columbia University Press, 1973.

Follows the pattern of the fourth and fifth editions.

———. *Granger's Index to Poetry, 1970–77*. Ed. William James Smith. New York: Columbia University Press, 1978.

A major supplement.

———. *Granger's Index to Poetry*. 7th ed., ed. William James Smith and William F. Bernhardt. New York: Columbia University Press, 1982.

Covers 1970–81 and drops much earlier material.

———. *Granger's Index to Poetry*. 8th ed., ed. William F. Bernhardt. New York: Columbia University Press, 1986.

Retains a good deal from the sixth and seventh editions and adds new coverage.

———. *The Columbia Granger's Index to Poetry*. 9th ed., ed. Edith P. Hazen and Deborah J. Fryer. New York: Columbia University Press, 1990.

Hoffman, Herbert H., comp. *Hoffman's Index to Poetry: European and Latin American Poetry in Anthologies*. Metuchen, N.J.: Scarecrow Press, 1985.

Author, title, and first-line indexes to 14,000 anthologized poems in foreign languages.

Hoffman, Herbert H., and Rita Ludwig Hoffman, comps. *International Index to Recorded Poetry*. New York: H. W. Wilson Co., 1983.

Author, title, and first-line indexes to some 15,000 poems in many languages.

Index of English Literary Manuscripts. London: Mansell; New York: R. R. Bowker Co., 1980– .

The fifth volume of this work, still in progress, will include indexes to titles and first lines.

Johnson, Samuel, ed. *The Works of the English Poets, with Prefaces, Biographical and Critical, by Samuel Johnson*. Vols. 57–58. London: H. Hughs for C. Bathurst [etc.], 1779–80.

A two-volume keyword and subject index to memorable poems, lines, and phrases in the collection. The word indexed is usually a noun or an adjective used as a noun. Reference is to author, volume, and page but not to the name of the poem.

———. *The Works of the English Poets, with Prefaces, Biographical and Critical, by Samuel Johnson*. Vols. 74–75. London: J. Nichols for J.

Buckland [etc.], 1790.

Index volumes.

Kline, Victoria, ed. *Last Lines: An Index to the Last Lines of Poetry.* New York: Facts on File, 1990.

Unlike *Granger's*, Kline indexes poems by their last lines. Some 174,000 poems from some 450 poetry anthologies, including most of the anthologies from the eighth edition of *Granger's* and many recent anthologies, are indexed. Includes indexes to poems and last lines, authors, and keywords. Should prove to be an important reference tool for the quotation tracer.

Lemay, J. A. Leo, ed. *A Calendar of American Poetry in the Colonial Newspapers and Magazines and in the Major English Magazines through 1765.* Worcester, Mass.: American Antiquarian Society, 1972.

Contains first-line and other indexes to American poetry of the colonial period.

Shaw, John Mackay, ed. *Childhood in Poetry: A Catalogue, with Biographical and Critical Annotations, of the Books of English and American Poets Comprising the Shaw Childhood in Poetry Collection in the Library of the Florida State University, with Lists of the Poems That Relate to Childhood, Notes, and Index.* 5 vols. Detroit: Gale Research Co., 1967.

Poems that relate to childhood or that have been enjoyed by children are indexed by keywords from titles, first lines, or characteristic phrases. Provides references to books and periodicals in which the poems are printed. Contains material not indexed elsewhere.

———. *Childhood in Poetry: Supplement.* 3 vols. Detroit: Gale Research Co., 1972.

———. *Childhood in Poetry: Second Supplement.* 2 vols. Detroit: Gale Research Co., 1976.

Vol. 2 of the *Second Supplement* is an extended, cumulative index to the main volumes and to the first two supplements.

———. *Childhood in Poetry: Third Supplement.* Detroit: Gale Research Co., 1980.

Song Indexes

Bloom, Ken, ed. *American Song: The Complete Musical Theatre Companion.* 2 vols. New York: Facts on File, 1985.

Contains a title index to more than 42,000 songs from American musicals.

Brunnings, Florence, comp. *Folk Song Index: A Comprehensive Guide to the Florence E. Brunnings Collection.* New York: Garland Publishing, 1981.

A title index to 50,000 songs from song books and records.

Cushing, Helen Grant, comp. *Children's Song Index*. New York: H. W. Wilson Co., 1936.

Indexes more than 22,000 songs by first lines, titles, authors, and composers.

De Charms, Desiree, and Paul F. Breed, comps. *Songs in Collections: An Index*. Detroit: Information Coordinators, 1966.

Contains an index to first lines and titles of more than 9,000 solo songs.

Diehl, Katharine Smith, ed. *Hymns and Tunes: An Index*. New York: Scarecrow Press, 1966.

Lists first lines of every first stanza and every refrain of the hymns from seventy-eight hymnals in use in this century.

Gargan, William, and Sue Sharma, comps. *Find That Tune: An Index to Rock, Folk-Rock, Disco, and Soul in Collections*. New York: Neal-Schuman Publishers, 1984.

Contains first-line, title, and other indexes to over 4,000 songs.

Havlice, Patricia Pate, ed. *Popular Song Index*. Metuchen, N.J.: Scarecrow Press, 1975.

An excellent reference work containing an index of titles and first lines of thousands of songs in 301 song books published between 1940 and 1972.

———. *Popular Song Index: First Supplement*. Metuchen, N.J.: Scarecrow Press, 1978.

———. *Popular Song Index: Second Supplement*. Metuchen, N.J.: Scarecrow Press, 1984.

Julian, John, ed. *A Dictionary of Hymnology*. Rev. ed. London: J. Murray, 1907; reprint, 2 vols., New York: Dover Publications, 1957; reprint, 2 vols., Grand Rapids: Kregel Publications, 1985.

Includes a first-line index to thousands of hymns in several languages.

Lax, Roger, and Frederick Smith, eds. *The Great Song Thesaurus*. 2d ed. New York: Oxford University Press, 1989.

Contains title indexes to thousands of American and British songs and an index to song titles by subject, keyword, and category.

Leigh, Robert, ed. *Index to Song Books*. Stockton, Calif.: Robert Leigh, 1964.

A title index to almost 7,000 songs.

Lewine, Richard, and Alfred Simon, comps. *Songs of the Theater*. New York: H. W. Wilson Co., 1984.

Contains a title index to about 17,000 songs from the theater.

Methodist Church (England). *Subject, Textual, and Lineal Indexes to the Methodist Hymn Book*. London: Methodist Conference Office, 1934.

Contains an index to every line of the hymns in this old British hymnal.

Sears, Minnie Earl, comp. *Song Index*. New York: H. W. Wilson Co., 1926.

An index by author, title, and first line, interfiled, to more than 12,000 songs in 177 collections.

——. *Song Index Supplement*. New York: H. W. Wilson Co., 1934.

An index to some 7,000 songs in 104 collections.

Indexes to Queries and Replies

Anderson, Charles R., comp. *Index to "The Exchange."* Northfield, Ill.: Charles R. Anderson, 1988.

A slim but important keyword index covering volumes 1–26 of *RQ*. Indexes quotations and other things that have been the subjects of questions or of questions and answers.

"Notes and Queries": General Index. London: [publisher varies], 1856–1955.

Fifteen separate cumulations of the annual indexes to the journal from 1849 to 1947, one for each series; annual indexes thereafter. Under the heading "Quotations" are alphabetically listed first lines and opening words of quotations queried or identified in the journal, with references to appropriate volumes. Initial definite and indefinite articles are treated as main words. Other useful headings are "Proverbs and Phrases," "Songs and Ballads," and, in the fifteenth series, "Phrases" and "Proverbs."

Detective Work: Names, Titles, Clues

Benét, William Rose, ed. *The Reader's Encyclopedia*. New York: Thomas Y. Crowell Co., 1948.

A basic handbook of useful and varied information. Entries include titles, characters, and persons.

Berger, Thomas L., and William C. Bradford, Jr., comps. *An Index of Characters in English Printed Drama to the Restoration*. Englewood, Colo.: Microcard Editions Books, 1975.

Identifies all the characters in English printed drama of the Tudor, Elizabethan, Jacobean, Caroline, and Commonwealth periods.

Bergquist, G. William, ed. *Three Centuries of English and American Plays: A Checklist*. New York: Readex Microprint Corp., 1963.

Lists some 5,500 English (to 1800) and American (to 1830) plays, by title and author.

Brewer, Ebenezer Cobham. *The Reader's Handbook of Allusions, References, Plots, and Stories*. Philadelphia: J. B. Lippincott Co., 1895.

A fine old literary handbook. Entries include titles, literary characters, and persons. An appendix lists plays by title.

Carpenter, Humphrey, and Mari Prichard, eds. *The Oxford Companion to Children's Literature.* Oxford and New York: Oxford University Press, 1984.

Entries include titles, characters, and authors.

The Century Cyclopedia of Names. Ed. Benjamin E. Smith. New York: Century Co., 1894.

A good old source for the identification of names of all kinds, including characters, titles, and persons. Contains some information not found in the later *New Century Cyclopedia of Names* and lacks some that is found there.

Eldredge, H. J. [Reginald Clarence, pseud.], comp. *"The Stage" Cyclopaedia: A Bibliography of Plays.* London: "The Stage," 1909; reprint, New York: Burt Franklin, 1970.

A good source for the identification of play titles.

Freeman, William, ed. *Everyman's Dictionary of Fictional Characters.* Rev. ed., ed. Fred Urquhart. London: J. M. Dent and Sons, 1973. Also published as the *Dictionary of Fictional Characters.* Boston: The Writer, 1974.

Identifies about 22,000 characters from British and American fiction, drama, and even poetry. Contains a title index.

Harvey, Sir Paul, ed. *The Oxford Companion to English Literature.* 3d ed. Oxford: Clarendon Press, 1946.

A very useful book. Entries include characters, titles, and persons.

Mortimore, Arthur D., comp. *Children's Literary Characters Index, 1981: The First Supplement to "Index to Characters in Children's Literature."* Bristol: D. Mortimore, 1981.

———. *Index to Characters in Children's Literature.* Bristol: D. Mortimore, 1977.

A slim index to characters from children's literature.

Mossman, Jennifer, ed. *Pseudonyms and Nicknames Dictionary.* 3d ed., 2 vols. Detroit: Gale Research Co., 1987.

Useful for identification of persons known by nicknames or epithetical characterizations.

The New Century Cyclopedia of Names. 3 vols., ed. Clarence L. Barnhart. New York: Appleton-Century-Crofts, 1954.

Successor to the old *Century Cyclopedia of Names.* Entries include titles, literary characters, and persons.

Sharp, Harold S., and Marjorie Z. Sharp, eds. *Index to Characters in the Performing Arts.* 4 pts. in 6 vols. New York: Scarecrow Press, 1966–73.

An important, not to be overlooked reference work for the identification of characters from plays, operas, radio and television dramas, and ballets. For the quote sleuth, the most useful part is part 1, which identifies 30,000 characters from nonmusical plays.

Sifakis, Carl, ed. *The Dictionary of Historic Nicknames.* New York: Facts on File, 1984.

One of the places to look when all you know about a person is his or her nickname.

Tracing Classical and Foreign Quotations

Guides to Reference Materials

Sheehy, Eugene P., ed. *Guide to Reference Books.* 10th ed. Chicago: American Library Association, 1986.

Walford, Albert John, ed. *Walford's Guide to Reference Material.* 4th ed., 3 vols. London: Library Association, 1980–87.

General Dictionaries of Quotations

Bartlett, John, ed. *Familiar Quotations.* 15th ed., ed. Emily Morison Beck. Boston: Little, Brown and Co., 1980.

A weak collection of Latin and foreign quotations in their original languages, combined with a strong collection of anglicized Latin, Greek, and foreign quotations, arranged chronologically by author. Original texts appear in footnotes. Excellent index and good texts, citations, and translations.

Evans, Bergen, comp. *Dictionary of Quotations.* New York: Delacorte Press, 1968.

Includes quotes from many languages, but they are all given in English. Excellent index. Useful for tracing anglicized quotations.

Hoyt, Jehiel Keeler, comp. *Hoyt's New Cyclopedia of Practical Quotations.* Rev. ed., ed. Kate Louise Roberts. New York and London: Funk and Wagnalls Co., 1922.

Includes a large number of Latin quotations and a less-impressive number of foreign quotations, organized by subject. Good source citations and translations. The indexing of Latin and foreign quotations is not strong, with less than three entries for each passage, but you can compensate for this by thorough checking.

Mencken, H. L., ed. *A New Dictionary of Quotations on Historical Principles from Ancient and Modern Sources.* New York: Alfred A. Knopf, 1942.

Thousands of interesting quotes, all in English, appear under hundreds of rubrics. No index.

The Oxford Dictionary of Quotations. 2d ed. London, New York, and Toronto: Oxford University Press, 1953.

Contains a large number of classical and foreign quotations, organized by author. Reliable texts, source citations, and translations. The index is not strong for Latin and foreign quotations, with about two entries for each passage, but you can compensate for this by checking under every likely word. Separate Greek index.

The Oxford Dictionary of Quotations. 3d ed. Oxford and New York: Oxford University Press, 1979.

A fair collection of classical and foreign quotations, organized by author, with a strong collection of anglicized quotations. The index is weak and must be compensated for by careful checking under every likely word. Good citations and modern translations.

Stevenson, Burton, ed. *The Home Book of Quotations, Classical and Modern.* 10th ed. New York: Dodd, Mead and Co., 1967.

Contains a large number of Latin quotations. Greek and foreign quotations are mainly anglicized, often with the original text supplied parenthetically. Organized by subject, with good source citations and translations. The index is weak, with usually one entry—ordinarily a noun, the subject of the sentence—for each passage.

Tracing Latin Quotations

See also Bartlett, Evans, *Hoyt's,* Mencken, the *ODQ2,* the *ODQ3,* and Stevenson, in the previous section.

SPECIALIZED QUOTATION COLLECTIONS

Collison, Robert, and Mary Collison, comps. *Dictionary of Foreign Quotations.* New York: Facts on File, 1980.

Some 6,000 quotations in several languages, organized by English subject. Good translations. Source citations provide only author and title. Indexes to authors and subjects but not to keywords or initial words. Useful for tracing anglicized Latin quotations and Latin quotations you can easily anglicize.

Cree, Anthony, comp. *Cree's Dictionary of Latin Quotations.* Topsfield, Mass.: Newbury Books, 1978.

A weak collection of perhaps 2,000 Latin quotations, arranged alphabetically by initial word. Good translations and source references. Provides pronunciations. No index.

Guterman, Norbert, comp. *A Book of Latin Quotations, with English Translations.* Garden City, N.Y.: Anchor Books, 1966.

A useful small collection, organized by author. Good translations and detailed source citations. Keyword index.

Harbottle, Thomas Benfield, comp. *Dictionary of Quotations (Classical).* 2d ed. London: S. Sonnenschein, 1902; reprint, New York: Frederick Ungar, [1958].

Contains one of the strongest collections of Latin quotations. Each language section is arranged alphabetically by opening word. Good translations and detailed source citations. Latin and English subject indexes and an author index.

Jones, Hugh Percy, comp. *Dictionary of Foreign Phrases and Classical Quotations*. Rev. ed. Edinburgh: John Grant, 1908.

Includes an insubstantial collection of Latin quotations, proverbs, and phrases, organized alphabetically by opening word. Source citations, when provided, are names of authors.

King, W. Francis H., comp. *Classical and Foreign Quotations*. 3d ed. London: J. Whitaker and Sons, 1904; reprint, Detroit: Gale Research Co., 1968.

An excellent collection of quotations in several languages, especially Latin, interfiled alphabetically by initial word. Includes an important supplementary index to quotes that are not findable in the main alphabetical sequence. Good source citations and interesting translations, many of them poetical. Author and English subject indexes.

Ramage, Craufurd Tait, comp. *Familiar Quotations from Latin Authors*. 3d ed. London: George Routledge and Sons, n.d. Also published as *Beautiful Thoughts from Latin Authors*.

A substantial collection of Latin quotations, organized by author, with detailed though abbreviated source citations. A Latin index to opening words and an English index that includes subjects, keywords, and opening words.

Stevenson, Burton, comp. *The Home Book of Proverbs, Maxims, and Familiar Phrases*. New York: Macmillan Co., 1948. Also published as *The Macmillan Book of Proverbs, Maxims, and Famous Phrases*. New York: Macmillan Co., n.d.

Includes a large number of Latin proverbs and literary restatements of proverbs. Good translations and source references. The index contains at least one keyword entry for every proverb, maxim, or familiar phrase.

LATIN DICTIONARIES

Andrews, Ethan Allen, ed. *Harpers' Latin Dictionary: A New Latin Dictionary Founded on the Translation of Freund's Latin-German Lexicon*. Rev. ed., ed. Charlton T. Lewis and Charles Short. New York: American Book Co., 1907.

A fine old one-volume dictionary, excellent for Latin quotations. Source citations are abbreviated but detailed.

Glare, P. G. W., ed. *Oxford Latin Dictionary*. Oxford: Clarendon Press, 1982.

An excellent, easy-to-use one-volume dictionary, a third longer than Lewis and Short. Contains hundreds of thousands of quotations, based on a completely new reading of sources over half a century. Source citations are abbreviated but detailed.

Forcellini, Egidio, ed. *Totius Latinitatis Lexicon.* 10 vols. Prati: Typis Aldinianis, 1858–87.

For the quote sleuth, a very useful supplement to the *Oxford* and to *Harpers'.* The last four volumes are an onomasticon, a work filled with quotations containing proper names.

Thesaurus Linguae Latinae. Lipsiae: B. G. Teubneri, 1900– .

A recent, not-yet-complete multivolume dictionary with an excellent collection of Latin quotations.

Selected Concordances and Indexes

Cooper, Lane, comp. *A Concordance of the Works of Horace.* Washington, D.C.: Carnegie Institution of Washington, 1916; reprint, New York: Barnes and Noble, 1962.

Deferrari, Roy J., Sr. M. Inviolata Barry, and Martin R. P. McGuire, eds. *A Concordance of Ovid.* Washington, D.C.: Catholic University of America Press, 1939.

Dutripon, François Pascal, comp. *Concordantiae Bibliorum Sacrorum Vulgatae Editionis.* 4th ed. Barri-Ducis: L. Guerin, 1873.

Fasciano, Domenico, ed. *Virgile Concordance.* 2 vols. Rome: Edizioni dell'Ateneo; Montreal: Les Presses de Université de Montréal, 1982.

Fischer, Bonifatius, comp. *Novae Concordantiae Bibliorum Sacrorum iuxta Vulgatam.* 5 vols. Stuttgart-Bad Cannstatt: Frommann-Holzboog, 1977.

Warwick, Henrietta Holm, comp. *A Vergil Concordance.* Minneapolis: University of Minnnesota Press, 1975.

Wetmore, Monroe Nichols, ed. *Index Verborum Vergilianus.* New Haven: Yale University Press, 1911.

May be used for tracing quotations known or thought to be by Virgil, if a concordance to Virgil is not available.

Bibliography of Latin Concordances

Quellet, Henri, ed. *Bibliographia Indicum, Lexicorum, et Concordantiarum Auctorum Latinorum.* Hildesheim and New York: Georg Olms, 1980.

Handbooks

Harvey, Sir Paul, ed. *The Oxford Companion to Classical Literature.* Oxford: Clarendon Press, 1937.

Lemprière, John, ed. *Lemprière's Classical Dictionary of Proper Names Mentioned in Ancient Authors Writ Large.* 3d ed. London: Routledge

and Kegan Paul, 1984.
Older editions, writ less large, will do as well.

Tracing French Quotations

See also Bartlett, Evans, *Hoyt's*, Mencken, the *ODQ2*, the *ODQ3*, and Stevenson in the earlier section on general dictionaries of quotations.

SPECIALIZED QUOTATION COLLECTIONS

Collison, Robert, and Mary Collison, comps. *Dictionary of Foreign Quotations*. New York: Facts on File, 1980.

Some 6,000 quotations in several languages, organized by English subjects, with good translations. Source citations provide only authors and titles. Indexes to authors and subjects but not to keywords or opening words. Useful in tracing anglicized French quotations and French quotations you can easily anglicize.

Dictionnaire de Citations Françaises. Paris: Robert, 1978.

A good collection of quotations, arranged by author. Minimal keyword index supplies page references but does not list phrases. Because of its poor index, this collection is useful only when authorship of the quotation is known.

Dupré, P., ed. *Encyclopédie des Citations*. Paris: Éditions de Trévise, 1959.

Better than most French compilations. Contains several sections of quotations in French, organized by country of origin. The largest section consists of genuine French quotations, organized by authors in chronological sequence. Detailed source citations and a good subject and keyword index in which phrases from quotations are repeated.

Genest, Émile, comp. *Dictionnaire des Citations*. Paris: Fernand Nathan, n.d.

Some 4,000 French quotations arranged alphabetically by opening word, with detailed source citations. Author and keyword indexes give references to quotations but do not repeat phrases from quotations.

Guerlac, Othon, comp. *Les Citations Françaises*. 7th ed. Paris: Librairie Armand Colin, 1961.

A good collection of French quotations, arranged by author, with detailed source citations. The excellent keyword index contains phrases from quotations.

Guterman, Norbert, comp. *A Book of French Quotations, with English Translations*. London: Alvin Redman, 1963.

Arranged by author, with French and English on opposite pages.

Source citations and translations are adequate. French and English indexes to first lines.

Harbottle, Thomas Benfield, and Philip Hugh Dalbiac, eds. *Dictionary of Quotations (French and Italian)*. London: Swan Sonnenschein and Co.; New York: Macmillan Co., 1904.

Contains a substantial collection of French quotations, arranged alphabetically. Adequate translations, many of which are poetical, and references to sources. Indexes of authors, French subjects and keywords, and English subjects and keywords.

Jones, Hugh Percy, ed. *Dictionary of Foreign Phrases and Classical Quotations*. Rev. ed. Edinburgh: John Grant, 1908.

Includes a large number of French quotations and expressions, in alphabetical order. Source citations, when they are provided, give only authors' names. Adequate translations. No subject or keyword index.

King, W. Francis H., comp. *Classical and Foreign Quotations*. 3d ed. London: J. Whitaker and Sons, 1904; reprint, Detroit: Gale Research Co., 1968.

An important collection of French quotations interfiled with quotations in other languages. Good translations and detailed source citations. Supplemental index to quotations and parts of quotations not findable in the main alphabetical sequence. English subject index includes anglicized phrases from quotations.

Larousse des Citations Françaises et Étrangères. Paris: Larousse, 1976.

The largest section consists of French quotations arranged alphabetically by author. Source citations are less than complete, usually consisting of author and title. A subject and keyword index contains phrases from the quotations.

Nouveau Dictionnaire de Citations Françaises. Ed. Jeanne Matignon, Denis Hollier, Aude Matignon, and Pierre Oster. Paris: Hachette-Tchou, 1970.

Almost identical to the *Dictionnaire de Citations Françaises*. Quotes are arranged by author. Because of its poor index, this work is useful only when authorship is known.

Ramage, Craufurd Tait, ed. *Familiar Quotations from French and Italian Authors*. London: George Routledge and Sons, 1904; reprint, Detroit: Gale Research Co., 1968.

Contains a substantial collection of French quotations, organized alphabetically by author. Good translations and detailed source citations. A detailed English index contains anglicized keywords.

SELECTED CONCORDANCES AND INDEXES

Freeman, Bryant C., comp. *Concordance du Théâtre et des Poésies de Jean Racine*. 2 vols. Ithaca: Cornell University Press, 1968.

Leake, Roy E., David B. Leake, and Alice Elder Leake, comps. *Concordance des Essais de Montaigne.* 2 vols. Geneva: Librairie Droz, 1981.

FRENCH DICTIONARIES

Grand Larousse de la Langue Française. 6 vols. Paris: Librairie Larousse, 1971–78.
 Contains a large number of French quotations of all periods.
Huguet, Edmond, ed. *Dictionnaire de la Langue Française du Seizième Siècle.* 7 vols. Paris: Didier, 1925–67.
 An important collection of French quotations of the sixteenth century.
Imbs, Paul, ed. *Trésor de la Langue Française: Dictionnaire de la Langue du XIXᵉ et du XXᵉ Siècle (1789–1960).* Paris: Éditions du Centre National de la Recherche Scientifique, 1971– .
 An important collection of French quotations from the late eighteenth, nineteenth, and twentieth centuries.
Littré, Émile, ed. *Dictionnaire de la Langue Française.* 7 vols. Paris: Jean-Jacques Pauvert, 1956–58.
 A basic reference work for quotation tracers.
Robert, Paul, ed. *Dictionnaire Alphabétique et Analogique de la Langue Française.* 2d ed., ed. Alain Rey. 9 vols. Paris: Robert, 1985.
 A multivolume work containing a large number of French quotations.

HANDBOOKS

Harvey, Sir Paul, and J. E. Heseltine, eds. *The Oxford Companion to French Literature.* Oxford: Clarendon Press, 1959; reprint, with corrections, 1969.
 Will enable you to identify names found in French quotations or in contextual information.

Tracing Italian Quotations

See also Bartlett, Evans, *Hoyt's*, Mencken, the *ODQ2*, the *ODQ3*, and Stevenson in the earlier section on general dictionaries of quotations.

SPECIALIZED QUOTATION COLLECTIONS

Collison, Robert, and Mary Collison, comps. *Dictionary of Foreign Quotations.* New York: Facts on File, 1980.
 About 6,000 quotations in several languages, organized by English subjects. Good translations. Source citations provide authors and titles. Indexes to authors and English subjects but not to keywords or opening words. Useful in tracing anglicized Italian quotations and Italian quotations that you can easily anglicize.

Finzi, Giuseppe, ed. *Dizionario di Citazioni Latine ed Italiane.* Palermo, 1902; reprint, n.p.: Arnaldo Forni, n.d.

> Organized by topics, with a keyword index. Source citations are authors and titles.

Fumagalli, Giuseppe, ed. *Chi l'ha Detto?* 10th ed. Milan: Ulrico Hoepli, 1968.

> Includes quotations in several languages but chiefly Italian, organized according to broad topics. Detailed source citations and discussions. Good index to opening words.

Harbottle, Thomas Benfield, and Philip Hugh Dalbiac, comps. *Dictionary of Quotations (French and Italian).* London: Swan Sonnenschein and Co., 1904.

> Contains a substantial collection of Italian quotations, organized alphabetically. Adequate source citations and good translations, many of them poetical. Italian and English subject and keyword indexes.

Jones, Hugh Percy, comp. *Dictionary of Foreign Phrases and Classical Quotations.* Rev. ed. Edinburgh: John Grant, 1908.

> Includes a small number of Italian quotations and expressions, arranged alphabetically by opening word. Adequate translations. Source citations, when they are provided, give only the names of the authors.

King, W. Francis H., comp. *Classical and Foreign Quotations.* London: J. Whitaker and Sons, 1904; reprint, Detroit: Gale Research Co., 1968.

> Contains Italian quotations interfiled with quotations in other languages, in alphabetical order. Good translations and detailed source citations. Important supplementary index to quotations and parts of quotations not findable in the main alphabetical sequence. English subject index.

Ramage, Craufurd Tait, ed. *Familiar Quotations from French and Italian Authors.* London: George Routledge and Sons, 1904; reprint, Detroit: Gale Research Co., 1968.

> Includes a small collection of Italian quotations, many of which are lengthy, arranged by author. Citations and translations are adequate. Italian index to opening words and English index to subjects and keywords.

Selected Concordances

Accademia della Crusca, Florence—Opera del Vocabolario. *Concordanze del Canzoniere di Francesco Petrarca.* 2 vols. Firenze, 1971.

Fay, Edward Allen, ed. *Concordance of the "Divina Commedia."* Boston: Little, Brown and Co.; London: Trübner and Co., for the Dante Society, 1888.

Wilkins, Ernest Hatch, and Thomas Goddard Bergin, comps. *A Concordance to the "Divine Comedy" of Dante Alighieri.* Cambridge: Belknap Press of Harvard University Press, 1965.

ITALIAN DICTIONARIES

Accademici della Crusca. *Vocabolario degli Accademici della Crusca.* 5th ed., 11 vols. Firenze: Nella Tipografia Galileiana, 1863–1923.
   Goes through the letter O. Detailed source citations.
Battaglia, Salvatore, ed. *Grande Dizionario della Lingua Italiana.* Torino: Unione Tipografico-Editrice Torinese, 1961– .
   About half complete. Detailed source citations.
Tommaseo, Nicolò, and Bernardo Bellini, eds. *Dizionario della Lingua Italiana.* 4 vols. in 7. Torino: Dalla Società L'Unione Tipografico-Editrice, 1865–79.
   Contains a large number of quotations. Citations are not sufficiently detailed.

Tracing German Quotations

See also Bartlett, Evans, *Hoyt's*, Mencken, the *ODQ2*, the *ODQ3*, and Stevenson in the earlier section on general dictionaries of quotations.

SPECIALIZED COLLECTIONS OF QUOTATIONS

Büchmann, Georg, ed. *Geflügelte Worte: Der Zitatenschatz des Deutschen Volkes.* Ed. Walter Robert-tornow et al. 32d ed., ed. Gunther Haupt and Winfried Hofmann. Berlin: Haude und Spenersche Verlagsbuchhandlung, 1972.
   Includes quotations from several languages but is important to the tracer because of its German collection. Adequate source citations, though explanations are in German. Good index to opening words of German quotations.
Collison, Robert, and Mary Collison, comps. *Dictionary of Foreign Quotations.* New York: Facts on File, 1980.
   Some 6,000 quotes in several languages, organized by English subject. Good translations. Source citations provide only author and title. Indexes to authors and subjects but not to keywords or initial words. Useful for tracing anglicized German quotations and German quotations you can easily anglicize.
Dalbiac, Lilian, comp. *Dictionary of Quotations (German).* London: Swan Sonnenschein, 1906.
   A large collection of German quotations, arranged alphabetically by opening word. Adequate English translations and source citations. German subject and keyword index repeats phrases from quotations. Author and English subject indexes.

King, W. Francis H., comp. *Classical and Foreign Quotations.* 3d ed. London: J. Whitaker and Sons, 1904; reprint, Detroit: Gale Research Co., 1968.

Contains German quotations interfiled with quotations in other languages, in alphabetical order. A supplementary index contains quotations and parts of quotations not findable in the main alphabetical sequence. Good translations and source citations. English subject index.

Lipperheide, Franz Joseph, freiherr von, comp. *Spruchwörterbuch.* Munich: Verlag von F. Bruchmann, 1909.

A classic collection of German quotations, including many proverbs, organized by topics that are also keywords. Lacks a separate index.

Peltzer, Karl, comp. *Das Treffende Zitat.* Thun and Munich: Ott Verlag, 1957.

Consists of quotations in German that were originally in several languages, arranged alphabetically by keyword. Source citations are adequate. Detailed author index, in which words or subjects of quotations are noted.

Ramage, Craufurd Tait, comp. *Familiar Quotations from German and Spanish Authors.* London: George Routledge and Sons, 1904; reprint, Detroit: Gale Research Co., 1968.

Contains a large collection of somewhat lengthy German quotations, arranged by author. Documentation is less than complete. The book has an author index, a German index to opening words, and an English index to subjects and keywords.

SELECTED AUTHOR INDEXES AND LEXICONS

Dannhauer, Heinz-Martin, Hans Otto Horch, and Klaus Schuffels, eds. *Wörterbuch zu Friedrich Hölderlin.* Tübingen: Max Niemeyer Verlag, 1893.

Dobel, Richard, ed. *Lexikon der Goethe-Zitate.* Zurich and Stuttgart: Artemis Verlag, 1968.

A major resource for tracing quotations attributed to Goethe or thought to be from Goethe. Quotations occur under keywords in alphabetical sequence. Citations are detailed.

Fischer, Paul, ed. *Goethe-Wortschatz.* Leipzig: Emil Rohmkopf, 1929.

A detailed glossary of words used by Goethe, with explanations, examples, and citations.

Goethe Wörterbuch. Stuttgart: Verlag W. Kohlhammer, 1978– .

For the early part of the alphabet, this is the definitive Goethe dictionary, filled with illustrative quotations.

Schmidt, Heinrich, ed. *Goethe-Lexikon*. Leipzig: Alfred Kröner Verlag, 1912.

A book of Goethe quotations arranged under general catchwords and traced to titles of the author's works.

GERMAN DICTIONARIES

Grimm, Jacob, and Wilhelm Grimm, eds. *Deutsches Wörterbuch*. 16 vols. in 32. Leipzig: Hirzel, 1854–1960.

In addition to its other purposes, this is a major resource for tracing German quotations.

———. *Deutsches Wörterbuch*. Rev. ed. Leipzig: S. Hirzel Verlag, 1965– .

Tracing Greek Quotations

See also Bartlett, Evans, *Hoyt's*, Mencken, the *ODQ2*, the *ODQ3*, and Stevenson in the earlier section on general dictionaries of quotations.

SPECIALIZED COLLECTIONS OF QUOTATIONS

Collison, Robert, and Mary Collison, comps. *Dictionary of Foreign Quotations*. New York: Facts on File, 1980.

About 6,000 quotations from several languages, arranged alphabetically under English subjects. Greek quotations are transliterated. Good translations, but source citations consist only of authors and titles. Useful in tracing anglicized Greek quotations and Greek quotations that you can easily translate. Lacks an index to keywords or initial words.

Harbottle, Thomas Benfield, comp. *Dictionary of Quotations (Classical)*. 2d ed. London: S. Sonnenschein, 1902; reprint, New York: Frederick Ungar Publishing Co., [1958].

Contains a large collection of Greek quotations, arranged alphabetically. Good translations and detailed source citations. Greek subject and keyword index as well as English subject index.

Jones, Hugh Percy, comp. *Dictionary of Foreign Phrases and Classical Quotations*. Rev. ed. Edinburgh: John Grant, 1908.

Includes a section of Greek quotations, proverbs, and phrases, arranged alphabetically. Good translations, but source citations, when they are given, consist only of names of authors. Lacks a keyword index.

King, W. Francis H., comp. *Classical and Foreign Quotations*. 3d ed. London: J. Whitaker and Sons, 1904; reprint, Detroit: Gale Research Co., 1968.

Contains Greek quotations interfiled with quotations from several other languages, in alphabetical sequence. Translations and source citations are competent. Has a separate Greek index to quotations, an author index, and an English subject and keyword index.

Ramage, Craufurd Tait, comp. *Familiar Quotations from Greek Authors.* 2d ed. London: George Routledge and Sons, n.d. Also published as *Beautiful Thoughts from Greek Authors.*

A substantial collection of Greek quotations, some of them lengthy, arranged alphabetically by author. Competent translations and detailed source citations. Detailed English index.

SELECTED CONCORDANCES AND INDEXES

Allen, James Turney, and Gabriel Italie, comps. *A Concordance to Euripides.* Berkeley: University of California Press, 1954.

Dunbar, Henry, comp. *A Complete Concordance to the "Odyssey" and Hymns of Homer.* Oxford: Clarendon Press, 1880.

Prendergast, Guy Lushington, comp. *A Complete Concordance to the "Iliad" of Homer.* Rev. ed., ed. Benedetto Marzullo. Hildesheim: Georg Olms, 1962.

GREEK DICTIONARIES

Estienne, Henri, ed. *Thesaurus Graecae Linguae.* 8 vols. in 9. Paris: Didot, 1831–65.

Contains a large number of well-referenced quotations, longer than those in Liddell and Scott and thus easier to recognize. Detailed but abbreviated source references.

Liddell, Henry George, and Robert Scott, eds. *A Greek-English Lexicon.* 9th ed., ed. Henry Stuart Jones. Oxford: Clarendon Press, 1940.

A fine one-volume dictionary with thousands of illustrative quotations, many of which are shortened to the bare essentials. Source references are detailed but abbreviated.

Passow, Franz, ed. *Handwörterbuch der Griechischen Sprache.* 2 vols. in 4. Leipzig: F. C. W. Vogel, 1841–57; reprint, Darmstadt: Wissenschaftliche Buchgesellschaft, 1970.

Contains short illustrative quotations. Source references are abbreviated, and explanations are in German. As Sheehy points out, this work includes place-names omitted in Liddell and Scott.

Index

This index covers the ten chapters of the text and all the concordance subjects of the bibliography. To retrieve any bibliographical item, locate it first in the text and then turn to the corresponding section of the bibliography.

Who among us has not encountered that elusive phrase, that perfect epigram whose source escapes us, that well-chosen *bon mot* that defies identification? And who has not been frustrated by the attempt to determine the provenance of some obscure but absolutely vital literary or historical allusion? All of us, whether scholars, librarians, researchers, or serious readers, find ourselves in these vexing situations with some frequency.

Our quest to locate and verify lost quotations will be made immeasurably easier thanks to the guidelines and helpful hints in *The Quote Sleuth*. Anthony W. Shipps, a noted practitioner of the noble art of quotation tracing, devotes an entire book to the tools and methods used in the identification of the sources of quotations. Shipps discusses old and recently published reference materials he has employed in his pursuit of quotation sources. Using as examples real quotations and misquotations, he also demonstrates the strengths, special characteristics, and deficiencies of various reference works.

Shipps provides information on several kinds of quotation compilations, on a number of useful indexes, on the recognition and pursuit of clues, on important but overlooked reference works that should be used by the zealous quotation tracer, and on how to scout out classical and foreign quotations. He concludes